MAKE IT HAPPEN

SIMPLE BLUEPRINTS FOR BOLD LEADERSHIP

Robert L. Kistner
Cami Nelson

ISBN: 979-8-9891409-0-9
Library of Congress Control Number: 2023922966

Cover design by Cami Nelson
Book design, composition, and editing by Cami Nelson
Website: www.makeithappenleadership.com

Printed in Houston, Texas, United States of America
First Edition

ACKNOWLEDGMENTS FROM ROBERT KISTNER

To my wife, Ana, and my children, Bobby, Bryan, Natasha, and Steven. I am grateful for your undying support of my leadership career and my journey through life.

To my business partners, Fernando Gonzalez, Sr., Owen Perry, and Luz Maria Torres Gonzalez, who have been my mentors and my family. I owe each of you gratitude for years of growth, friendship, and success.

ACKNOWLEDGMENTS FROM CAMI NELSON

To Robert Kistner, who invited me to collaborate with him on this project. I have learned a great deal from our conversations. The past few years of researching and writing have been highly rewarding.

To Mark Nelson who provided brilliant suggestions and collaborated to generate vision for this project. Most importantly, to my three talented teenagers, who are my teachers and my inspiration.

CONTENTS

INTRODUCTION

Overview of Bold Business Leadership

Effective business leadership is crucial for the success and growth of any organization. Within an organization, business leadership refers to the ability of an individual to influence others toward achieving common goals and objectives. Each day, leaders make strategic decisions, provide direction, motivate employees, and foster a positive work environment. Vibrant leaders also dedicate time to improving themselves so that they can provide an example worth following. For example, leaders may create and review personal mission statements, refine communication skills, and develop emotional intelligence.

Talented leaders exhibit several qualities:

- Vision: Strong leaders have a clear vision for the organization's future. They articulate this vision to others and inspire them to work towards its realization. They set ambitious yet achievable goals and communicate them effectively to the team.

- Strategic Thinking: Bold leaders can think critically and strategically. They analyze market trends, identify opportunities, and make informed decisions to stay ahead of the competition. They are proactive in adapting to changes and developing innovative strategies.

- Communication Skills: Effective communication is vital for business leaders. They must be able to clearly convey their ideas, expectations, and feedback to their team members. They listen actively, encourage open dialogue, and ensure that everyone understands the organization's objectives.

- Emotional Intelligence: Great leaders understand and manage their emotions and those of others. They are empathetic, approachable, and supportive. They build relationships, inspire trust, and create a positive work culture that fosters collaboration and productivity.

- Decision Making: Leaders face numerous decisions daily. They evaluate information, consider various perspectives, and make timely decisions. They are not afraid to take calculated risks, but they also learn from failures and adjust their strategies accordingly.

- Delegation and Empowerment: Effective leaders delegate tasks and responsibilities to their team members based on their strengths and abilities. They trust their employees and empower them to make decisions and take ownership of their work. This fosters a sense of accountability and promotes individual growth.

- Continuous Learning: Business leaders understand the importance of continuous learning and personal development. They stay updated with industry trends, seek feedback, and actively seek opportunities for self-improvement. They encourage a learning culture within the organization and support the professional growth of their employees.

- Integrity and Ethics: Good leaders lead by example and demonstrate high ethical standards. They act with integrity, honesty, and transparency. They make decisions that align with the organization's values and consider the long-term impact on all stakeholders.

- Resilience and Adaptability: Leaders face challenges and setbacks, but they remain resilient and adaptable. They maintain a positive attitude, motivate their team during tough times, and find solutions to overcome obstacles. They embrace change and inspire others to do the same.

- Collaboration and teamwork: Business leaders recognize the value of collaboration and teamwork. They foster a culture that promotes cooperation, open communication, and synergy among team members. They build diverse and inclusive teams, leveraging the strengths of each individual to achieve collective success.

Leadership is a journey, and it requires continuous development and refinement of skills. This leadership book is built on the wisdom of great leaders including Robert Kistner. It harnesses pro tips, cutting-edge research, and wisdom to help leaders inspire their teams, drive innovation, and navigate through complex challenges to achieve long-term success.

Book Structure

Envision an urban skyline, jaggedly defined by tall buildings that reflect bright blue sky and passing clouds—you might think of Singapore, Dubai, New York City, Hong Kong, or Los Angeles. Until the mid-twentieth century, high-rise buildings were constructed with boxy exoskeletons made of brick, concrete, or stone. As technology advanced, internal central steel supports enabled newer "slick skin" skyscrapers to boldly shed their heavy exteriors and reach heavenward wearing just a curtain of exterior glass. Such modern skyscrapers represent thriving global businesses and powerful leadership.

Because this book provides simple blueprints for bold leadership, we will lean on two main architectural features of slick skin skyscrapers as metaphors for bold business leadership: 1) the sleek, glassy exterior, and 2) the strong, load-bearing interior. Around these metaphors, this book is organized into two parts. Put simply, Part One focuses on the leader's role within the organization and with others, and Part Two focuses on the leader as an individual.

Part One: Leadership as Strategic Performance
Or, The Sleek, Glassy Exterior of Business Leadership
Part One represents what people see from the outside of the skyscraper. People walking by and craning their gaze upward are aware

of the rush of rising glass, concrete, metal, and decorative facades. Depending on the time of day and lighting, passersby can sometimes see through the exterior glass into offices and entryways, where people are busy at work.

In this first part of the book, we discuss what people see when they think of bold leadership: managers, teams, performance metrics, etc. Part One provides simple blueprints for bold leadership within the organization, offering strategies for when leaders interface with colleagues and with people they manage. We characterize good leaders as coaches and provide tips that leaders can use to inspire responsibility, measure results, and motivate peak performance. Two chapters in this section are dedicated to sparking creativity, which bold leaders nurture in the workplace, in their teams, and in themselves.

Additionally, this section devotes three chapters to the power of business culture, including methods leaders can use to spark cultural evolution and anchor culture in values. Finally, because innovation and negotiation are critical to bold leadership, we provide multiple strategies for each.

In short, Part One focuses on the leader's role and skills within the organization. It provides tips and methods for improving performance, creativity, and business culture with teams and colleagues.

Part Two: Leadership as Transformation Catalyst
Or, The Strong, Load-Bearing Interior of Business Leadership

If Part One represents the externally visible sleek and shiny aspects of business leadership, Part Two focuses on the inner core steel support structure that supports the weight of the business: the leaders themselves. Part Two provides simple blueprints for becoming a better, bolder leader from the inside out. In this part, we discuss leadership as stewardship and finding success through happiness. We have dedicated a chapter each to the critical topics of resilience, mindfulness in management, and meditation for business leaders. Finally, this section boasts three chapters that discuss making smart leadership decisions by understanding values and tradeoffs, brain evolution, and subconscious drivers.

While it is natural for leaders to focus on the external manifestations of leadership within the organization, we find that leaders who also dedicate time to cultivating inner strength are more successful when they are interfacing with members of the organization. Such leaders are inherently more centered, more kind, and more insightful. In short, they are bold leaders and they serve as the core support for the whole organization.

In short, Part Two turns the lens inward, so to speak, by providing strategies for improving oneself to become a more talented leader. It addresses skills and practices like mindfulness, vision, and smart decision making.

Conclusion

Finally, as a case in point, we conclude with a narrative describing Bob Kistner's journey into leadership, highlighting ten specific leadership lessons. From street salesman through mid and upper-level management, Bob gained skills and motivated people for decades. Now in the top echelons of leadership, Bob has invested time and energy in a legacy project encapsulating his wisdom. He has created these simple blueprints to assist other leaders in walking their bold leadership journey.

PART ONE.
LEADERSHIP AS
STRATEGIC PERFORMANCE

SIMPLE BLUEPRINTS FOR
BOLD LEADERSHIP
WITHIN THE ORGANIZATION

1

Leaders as Coaches

In years past, people often began successful careers by developing expertise in a technical, functional, or professional industry. If you had the right information and techniques, you could do a job well. As you proved yourself, you would climb the ladder of success and move into management. As a manager, you would teach others how to do what needed to be done, and you'd evaluate their performance.

However, Harvard Business Review illuminates evolution in the trajectory of management: "Command and control was the name of the game, and your goal was to direct and develop employees who understood how the business worked and were able to reproduce its previous successes. Not today. Rapid, constant, and disruptive change is now the norm, and what succeeded in the past is no longer a guide to what will succeed in the future."[1] In short, today's business management is not about having all the right answers. Rather, it is about coping with an ever-changing reality by supporting and guiding employees so that they can "adapt to constantly changing environments in ways that unleash fresh energy, innovation, and commitment. The role of the manager, in short, is becoming that of a coach."[2] In fact, coaching is "the most critical skill that any leader can master in order to ensure career success."[3]

Evolution in Leadership from Guiding to Coaching

This fundamental shift is as new as it is dramatic. Research shows that as organizations are rapidly transforming themselves to match the demands and opportunities posed by the advancing digital age, business leaders have taken on the role of managing change.[4] For example, in years gone by, leaders were tasked with guiding the organization in following a pre-charted, time-tested course toward achieving business success. However, in today's business environment, leaders are navigating globally networked, cloud-based, artificial intelligence-laden applications where no pre-charted course exists.

Robert Kistner explains: "Everything is changing; we have to change with it."[5] This high-paced change has prompted business leaders to adopt coaching techniques. Gary Collins says that "coaching might have stayed in the realm of sports" but it moved into the corporate world because, "faced with the unsettling impact of galloping change, rapid technological advances, and tidal waves of information glut, business leaders began to see that no one person could keep abreast of everything."[6]

Thus, leadership skills of today have a lot to do with adapting to change to stay on top of the wave of transformation. In response, companies are "investing in training their leaders as coaches. Increasingly, coaching is becoming integral to the fabric of a learning culture—a skill that good managers at all levels need to develop and deploy."[7] "The power of coaching is this," says Tom Mahalo, "You are expected to give people the path to find the answers, not the answers."[8]

Definition of Coaching: Sparking Insight

What does coaching mean in the context of business? It's easy to see how coaching works in the world of athletics, but how does that translate into the office?

While leader-coaches perform traditional roles associated with coaching, such as mentoring less-experienced employees and answering questions, they take coaching one step further to spark insight. For example, Sir John Whitmore defined skilled coaching in business as "unlocking people's potential to maximize their own performance." In other words, coaches who get the best results create a balance between imparting knowledge and helping employees discover knowledge.

Chapter Roadmap

In this chapter, we will cover three key aspects of leadership and coaching.

1. First, we'll differentiate coaching from consulting in business and focus on coaching language through the lens of conversational leadership.
2. Second, we will outline two models that leaders can implement when coaching employees: GROW and communication loops. These highlight the role of attention in coaching. We've also put together a Top Ten list of leadership-coaching tips.
3. Finally, we'll conclude by discussing extrinsic and intrinsic motivation, as well as the importance of seeking out coachable moments.

Coaching vs. Consulting

In business, coaching is different from consulting. Harvard Business Review explains: "When we talk about coaching, we mean something broader than just the efforts of consultants who are hired to help executives build their personal and professional skills. That work is important . . . but it's temporary and executed by outsiders." Rather, the coaching "that creates a true learning organization is ongoing and executed by those inside the organization. It's work that all managers should engage in." For example, where consulting often begins with 'Chapter 1' of whatever method, coaching begins by analyzing the specific needs of each employee or situation. To build an action plan, coaches do specific diagnostic work: "Coaches have to watch for what they don't want to see and listen to what they don't want to hear."[9]

Further, coaching points employees to their personal resources, rather than directing them to outside resources. Instead of teaching employees to rely on scaffolding, leader-coaches help employees tap into their own understanding and innovate to resolve situations. Coaching is tailored to the person being coached and it is about sparking innovation. Leaders can draw out "the best effort from others not by lighting a fire beneath them, but by building a fire within."[10]

In the role of coaches, managers engage with their people and help define the organization's culture to be conducive to growth and goal advancement. Instead of simply providing answers, leader-coaches ask questions and listen. Instead of simply evaluating employees and dictating what must be done—thereby eliciting employee obedience—leader-coaches ask questions that elicit employee growth and development. In the coaching role, leaders ask questions and rely on their staff as experts to provide information.[11] Harvard Business Review notes that when an organization is "open to constant learning and risk-taking . . . the leaders of the company [have] to shift from being know-it-alls to being 'learn-it-alls.'"[12]

Despite the positive research about applied coaching in business, certain leaders resist taking on the role of coach. For some, coaching may feel too 'soft'—like a tedious use of time because it seems more efficient in the moment to tell people what to do than to ask them questions to spark longer-term knowledge, skills, and growth. For others, coaching may feel psychologically squeamish because it deprives managers of "their most familiar management tool: asserting their authority."[13]

Conversational Leadership

In business, leaders enact coaching in their conversations throughout the day. A typical day may require a leader to navigate various conversations and respond nimbly with coaching. For example, in a team huddle, leaders may take on the goal of motivating and inspiring employees to achieve objectives by sharing recent successes and future plans. In management meetings, leaders may encounter conflict thoughtfully and professionally, asking questions to discern key issues and needs.

Madison says it this way: "Coaches in the office do not teach accountants how to balance ledger books [nor] sectaries how to use letterheads. No. Rather, they have a way of beginning an informal conversation with employees" where everyone gets on the same page regarding "prevailing challenges."[14] Conversation is the means of constructing strategic action. Phil Dixon reiterates: "Probably my best quality as a coach is that I ask a lot of challenging questions and let the person come up with the answer."[15]

As coaches, leaders use language to calibrate team and individual performance. To inspire confidence in employees, leaders may coach with positive reinforcement, focusing on effort and progress rather than on what went wrong in the past. To help bring over-confident employees back down to earth, leaders may coach awareness surrounding transforming perceived arrogance into a team player attitude. As part of coaching, leaders need to share bad news. The goal in this situation is to "communicate with the objective of guidance" and language is key to this messaging. Helpful words for framing bad news may include "visibility," "perspective," "share," and "opportunity."[16]

David Gurteen defines Conversational Leadership as "appreciating the extraordinary but underutilized power of conversation, recognizing that we can all lead, and adopting a conversational approach to the way in which we live and work together in an increasingly complex world."[17]

Two Models: GROW and Communication Loops

This section covers two useful models for coaching: GROW and Communication Loops. We describe the steps of each model and provide practical information about implementing them. Finally, this section concludes with a discussion of the role of attention.

A. GROW Model for Nondirective Coaching

One model for nondirective coaching helps managers draw wisdom, insight, and creativity out of the people they're coaching. It is built on listening, questioning, and withholding judgment. The goal of this energizing method is to help employees build skills for resolving problems and addressing challenging situations independently. Although this is a simple model, it can be challenging to implement because most managers naturally prefer to give direction rather than to ask questions. Further, implementing this model invites leaders to reassess their role and value in conversations. The four steps are: 1) Goal, 2) Reality, 3) Options, and 4) Will.[18] To envision these steps, consider a leader having a coaching conversation with an employee.

G: Goal

At the outset of the conversation, this model asks a leader to establish with an employee what that individual wants to accomplish during the conversation. Rather than articulating goals for a project or role, the employee must zoom in and articulate what he or she wants to take away from this conversation. Because employees may not articulate this naturally, leaders should support them using questions like: "What would be most helpful to you in this conversation? Is there something you're looking to take out the door with you that you don't have or know already?"

R: Reality

After establishing a goal for the conversation, the leader-coach should ask specific, fact-based questions that help the rubber meet the road. What information do we need? What are we missing? What have you already thought of? These questions may include *what, when, where,* and whom to invite employees to engage with the problem in a new way. This model recommends that leaders don't need to ask *why* because asking why demands that people explore reasons and motivations rather than facts, and this can carry overtones of judgment or trigger self-justification, both of which can be counterproductive. The leader's job "is to just raise the right questions and then get out of the way."[19]

O: Options

During the conversation, a leader may notice that the employee feels stuck, or is debating between two options that present a false juxtaposition. Because there's rarely only one or two real options to approaching a situation, leaders can help employees broaden and deepen their thought processes. Harvard Business Review suggests a simple question to explore options: "If you had a magic wand, what would you do?" This question can be freeing and can spark fresh, productive thinking. Then, instead of evaluating options, leader-coaches using the GROW model help employees explore the various angles, upsides, and risks related to viable options.

W: Will

As the conversation concludes, leaders can ask two questions using the word "will." First, to encourage the employee to re-cap the action plan, a leader may ask, "So, at this point, what will you do?" If the employee's answer isn't clear or doesn't match the leader's understanding of the conversation, then the leader can cycle back through the steps to help define the plan more clearly.

Second, to assess the employee's motivation, a leader could ask, "On a scale of 1-10, how likely is it that you will do this plan?" Harvard Business Review suggests that if the employee answers between 8 and 10, then he or she will likely follow through on the defined plan. However, if the employee predicts less than 7, then the leader may want to go back through the steps to help create a more actionable solution. Gordon Dryden teaches that "people will exceed targets they set themselves."[20]

B. Five-Step Coaching Communication Loop

In many arenas, coaching often works via a loop of communication, practice, and feedback. For example, Nick Winkleman, Ph.D., describes five stages of this loop,[21] including:

- Describe
- Demonstrate
- Cue
- Do
- Debrief

To illustrate the process, we will describe each of the phases of this loop using two examples—one from athletics and one from business. This should help clarify and spark your insight as a leader in implementing this coaching communication loop with your teams.

Describe: "Here's what I want."
In the first phase of this step, coaches describe the activity in detail. For example, they might explain the specific steps of the process and what occurs at each step. They might provide overviews and rationale to help coachees formulate the picture in their minds. For simple tasks, this description phase might be quite short.

Athletics Example
When describing a skill to a soccer/futbol athlete, a coach might say something like: "I want you to strike the ball below its midline to lift it because that contact point will help the ball arc higher into the air. Be sure you are behind the ball, not over it, and lean back."

Business Example

In the realm of business, perhaps a manager would describe a skill improvement for a salesperson: "When you're getting to this point in the sales process, I'd like you to spend more time assessing the customer's interests using open-ended questions. The more you know about the person, the more you can tailor the sales presentation later to exactly what they need."

Demonstrate: *"You do it like this."*

To help the coaching description stick, the coach moves into phase two by demonstrating the activity. A demonstration can provide critical information that reinforces the description because it shows the person how to do what the coach has asked. In other words, if the description teaches the *what*, then the demonstration teaches the *how*. Depending on what the coach wants the coachee to do, the coach may demonstrate the activity physically.

Athletics Example

Demonstration makes sense in an environment of athletics because a coach can show the player how to perform the move or drill. "Look at my foot placement: when you step up to the ball, lock your ankle down and use the instep to strike the ball. Try it."

Business Example

Demonstration is also important in the business world because a leader might show a manager how to use open-ended questions effectively. As the coach demonstrates the desired skill, he or she can show nuances that simple description misses. For example, the leader may show the salesperson: "Here's what I do. I ask open-ended questions like, 'Tell me more.' Or, 'How did you get interested in that?' Then, when the person tells me information, I respond with another validating and open-ended question like, 'Wow, I hadn't thought of that. How long have you been using that strategy?' This invites the person to share more and it shows that I am interested in what they are saying. Our shared interest builds trust and reinforces our relationship throughout the sales process."

Cue: *"Consider your position relative to the things around you."*

The cueing phase begins as the coach provides brief phrases and ideas to focus the coachee on certain aspects of the skill. This cueing enables extra explanation and demonstration where needed to ensure that the coachee understood the coach's description of what the coach wants to see happen. Experienced leader-coaches harness the difference between internal-focused cues and external-focused cues to generate best results. External-focused cues highlight the objects and things around the body and nearby, such as a ball, goal, person, or table. Internal-focused cues turn attention to what happens inside the body, such as breath, posture, and mindset.

Athletics Example
For example, in soccer, the coach may cue simply after demonstrating, saying: "Strike the ball toward the target as if passing to another player." [External cue] "Feel your leg extend completely as you strike." [Internal cue]

Business Example
In business, the coach might say, "What open-ended questions do you like to use during the sales process when you're sitting at the table with a client?" [External cue] "Have you considered nodding your head and smiling as you listen to the answers?" [Internal cue]

Do: *"Your turn. Try it ten times."*
After the coach invests time describing, demonstrating, and cueing to refine understanding, the coachee is ready to try out the skill. In the "do" phase, the coachee focuses on the skill and performs the activity. Because new skills and refinements take time to implement successfully, the "do" phase may extend to several iterations of the activity.

Athletics Example
When the coach turns the athlete loose, it's time to take cover because balls will be flying. At this point, the player tries to implement the exact foot positioning that the coach described. Several tries can be helpful because conditions change during a dynamic game and the exact thing that the coach described may not materialize on every iteration. Further, some kicks go perfectly and others go wild, so it takes some 'doing' to build up consistency.

Business Example
The same is true in business. As the salesman begins implementing the manager's suggestions for open-ended questions, he or she may need

several times through the sales process to begin to see improvements. The salesman might role play with a colleague (or with the manager), but then, when it's the real deal with customers who will either buy or walk away, the salesperson can try out his or her new technique, see what works, and implement the manager's suggestions. Like dynamic athletics, conditions in sales are ever changing: the customer's preferences and even the product condition can all make a difference in a salesperson's ability to close a sale.

Debrief: "That was great. Here's some feedback to help you improve."
Finally, the coaching communication loop closes with feedback. Here, the coach and coachee reconnect to assess the process and results. This phase involves sharing openly, listening patiently, answering questions, and providing further refinements. In all reality, the debrief phase may become a new "describe" phase to kick off the next coaching communication loop.

Athletics Example
After the soccer player has practiced the new kicking technique several times with the coach watching, the coach may call the player over and provide feedback like, "Nice job! I noticed that you worked on doing exactly what I asked with the ankle position. How did you feel about it? I saw that sometimes it worked like we thought but other times things didn't quite go according to plan. What do you think made the difference? Here are my thoughts going forward . . ." Former UCLA basketball coach John Wooden notes: "A good coach can change a game. A great coach can change a life."[22]

Business Example
After the salesperson has practiced implementing the refined open-ended question technique, the manager might provide critical and improvement-oriented debrief feedback like, "I overheard you ask three open-ended questions and follow-up questions during your last sales meeting. How did that go for you? Did you notice a difference from the way you were doing it beforehand? Well, here's what I observed: I saw that this element improved, but I think there's still a little more room to grow on that element. Here's what I suggest we try next . . ."

During the debrief, coaches and coachees recognize success, open the door for whatever else needs to be said, and determine how to move forward. No matter how good a person's technique is currently, there is always room for improvement. Throughout this communication loop, perhaps the most helpful characteristic that coaches can demonstrate is genuine listening and curiosity.

Understanding the Role of Attention

Employees can only learn from the experiences and information that they pay attention to; thus, the leader-coach's first responsibility is to capture, keep, and direct attention. Although multitasking is a popular concept, attention has a limited capacity because our human brains can only pay attention to one thing at a time. Multitasking is about switching rapidly from thing to thing, but it doesn't change that our attention can only focus on one task at a time. Therefore, good coaches help guide employees' "attentional investments"[23] by providing a single focus point at a time.

For example, in the realm of golf, coaches often provide golfers with one "swing thought"—or one specific element of the swing that the golfer tries to focus on while hitting a shot. Often, swing thoughts take the form of metaphors that lead the brain and muscles into executing specific actions. A swing thought might be as simple as "arms straight," "belt buckle facing the target," or "head down; eyes on the ball." Or, it might be more complex, like "club face open on the backswing," or "weight in the back heel on the backswing." If a golfer tries to hold in mind more than one thought per swing, he or she won't be able to implement many of those things because the swing is over so quickly. These minor adjustments help golfers return to the basics, correct specific errors, or develop core elements. With time, attention to a single swing thought can dramatically improve the golfer's game overall.

Similarly, in business, the most effective coaching enables employees to take a single-minded approach and focus on improving one concept at a time. Note that those moments in time can be quick—a golf swing is over in seconds and the golfer could hold a different swing thought in mind for the next swing. Employees may focus on one 'sales thought' per sales contact, such as using open-ended questions, and then may focus on a different thought/technique during the next sales contact. The point is that leader-coaches can direct employees' attention to the best investments and adjustments. Practicing small, specific, and even minor corrections over time can make a tangible difference in the employee's overall 'sales game' or ability to succeed.

Ten Tips for Improving Leadership Coaching Skills

Here are ten tips to help business leaders improve their coaching skills:

1. Generate insight. By helping employees seek out discoveries, managers boost employee engagement and harness new creativity that can benefit the entire organization. Whenever you encounter conscious or unconscious limiting beliefs—such that something is 'impossible'—look to create a new vantage point and possibility. Doing so generates both innovation and commitment.

2. Notice micromanagement and question it. If you hear yourself directing the details of a situation where the employee could generate his or her path, get quiet and listen. Sometimes driving the details is important, but sometimes it slows down the entire machine. As a specific measurement, if you find yourself doing more than 50% of the talking in a conversation, ask yourself whether you might be micromanaging the details.

3. Listen for understanding. Employees who feel like their voices are heard "are 4.6 times more likely to feel empowered to do their best work."[24] When you are listening, it's natural to form judgments, but try to set those judgments on the shelf while you are listening so that you can hear more deeply. Effective coaches listen for understanding because hearing other viewpoints can build a sense of shared perspective, and thereby improve collaboration and efficiency in teams.

4. Trade constructive criticism for safety where feasible. Forbes notes: "Coaches realize what managers don't: there's no such thing as constructive criticism. The only thing that criticism constructs is defensiveness."[25] Often, managers invite

employees to share openly, and then managers respond with constructive critique. However, what managers lose in that moment is an atmosphere of safety. How would teams transform if they knew that they could say and explore any idea without fear of retribution, criticism, or correction? Would that transform relationships over time? In creating an environment of safety, manager-coaches empower employees and foster creativity. John Wooden notes that a good coach "is someone who can give correction without inspiring resentment."[26] The coach-coachee relationship must rest on a foundation of trust so the coaching dialogue can take place productively and positively.

5. Measure everything. Robert Kistner advises leaders, "Measure, measure, measure everything you do every day, everything you can. The more you measure, the more you accomplish. Measure it so you can correct it." Coaches instinctively measure skills so that they can assess baselines and progress. As leaders measure their employees' progress, they can celebrate specific achievements and they can focus on areas that need more support.

6. Model enthusiasm for learning. As leaders walk the talk, they build momentum and set an example for employees who are likely to mimic the behavior of those who are higher up in the company. Robert Kistner describes leadership by engagement: "In your career path, you create enthusiasm. That's been the biggest key to our success over the years."[27] When leaders take on an attitude of constant learning, they invite the people they manage to do similarly.

7. Set a groundwork of positivity. People achieve more when they're in a positive state psychologically and physically. When leaders hear employees describe problems, they often drill into details and respond with advice or solutions, rather than with compassion. This can trigger stress rather than invite progress. The best tool for helping employees get into the right mindset is to coach with compassion—showing care and curiosity.[28]

8. Try "humble inquiry." At a fundamental level, leadership coaching is about helping employees develop their ideal versions of themselves in their roles—bringing their values and passions to their work every day. As leaders set aside their biases, assumptions, and experiences to simply listen and convey empathy, they demonstrate "humble inquiry."[29] And this is what will motivate employees to change and grow far more than will pushing or directing. Directive leadership motivates compliance, whereas humble inquiry motivates growth.

9. Choose the best people. If you have control over hiring, choose the people who will engage in training and come away with motivation. Robert Kistner's advice for leaders is something he follows in his organization: "'HTM:' Hire, train, and motivate. We're hiring the right people to do the right job and we're giving them the tools to do the job. We're going to motivate those people."[30] Leadership coaching creates the necessary motivation.

10. Take responsibility. Given today's rapidly evolving business environment, leadership coaching skills are urgently needed. Kistner encourages leaders to take responsibility for making this happen each day: "There is no tomorrow. If it needs to be done, it needs to be done now. I get up every morning somewhere between 4 and 4:15 AM. I walk into the bathroom and the first thing I do is look in the mirror and say to myself, 'I am responsible. Anything that's going to happen is going to happen because you went out and made it happen. Do it now.'"[31]

Growth Creates Opportunities

With business industries constantly in flux, successful executives supplement their "industry and functional expertise with a general capacity for learning—and they must develop that capacity in the people they supervise."[32] Beyond simply directing the troops and rewarding obedience, today's managers "need to reinvent themselves as coaches whose job it is to draw energy, creativity, and learning out of the people with whom they work."[33] Each day in leadership is a process of developing self and others, and Robert Kistner reiterates: "As you keep growing, you keep creating opportunities."[34]

Extrinsic vs. Intrinsic Motivation

According to Chief Learning Officer Magazine, the "top desired skill for front-line managers is coaching."[35] There are several key differences between managing and coaching. For example, where managing may provide directions or directive motivation by telling people what needs to be done, coaching sparks intrinsic motivation. This means "inspiring the self-directed willingness to try new things and make new discoveries."[36]

In other words, under directive management, employees must ask for permission or direction regarding every step, which limits efficiency overall. However, when managers take on more of a coaching style, they collaborate with and empower team members to harness their resourcefulness and insight to resolve problems. Instead of directing the processes, procedures, or tasks, the "coach asks the employee to self-identify and self-direct toward what's missing. The idea is to make the unconscious conscious, as the employee discovers blind spots and opportunities."[37] With a coaching agenda, leaders inspire insight that creates behavioral change. And there's a substantial payoff: statistics regarding job commitment and satisfaction show that "when employees find greater intrinsic motivation, they are 32% more committed to their work and 46% more satisfied with their jobs."[38]

While directing employees is "a necessary part of the chain of command" in an organization, breaking "that chain doesn't create anarchy or disaster. It creates greater freedom for the leader and greater empowerment for the employee."[39] When done well, leader-coaches motivate employees to change behavior from the inside, which is the most powerful place to focus attention and drive results. Week by week, day by day, leaders help employees stay focused.[40] This style of coaching interaction ensures that "team members know they are working with you, not for you."[41]

Seek Out Coachable Moments

Contrary to traditional management of pushing, leading, or even guiding, coaches "help" employees through the process of intentional change. Instead of telling employees what to do, leaders ask questions, listen, offer compassion, explore individual vision, and build a caring relationship. Instead of coaching solely for career advancement, leaders who center their coaching on a vision of a positive future help employees feel happier, express higher aspirations, and are willing to exert more effort in pursuing goals.[42]

As a leader, "Your asset is your time. You only have so many hours a day. Using your time in your areas of opportunity is huge."[43] Look for "coachable moments," wherein people realize that they need to shift gears. Maybe they're facing a challenge, a significant project, or even a promotion and they realize that they need support in the face of this wake-up call. As leaders help employees spot specific learning opportunities, they can then help employees envision the ideal results, explore options, fill gaps, and develop an agenda. Brian Cagneey said: "Coaches are aware of how to ignite passion and motivate people. They have an energy that is contagious."[44] Coaching is the way that leaders empower employees and build their confidence.

Even in these challenging times, leaders can step up to the task and know that their actions can make all the difference. Brian Tracy says, "You have within you right now everything you need to deal with whatever the world can throw at you."[45] More than ever, now is the time for consistent, hope-building, skill-growing coaching from business leaders.

Key Takeaways

In conclusion, when leaders take on the role of coaches, they generate motivation in employees. Synonymous with the desire to accomplish, real motivation only comes from one place: inside. Thus, leaders who are successful at changing behavior focus attention on internal motivators. Robert Kistner echoes: "Leadership happens by objectives and results, not by assumptions or simply filling space."[46] It's critical for leaders to show the way with their behavior and commitment— Don McGannon reiterates: "Leadership is not a position or a title; it's an action and example."[47]

2

Accountability and Measuring Results

The word "accountability" often evokes a grimace in the workplace—from managers and employees alike. Harvard Business Review notes: "Fewer words in corporate vernacular induce a tighter wince than 'accountability,' and for good reason. Companies and leaders have grappled with what it is and how to achieve it effectively for decades."[48] Research indicates that a high percentage of managers believe they are limited in their abilities to successfully hold their teams and employees accountable even though accountability is one of the top leadership needs in any thriving company.

Further, Gallup found that employees often feel their accountability is managed in a way that doesn't motivate top performance—many indicate they receive feedback less than once per year and don't feel that their performance metrics are within their control.[49]

At a fundamental level, accountability is the glue that links employees together as teams, and teams at all levels together as a thriving company. It cements relationships at all levels of an organization, both internal and external, and it is the driving force behind achieving results. Leaders are accountable to those they manage, as well as to their bosses and the company's shareholders. Employees are accountable to their leaders, as well as to their colleagues and teams. To improve business results, leaders must shift the way they think about and manage accountability.

Chapter Roadmap

This chapter is divided into two sections: 1) boosting business performance via accountability and honoring your word, and 2) targeting specific results based on harnessing a data-driven approach to measuring what matters. First, we'll define accountability as taking responsibility for honoring our commitments, and creating an environment for others to honor their commitments—thereby enabling them to deliver what they said they would do when they said they would do it. We'll discuss how honoring your word as a leader includes two functional actions, and how it impacts workability. We suggest here that as leaders honor their word, they increase personal and company performance and thus boost desirable results as defined by the company vision.

Second, using a metaphor of the evolution in American baseball recruiting techniques, we'll analyze how leaders can articulate specific, attainable results. Our focus will be on the idea that *the way that* leaders clarify their aims enables them to achieve better results. Finally, we will analyze the means of effective measurement, including utilizing data as the means for driving both measurement techniques and key results.

Boosting Performance Via Accountability and Honoring Your Word

Accountability in Business Increases Performance

In the realm of business, there is a direct correlation between improving performance and honoring your commitments. Leaders make commitments by giving and keeping their word. Research by Michael Jensen of the Harvard Business School shows that keeping your word is a "necessary condition for workability"[50]—for creating opportunity and boosting performance at all levels of the company. Honoring your word serves as the foundation for trust because employees and managers alike can rely on you to do what you said you'd do by the time you said you'd do it.

Any discussion of accountability prompts us to consider its opposite: lack of accountability. Does it matter if company leaders give their word and don't follow through? What if nobody is hurt? Does performance suffer if leaders perform a cost-benefit analysis before keeping their word? We will look at this in more detail below but suffice it to say that lack of positive accountability creates small cracks—often unseen given the overall perspective—that weaken the systems and relationships in a company over time. For example, such actions and decisions limit a team's ability to function as intended and limit a customer's ability to rely on the company.

Structural Integrity Increases Performance

Imagine for a moment the weight-bearing frame of a suspension bridge, which is responsible for holding up the entire structure. It can only perform as intended when all the pieces are in place and are balanced, right? In whole, perfect condition, the bridge can bear the weight of all anticipated auto traffic and pedestrians without falling or buckling. When the bridge engineering structure is soundly designed and constructed, it works perfectly and provides safe transit.

However, if cracks develop in the structure, the entire bridge may stand but its performance becomes subject to risk. Imagine if one length of the suspension cable broke. While the entire bridge may not fall, the performance of the bridge would be compromised. It might be able to carry some of the anticipated traffic, but not all. It might begin to buckle. Secondary problems might develop as a result, such as more cracks or fissures in the structure.

Over time, the bridge would struggle to hold its own frame, let alone the weight of the vehicles and people traveling over it. Invariably, unless structural repairs restore the bridge to sound condition and wholeness, the bridge will likely fail under stresses that it had been designed to withstand in unimpaired condition, such as high winds, cold snow and ice, hot summer heat expansion, etc. And if the bridge falls while cars or people are on it, human tragedy could result. In sum, structural integrity balances all forces and directly impacts the performance of the bridge.

Team Integrity Increases Performance

In the workplace, a 'whole and complete bridge' is analogous to a team where all members honor their word. We will discuss more what honoring one's word involves as we go on, but for now, consider how an environment of positive accountability automatically fosters trust. Colleagues know that they can rely on each other to do what they commit to do by the agreed-upon timeframes. This invisible trust forms the weight-bearing structure of the team, allowing them to lean on each other, get critical work done, and meet deadlines. Can you imagine how such an environment increases the performance of the team as a whole? Like a bridge in sound condition, this team is not subject to the emotional fissures of missed expectations, miscommunications, and let-down frustrations. They can work together for their intended purpose—safely and effectively carrying projects from start to finish.

Now, you're probably thinking something like: "Never in the history of my company have I seen a so-called 'perfect' team," but perfection is not the point. Humans are imperfect by nature. But they can perfectly honor their word to each other by keeping their word, by letting people know when they won't be keeping their word, and by picking up the pieces when they let others down. This restores balance to the team and maintains it in good working condition over time.

Accountability is Directly Linked to Results

This discussion of accountability and honoring our word is not a sermon on morality. We're not advocating here that leaders should honor their word because it's the 'right' thing to do or because it serves the greater 'good.' Instead, we are saying that leaders should honor their word because doing so improves performance. Period. A bridge in working condition performs better than a bridge with cracks in it. A team that honors their word to each other performs better than a team with miscommunications and unmet expectations. Period.

Now, honoring our word may well be a good and moral thing for leaders to do, but—in business terms—leaders are accountable for producing results. And improving performance improves results. Along these lines, Brian Tracy notes, "Just as your car runs more smoothly and requires less energy to go faster and farther when the wheels are in perfect alignment, you perform better when your thoughts, feelings, emotions, goals, and values are in balance."[51]

Here's How: Two Parts to Honoring Our Word

With that in mind, let's look at what it takes for leaders to honor their word. We propose honoring our word has two parts:

1. First, honoring our word means simply *keeping* our word. Do what we promised when we promised to do it. Unfortunately, since we don't live in a perfect world, it's not always possible to keep our word, so we have part two below.

2. Second, honoring our word means that when we cannot keep our word, we promptly tell the people who will be affected, acknowledge the impact they will experience because of this failure, clean up the mess, and make a new agreement with them for when we will keep our word.

Below, we will unpack what these two actions involve, and we propose that workability increases as leaders follow these actions.

Openly Acknowledging a Failure to Keep Our Word Engenders Trust

Although this may sound strange at the outset, employees benefit when leaders *honor* their word, even when they can't *keep* their word. For example, when we give our word to deliver a certain outcome but we realize after a while that we will not be able to deliver that outcome, we can preserve employees' trust by openly acknowledging that disparity. In such an acknowledgment, we should clearly state our view of the impact it has on the employees and the company, and then recommit to a new outcome.

For example, if we agreed to provide a document to our team by Tuesday at 5 PM but we realize on Monday that we will not be able to meet that deadline (preferably because of circumstances beyond our control), we could say in an email or call, "Team, I know that you are expecting me to deliver this document by Tuesday at 5 PM. At this point, because of an emergency project that came up on Monday and took priority over this document, I won't be able to meet the delivery timeframe that I had promised. I acknowledge that this means we will experience a delay in our bid process because you're waiting for the document I am to provide. I apologize for this delay and I'll take it upon myself to reach out to the customer to let them know about this so that you don't have to do so. At this point, I recommit to delivering the document to you by Wednesday at 3 PM and I foresee that this will only create a minimal delay with the overall project. Thank you for your understanding."

Can you see how such communication promotes open dialogue among leaders and teams, and re-establishes trust even when prior deadlines change? Put simply, honoring our word is accepting openly that we gave our word and didn't keep it, recognizing the impact this had on those involved, and giving our word to a new agreement that we will keep. Brian Tracy declares, "Trust is the lubricant of human relationships."[52]

Cleaning Up the Mess Engenders Trust

In the workplace, there can be huge 'messes' whenever leaders don't follow through on their commitments or honor their word. Leaders make mistakes and timeframes regularly change—it's the nature of having a high-profile job and trying to accomplish ambitious goals amid the shifting tides of economic conditions, public opinion, and even pandemics. Yet, when leaders are unable to deliver on outcomes they promised, trust is broken with employees and clients, deadlines are missed, and often employees must do more work to help clean up the mess.

In such situations, leaders have a few options when addressing a 'mess' in the workplace. Some prefer to ignore the mess, choosing denial as their happy place. Others try to cover it up, pretending there is no problem or that anyone who thinks there is a problem is mistaken. Others prefer to shirk responsibility, acknowledging that there is a problem but blaming other people or conditions for the problem. The leaders who are most effective when problems occur do not ignore, deny, cover up, or shirk responsibility for the mess; they openly and honestly state the problem and take responsibility for cleaning it up. They acknowledge the impact of the problem on those affected, and they recommit to their employees, clients, and all involved in creating a desirable outcome in the future.

By doing this, leaders 'honor their word' even when they didn't 'keep their word,' and they engender trust[53] internally in their organizations as well as externally with other businesses and clients. Brian Tracy says, "Your ability and willingness to discipline yourself to accept personal responsibility for your life are essential to happiness, health, success, achievement, and personal leadership. Accepting responsibility is one of the hardest of all disciplines, but without it, no success is possible."[54]

What is Your Word?

Because giving your word is the essence of being accountable, let's dive deeper into what is specifically involved when you give your word. Another way to think of 'your word' is anything you are responsible for delivering—or, in other words, what others expect you to deliver. Relying on Jensen's[55] research with Harvard, we find it helpful to define your 'word' in three parts. It includes:

1. *What you said you'd do.* Leaders are responsible for delivering anything they said they will or won't do. These are things that leaders deliberately, expressly, and openly state they will do. Note also that timeframes are inherent in your word: if you said you would do something by Friday but you don't do it until the following Monday, then even if you do the thing on Monday, you did not keep your word as you gave it.

2. *What you know you should do.* Leaders are on the hook for doing what they know they should do, and for doing it the way it was meant to be done—on time. Because leaders are also responsible for doing what they know they should do in the way that they know it should be done, this means that not only are people relying on what you promised, but they have an expectation for how you will deliver it. In colloquial terms, we might shorten this to: 'half-as* jobs don't cut it.'

3. *What society or the company expects you to do.* Leaders are on the hook for doing what others expect them to do, even if leaders never directly said they would do it. This includes following social/moral standards, laws, and community ethical standards, as well as acceptable associated timeframes. Countless examples are highlighted in the news of leaders being crucified for transgressing social standards even when they never gave their word to keep those specific standards. Such standards are simply expected of leaders and those standards are thus integrally part of 'your word' as a leader.

Failing to Honor Your Word Decreases Performance

Leaders can fail to keep their word in small ways and big ways, but the results are ultimately the same: erosion of trust and diminished performance overall. Regarding integrity in finance, Peter Forstmoser[56] presented several of the following ideas to the Swiss Banking Institute:

- *Big.* Examples of 'big' failures to keep your word include stealing from the company, falsifying expense reports, violating negotiated agreements, cheating on taxes, lying to shareholders, falsifying reports, engaging in insider trading, committing fraud, and so on.
- *Small.* Examples of 'small' failures to keep your word include failing to attend meetings or return calls when promised, or arriving later than promised.

Regarding impact on overall performance, it's easy to see how 'big' failures to keep our word cause big messes, but even 'small' failures reduce the workability and performance of a team or company because people cannot rely on each other to show up, let alone to deliver good work. Regardless of whether the effects of honoring our word are visible or invisible, they are critical to maximizing production and quality of workplace life. Ralph Waldo Emerson's words apply to this topic: "What you do speaks so loudly that I cannot hear a word you say."[57] Brian Tracy notes, "There is a direct link between self-discipline and self-esteem. Each time you discipline yourself to do what you should do, when you should do it, whether you feel like it or not, your self-esteem increases."[58]

Why People Fail to Honor Their Word

Although leaders implicitly give their word to upholding corporate ethics by virtue of their role in companies, leaders often justify unethical behavior as a means of generating desired results. Some leaders may errantly rationalize: Everyone is padding their expense reports a bit, so what's the worry? We've always reported our financial statements that way. It's how business works; doing it by the rulebook is too expensive. If we don't take advantage of this, we won't be able to deliver to the shareholders the prices they want. Nobody is going to notice or be hurt. The ends justify the means.

Think of the scandals created by leaders failing to honor their word with such rationale. Integrity is the source for building and maintaining a firm's most valuable asset: its reputation.[59] Warren Buffet says: "Lose money for the firm and I will be understanding; lose a shred of reputation for the firm, and I will be ruthless."[60] Brian Tracy adds, "Only your actions tell you—and others—what you truly value."[61]

If honoring our commitments as leaders is critical to the company's internal culture and society-wide reputation, why are we so often willing to be out of integrity with our commitments? Sometimes, it's about doing what's easy or what seemingly 'needs' to be done to achieve a desirable result.

Other times, it's about not being aware of what we're doing or deceiving ourselves because the failure seems 'not too bad' or 'not a big deal' in the context of the company. Quite often, leaders are motivated by fear of what could occur if they acknowledge that they haven't kept their word. Brian Tracy adds, "The habit of taking the easy way, doing what is fun and enjoyable, or eating dessert before dinner becomes stronger and stronger, and it leads inevitably to personal weakness, underachievement, and failure."[62]

Where a Cost-Benefit Analysis Is Most Helpful

What it comes down to is this: it's impossible to be accountable for results if we are not willing to perform a cost-benefit analysis in conjunction with honoring our word. As business leaders, we rely on cost-benefit analyses every day, so why couldn't it be helpful in this case? It turns out that we do need to use a cost-benefit analysis regarding our word, but the timing makes all the difference. Here's what we mean: our careful cost-benefit analysis should occur at the outset *before* we *give* our word, not *later* when it's time to *keep* our word.

Put another way, we should carefully consider whether we can or should commit, not whether we will deliver what we already committed to delivering. The difference in timing has everything to do with consistency, reliability, trust, and—yes—results. Elbert Hubbard reiterates the importance of cultivating "the ability to do what you should do, when you should do it, whether you feel like it or not."[63]

Targeting Specific Results Based on Measuring What Matters

In the 2011 nonfiction film "Moneyball," Brad Pitt portrays Billy Beane, general manager of the Oakland Athletics baseball team. Beane's team had experienced repeated losses, and he was given only a limited budget to build a competitive team for the 2002 season. The process of selecting and drafting players traditionally sat in the hands of experienced talent scouts, who relied heavily on their intuition about various players' abilities regarding hits, power, and throws. Ironically, scouts even assigned merit to the subjective metric of 'who looked the role' and who didn't, as though looks could impact performance.

Beane knew he needed to take a different approach to building a team because he couldn't afford to recruit players who were ranked highly by baseball talent scout metrics. He met Peter Brand, a young Yale graduate who had studied economics and developed a new, data-driven method for assessing player value. Specifically, Brand utilized sabermetrics, which is the empirical analysis of in-game statistics, and he discovered the overlooked importance of one statistic: a player's on-base percentage.

How many times a player would get on base wasn't one of the metrics that talent scouts intuitively felt was worth a lot of money, but Brand found that it was critical to overall 'runs,' which then influenced a team's overall 'wins.' Therefore, using this new, historically undervalued on-base metric, Brand and Beane were able to filter available candidates and 'cheaply' acquire players who had a strong record of getting on base but who were not highly valued by traditional talent scouts.

Although scouts mocked Beane for trusting Brand's data, Beane's method showed its merit as the Oakland As began to win game after game. Following a few refinements to the strategy, like juggling naysayer players and trainers, Beane's team kicked off a winning streak that took them to a record-breaking 20th consecutive win and ultimately the American League West title. That year, Beane received an offer to become the prestigious Red Sox general manager and implement sabermetrics for that team, which would have made him the highest-paid general manager in professional sports history.[64]

What's the key takeaway? By using data to measure what skills were most valuable to real-game performance and results, Brand and Beane transformed the way that American baseball teams recruited players.

Defining Specific, Achievable Results

Set a specific target: such as buying "runs" rather than buying "wins." This example highlights two factors related to performance: defining key desirable results and using data to measure those results. When Billy Beane in "Moneyball" re-defined the result he was seeking, he thereby re-engineered his team's ability to perform. At the outset, it would have been logical for him to prioritize "winning more games" or "hitting more home runs" as the desired result. But simply seeking to win games is too broad a result to be achievable: so many factors influence winning a game that it's hard to leverage and augment any specific factor without more focus.

Instead, by refining his recruiting goal to "buying runs" in terms of drafting players who got on base consistently according to statistics, Beane boosted team win performance significantly. Compared to trusting talent scout intuition, measuring "a player's ability to get on base was a much better predictor of how many runs he would score."[65] Put another way, buying "runs" according to sabermetrics was far more efficient than attempting to buy "wins" by recruiting high-value players per talent scout metrics. Beane's careful definition of key results—"buying runs"—enabled him to achieve a high return on investment financially and practically.

Likewise, in business, leaders must clarify exactly what results they're seeking and how they'll know if they've arrived at those results. "Good business leaders create a vision, articulate the vision, passionately own the vision, and relentlessly drive it to completion,"[66] said Jack Welch. At the outset of each year or period, the company's top minds come together to define the key results they are seeking and then delineate a strategy that will help achieve those results. Robert Kistner notes, "As a leader, I don't have the glory of sitting in a meeting and talking about all the reasons that the situation is not working because the buck stops with me."[67]

How shall leaders define specific results that add value? By analyzing data, trends, and patterns, leaders can articulate desired "SMART" results that are specific, measurable, achievable, relevant, and time-bound:

- *Specific.* Each desired result should be specific, simple, sensible, and significant. Ask: what do we want to accomplish? Why is it important? Which resources and people are involved? Where is it located?

- *Measurable.* Each desired result should be measurable, meaningful, and motivating. Ask: how much? How many? How will I know when it is accomplished? Which milestones are relevant along the way? A component of measurability is organization.

- *Achievable.* Each desired result should be achievable and attainable. Ask: how realistic is this result based on all constraints such as financial factors? What are the key steps?

- *Relevant.* Each desired result should be relevant, reasonable, realistic, resourced, and results based. Ask: why is this worthwhile? Is this the right time? Does this match my other efforts and needs?

- *Time-bound.* Each desired result should be time-bound, time-based, time-limited, timely, and time-sensitive. Ask: What can we do six weeks from now? What can we do six months from now? What can we do today? Brian Tracy advises: "If for some reason you don't achieve your goal by the deadline, simply set a new deadline. There are no unreasonable goals, only unreasonable deadlines."[68]

When all is said and done, results usually have dollars tied to them. Bottom lines are bottom lines for a reason. Business results are measures of the product and operational performance of a business. Results demonstrate the quality and value of products and services that lead to customer satisfaction and customer engagement. But note that desirable results can also be larger than revenues—they might include green planet initiatives, eco-friendly goals, or relationship-enhancement results, such as with employees or with the community. Results could focus on employee retention, growth, and well-being. Or giving back to the community. Such non-monetary results are defined by the company leaders and they define company culture.

Measuring What Matters Drives Results

After results have been defined, measurement is the means of driving results—measurement is informed by data. Mauboussin notes that, like talent scouts, many business executives, in their desire to create value, also "rely on intuition in selecting statistics. The metrics companies use most often to measure, manage, and communicate results . . . include financial measures such as sales growth and earnings per share (EPS) growth in addition to nonfinancial loyalty and product quality."[69] As we noted in our "Moneyball" metaphor, measuring for results—for on-base runs, for example—is far more effective than measuring for fuzzier, notional ideas of what might impact wins.

Unfortunately, time has shown that more intuitive metrics demonstrate "only a loose connection to the objective of creating value."[70] In other words, like old-time baseball talent scouts, executives lean heavily on metrics that don't always predict results. Intuition may be skewed by cognitive biases, such as "the overconfidence bias, the availability heuristic, and the status quo bias."[71] To counter the effect of such biases, which can limit leaders' ability to make effective business decisions, leaders would do well to lean on data.

The Data Quadrant

Some leaders use a data quadrant approach for sorting performance measures into four categories, or intersecting quadrants: quantity, quality, effort, and effect:

- Effort indicates what is done and how well it is done.
- Effect measures the change or impact that resulted.
- Quantity and quality are applied to the relevant effort or effect.

For example, a data quadrant enables leaders to ask: How much did we do? How many customers did we serve? How well did we do it? What activities or services did we perform well? Is anyone better off? What changed for the better regarding skills, attitudes, behavior, or circumstances? What are the factors that are supporting progress and the factors that are hindering progress? What are the root causes or proximate causes that have an impact on progress? Data regarding results helps leaders identify where performance measures are generating positive impact for clients.

To be credible, data must be consistent and reliable. When tapping into data for measurement focus, leaders should look at a historic baseline for least five years, if available. Examining historical data enables leaders to forecast the coming three to five years, assuming no change in the current level of effort. This answers the question, in essence, "Where will we be soon if we continue as we are doing now?" Also, the "alignment of a proposed option with a root cause provides the rationale for selecting that particular option: it is the link between the 'end' (as measured by the indicator or performance measure) and the 'means' (the strategy)."[72]

In addition to using data, leaders should ground their measurement strategies in evidence and research. To obtain maximum measurement leverage, consider what resources the proposed result will require and whether that intended impact will have a strong effect on progress, as compared with the baseline. To foster feasibility as the counterpart to leverage, consider whether the proposed strategy will limit or augment innovation. "Sometimes the consideration of an apparently infeasible option will be the catalyst in the thinking process that leads to a highly creative and feasible option."[73]

After exploring ways to improve feasibility in measurement, leaders should weigh the costs against desired outcomes to select the best option for action. This measurement strategy should be clear in terms of deliverables so that it addresses the relevant who, what, when, where, and how—like the process of defining specific desirable results as we discussed above. Finally, leaders should align the strategy with the core values of the company. Brian Tracy notes, "Leaders concentrate single-mindedly on one thing—the most important thing—and they stay at it until it's complete."[74]

Key Takeaways

Robert Kistner teaches, "We can be doing all this work, but at the end of the day, the numbers talk."[75] Leaders are accountable to their higher-ups to produce results. The company is accountable to its shareholders, if any, or to the ultimate owners to produce results. In his Harvard research, Jensen equates accountability—"honoring your word"—with "integrity" in business. He reiterates the correlation between integrity and performance: "Integrity is important to individuals, groups, organizations, and society because it creates workability. Without integrity, the workability of any object, system, person, group, or organization declines; and as workability declines, the opportunity for performance declines. Therefore, integrity is a necessary condition for maximum performance."[76]

Further, Jensen describes the connection between integrity and trust: "As an added benefit, honoring one's word is also an actionable pathway to being trusted by others."[77] That trust goes a long way toward maintaining reputation and generating results.

Experienced leaders know that accountability is not the same as 'accounting' or 'scorekeeping.' Rather, accountability involves "the formal and informal ways that leaders talk about, assess, and affirm the contributions of those they lead and the improvements they can make to strengthen those contributions."[78] Delivering results can be stressful when there's pressure, but as leaders create clarity about the end goal and utilize a data-informed means of measurement, accountability augments workability, and success rates overall.

In conclusion, to measure what matters most to performance, leaders should focus on data-driven indicators of performance. To produce wins in baseball, teams need runs. To produce sales in business, teams need strong contacts, tireless follow-through, and consistent closing techniques. Leaders are constantly measuring, checking in, and guiding teams and employees to produce the desired day-to-day actions. Measuring what matters most drives results. Welch opines: "A leader's job is to look into the future and see the organization not as it is, but as it should be."[79]

3

Motivating Peak Performance

Captain William Swenson was awarded the Congressional Medal of Honor for his actions on September 8, 2009. On that day, several American and Afghan troops were protecting a group of Afghan government officials who planned to meet with local village elders. Without warning, the group was ambushed—surrounded on three sides.

Captain Swenson was recognized for "running into live fire to rescue the wounded and pull out the dead." [80] One of the medics on the medevac helicopter had a GoPro camera on his helmet and captured the whole scene: Swenson and a comrade carried a wounded soldier who had received a gunshot to the neck. "They put him in the helicopter," Simon Sinek describes, "and then you see Captain Swenson bend over and give him a kiss before he turns around to rescue more. I saw this, and I thought to myself, where do people like that come from? . . . There's a love there." [81]

Simon Sinek is an author and researcher who studies how leaders can inspire trust, cooperation, and change. When he studied military heroes—those who bravely face fire to rescue a wounded compatriot, for example—he asked the hefty question: "Why?" What motivated these soldiers to risk their lives to save the life of someone on their team? From a business lens, that is serious dedication to workplace well-being, if you will.

Not surprisingly, when Sinek interviewed such heroes, none of them mentioned risking their lives to boost troop morale. At the moment that bullets were flying and team members were down, none of these heroes responded to mere duty in risking their lives. None of them even mentioned a self-interest in becoming a decorated war hero. The answer he received was unanimous: "I did it because they would have done it for me."[82]

In the military, people are rewarded for sacrificing themselves for others, but in business, we often see the reverse: people are rewarded when they sacrifice others for their own gain.[83] Thinking of Swenson's dedication to his team, business leaders might wonder why teams at work aren't as bonded and willing to sacrifice for each other. Does the military simply attract people who are willing to sacrifice? Or is there something in the environment that motivates this sort of behavior? Sinek's research showed that the answer lies in the environment.

As leaders set a tone of safety within the team or company, they foster an environment of trust and cooperation that supports strong relationships and productive work. Such an environment motivates people to make sacrifices of self for the well-being of others. For Captain Swenson, that environment of trust and cooperation among his soldiers meant that he risked his life to save others.

Employees in a less-life-threatening line of business might, for example, contribute accrued sick days to another employee who had to get surgery. They might help a co-worker get a promotion even when there's no direct reward for themselves. Or they might simply lift others up rather than putting others down.

Chapter Roadmap

In this chapter, we provide tips that leaders can use to create strong teams and environments that facilitate loyalty, commitment, integration, and success. We will also discuss strategies that leaders can use to motivate employees and teams toward peak performance. Some of these include setting specific and measurable performance standards, building mentoring relationships, and providing recognition.

Just as leaders need to recruit employees into teams, they also need to let team members go when things aren't working. Here, we provide strategies for such reorganization and/or "transparent separation" firing. In sum, this chapter supports leaders in mindfully building strong teams and positive environments, which are critical to both personal and company success.

Building Strong Teams

Recruiting: Getting the Right People

Business leaders are often responsible for drawing together teams to accomplish projects or spearhead campaigns. Leaders may collect talent from within the company or they may recruit new people with critical skills. This section provides tips for selecting and recruiting the best-suited people for your teams. Also, it covers clarifying roles, interviewing candidates, and integrating chosen team members.

Brian Tracy teaches: "Ninety-five percent of your success as a manager resides in your ability to select the right people."[84] It's about finding the right fit and then supporting those you select. Jim Collins, author of *Good to Great*, notes that executives who have transformed companies from good to great "did not first figure out where to drive the bus and then get people to take it there. No, they first got the right people on the bus—and the wrong people off the bus—and then figured out where to drive it."[85]

If business leaders start "who" rather than "what," then the company will be better at adapting to changing times because the problem of "how" to manage people largely goes away. If you don't have the right "who," it doesn't matter what you're trying to accomplish because the people will not identify with the company's core values or vision. The right people, on the other hand, can "get it" so they don't need as much management. Plus, the right people feel a sense of responsibility for achieving desired outcomes.

Hiring is a critical skill for executives that finds application throughout the lifetime of a career. Although your job may not involve hiring people into the company, a similar process applies whether you are selecting an external candidate or an internal candidate as you are building a team.

Clarifying the Role and Seeking Great Candidates

First, you should take time to clarify the role(s) you are trying to fill. What should this person be able to do? What responsibilities will he or she carry? When thinking about a candidate's ideal skills, decide what's essential, what's important, and what's merely a bonus. Are certain attributes, attitudes, or qualities essential? Think about the workload involved and who this person will be interfacing with or teaming up with. What sort of personality will be a good fit in that working environment? Taking a more subjective approach, Spike Jonze says: "I like hiring people based on a feeling—this person gets it—rather than what they've done in the past."[86]

Second, build a strategy for seeking the best candidates. Look carefully inside of your company (and outside, if you are bringing in new talent). Is there someone already in your realm who can fill the space? Who do you know who may know someone? How could you work with recruiters, placement agencies, and print or online ads? Sometimes it helps to think outside the box when looking for people who bring critical skills. For example, perhaps a designer might have key input for a new software systems plan. Perhaps a psychologist could bring the needed edge to your marketing team. Maybe a physicist could apply scientific ways of thinking to the creation of a new product.

Strategies for Interviewing

Third, spend time interviewing. Depending on the importance of the role—such as if he or she will be part of a critical team or leading a high-priority venture—you might choose to meet with the candidate several times or in many different locations. Have a plan for your interview and set expectations. Tell the person about yourself, the company, and the role. What is your gut feeling or intuition about them? Will this person fit in with the corporate environment? Will he or she be happy there? Does he or she seem responsible and positive? Some leaders employ a test to check the fit of personalities, asking: would I enjoy having this person come over to dinner?

Take your time in deciding and ask good questions. Hiring in haste can cost you time, money, and productivity while you let that person go and pay his/her salary while finding a replacement. Ask about past achievements that are proven. What experience qualifies you? What relevant training do you have? Analyze how candidates present themselves in person and on paper. Look for simplicity, honesty, and past performance. Look for motivation and willingness to contribute. Ask others—check references via phone calls and ask about strengths, weaknesses, accomplishments, and "anything else" with the promise of confidentiality.

Brian Tracy teaches that four things make a candidate stand out:[87]

- Achievement or results-oriented
- Intelligent questions
- Willingness to work hard
- Sense of urgency

Integrating the New Person

Finally, when you find the right fit, capitalize on eagerness. Give them plenty to do and even overload them to foster a sense of rising to the challenge. Provide feedback and discussions that match the intensity level of the work. Create a buddy system—link the new person with an experienced coworker and spend time introducing him or her around the company.

In the beginning, willingness and openness are high, while task ability and confidence are low. This early phase is where leaders and the candidates begin to form solid working impressions of each other—as such, this early phase is where support can go a long way toward facilitating positivity and growth. As the new candidates work to meet challenges, try to catch them doing something right and showcase their achievements to the company.

Motivating Peak Performance

Dwight D. Eisenhower said: "Motivation is the art of getting people to do what you want them to do because they want to do it."[88] After collecting the right people, a business leader's task switches to motivation. It's a daily, ongoing effort that is multifaceted: it involves intertwined aspects of performance and relationships.

Leaders motivate top performance by setting clear expectations and measurable standards. They take time to instruct and teach their people, and to provide recognition and rewards for small and large wins. Further, to truly motivate employees, leaders build mentoring relationships grounded in positive communication, listening, encouragement, and understanding. This personal level inspires employees to make great strides, as Captain Swenson did in our introductory story. Performance metrics are key to success, but relationships are the glue that holds people together and invites them to go above and beyond to get the job done. Zig Ziglar made this comparison: "People often say that motivation doesn't last. Well, neither does bathing. That's why we recommend it daily."[89]

Setting Clear Expectations and Measurable Standards

Research shows that one of the key motivators is having clear expectations. When people know what the boss expects, they thrive. Brian Tracy offers: "People want to feel like winners. A key role of the manager is to help them feel like winners. People need clear goals to aim at, or else they feel like losers."[90]

Leaders can set clear expectations by being specific about desired outcomes. Research shows that people report much higher levels of job satisfaction when they feel that they have a clear understanding of what is expected of them. On the other hand, people report low levels of job satisfaction when they struggle to understand what precisely their role involves, or how their performance will be measured. When leaders set clear but challenging expectations, employees are motivated to stretch. And, when they achieve those expectations, they gain positive self-concept and greater autonomy. To the extent possible, allow employees to determine the method and approach they think will be most effective. Then, mutually agree on objectives and schedules, and set workable deadlines.

It helps to set measurable performance standards because what gets measured gets done. Tracy counsels leaders to "Inspect what you expect. Monitor; check; and reassign the person if necessary."[91] By establishing a clear roadmap including measurable checkpoints along the way, leaders support employees in performing well.

Training, Mentoring, and Recognizing

"The average company spends 85 percent of operating costs on payroll and less than one percent on training those people."[92] Continuous training and education are the keys to performance, motivation, enthusiasm, and commitment. Effective business leaders take time to instruct and teach people, thereby helping them grow. A key management responsibility is teaching and training staff to do their jobs.

In this effort, you become a mentor and this attention builds self-esteem. Tracy notes: "The Gallup Organization has conducted research on tens of thousands of employees, and it found that perhaps the most profound issue driving employee engagement is their relationship with their boss."[93] To support employees, leaders must get the tone right: show respect, warmth, and belief in employees' capabilities. Listen patiently and show caring and courtesy.

When employees respond to training and perform well, business leaders and mentors invest time in providing recognition, including tangible and intangible rewards for work well done. A tangible reward might include a lunch celebration, bonus, or extra time off. Intangible rewards might involve reinforcement and public and private praise for a job well done. Celebrate achievement for both large and small wins. "What gets rewarded, gets done."[94]

Inspiring Loyalty and Commitment

To give their all at work, employees and teams need to know why they are doing what they're doing. If leaders define the work in terms of its meaning and significance to others, then teams will understand how what they are doing benefits others and enhances lives. This will instill a sense of meaning and purpose in work, which serves as a powerful motivation tactic. Also, it provides the big picture of why a business is doing what it's doing. An example from Harish Manwani, COO of the global corporation Unilever, illustrates this concept.

Uniting People by Focusing Beyond the Balance Sheet

One day, Manwani visited a small, impoverished village in India, which struggled with low standard of living conditions. He intended to visit a woman who was one of the small distributors for the Unilever company. He stopped by her modest but beautiful home and he joined her as she went out to promote the products and use of soap. Step by step, she made her way through the chaotic living spaces bringing a message of health and a practical action plan for reducing disease.

Two aspects stood out: first, the woman's message was much more expansive than mere soap sales. For example, research has shown that "five million children don't reach the age of five because of simple infections that can be prevented by an act of washing their hands with soap."[95] In this light, selling soap and promoting its use is about saving lives, not just gaining revenues. If the villagers began washing their hands with soap and thereby saved the life of even one child, all the woman's effort would be worthwhile. By acting as a soap distributor, this woman was slowly endeavoring to change the routines and health practices in her community and thus give local children born into poverty a better chance at survival.

Second, this woman's work improved society in another way. As she went about her sales route, the woman's husband followed in the back, as did her mother-in-law and sister-in-law. In a society where men are the traditional leaders and business owners, a woman who is a small business owner is unique. As Unilever supported women in starting and expanding their small businesses related to distribution, the gender gap in business began to shrink. Manwani explains: "The social order was changing because this lady is part of our Project Shakti that is teaching women how to do small business and how to carry the message of nutrition and hygiene. We have 60,000 such women now in India."[96]

Manwani believes that leaders must look beyond the balance sheet and bottom line to include value, purpose, and sustainability in top-level decision making. In his view, this is not just savvy, but it's the only way to run a 21st-century business responsibly. Thus, the woman selling soap in a rural village was not a simple salesperson; rather, she was a catalyst of social change. Her efforts improved the community's health by saving lives and created a tangible economic success model of a woman-led small business in a traditionally patriarchal society.

The key takeaway from this story is that success is enhanced as leaders not only consider financial statements but also inspire their people to change lives. Manwani advises leaders: we must move to a model of "how do we do well (make money) and do good (care for the communities around us)?"[97] (Emphasis added). Companies satisfy shareholders by creating economic value but they satisfy local communities by creating social value that is consistent, competitive, profitable, and responsible.

Cultivating an Environment of Safety and Growth

As teams and new candidates become established within the company or group, leaders should focus on creating an environment of trust and cooperation in the workplace. This harks back to the story of Captain Swenson: he exhibited bravery and sacrifice for his injured squad member because his team had the bonds of trust and cooperation. While his unit's physical environment of a war theater wasn't safe from attack or bullets, the team's emotional commitment to each other made each person feel safe. They knew that they had each other's back no matter what.

One way that leaders can build an environment of safety and cooperation is to behave more like a family than like a company. For example, if you've seen leaders shout and criticize, you've also seen that this undercuts real results because employees who feel emotionally safe will perform better than those who don't. Employees may deliver short-term results motivated by fear of punishment or termination, but they will expend more energy trying to protect themselves than trying to help others. Management by terror does not produce the highest results in the long run.

As another example, in a family, there are no layoffs. Lower performers instead receive coaching, support, and bolstering. Businesses can pull together in hard times to get through as well as possible. Sometimes layoffs are inevitable, but other times, a leader's willingness to think outside the box can create a sense of safety for employees and thus provide a higher return on investment than the layoffs would have accomplished.

A true story illustrates this concept. In 2008, a Midwestern manufacturing company was hit hard by the recession and fully 30 percent of their orders dried up overnight. Bob Chapman, the leader, saw that he could no longer afford his workforce and that he needed to save ten million dollars to save the company.

While many businesses took the route of layoffs, Chapman thought about things differently. Instead of letting people go, he asked his employees to pull together and work with a furlough plan wherein each employee—from secretary to CEO—took four weeks of unpaid vacation. He didn't mandate when and how they took this time, but he presented the plan this way: "It's better that we should all suffer a little than that any of us should have to suffer a lot."[98]

Surprisingly—or not—morale rose. Chapman saw that people began to cooperate because they felt protected by the organization's leadership. For instance, some people who could afford it were willing to take on an extra week of furlough for someone who couldn't, so some employees took five weeks to allow others to take only three. What was the outcome? The company ended up saving 20 million dollars and retaining the loyalty of its employees.[99] By creating an environment where employees feel safe and valued—even in hard times—leaders can motivate peak performance.

Troubleshooting Teams: Reorganizing and/or Firing

Chapman's inspirational story about preserving employees' jobs makes most sense when the critical challenge is externally imposed, like a nationwide emergency or global recession. In such cases, pulling together is often the best option.

However, there are times when the challenges that employees face are more internal, and layoffs or reorganization are the best solutions. While your role may not specifically involve firing, it may involve shuffling out team members who aren't the right fit or dissolving teams altogether. Leaders tap into similar reasoning, preparation, and methods when letting someone go from a position and when re-structuring teams.

Two Critical Problems

Research shows that two main employee problems are difficult or nearly impossible to resolve and may necessitate firing or reorganization. The first is an attitude issue: the employee has lost motivation. Essentially, it's the end of the road for this person in this role. Things are not working, and there seems to be no cure despite significant effort. Sometimes personalities on a team can generate enough friction that the work of the team grinds to a halt. In-fighting undercuts the sense of community and safety, and people must focus on choosing sides rather than focusing on getting the work done. Brian Tracy advises rather directly: "Get rid of difficult people. They poison the attitudinal climate and demotivate others."[100]

The second problem is related but different: the employee is failing because he or she is simply not competent and cannot reasonably deliver on job responsibilities despite support. Sometimes a person can't perform the tasks associated with the role, and all the coaching, training, and mentoring simply hasn't made a measurable difference. In this situation, leaders should try to help improve performance by explaining expectations clearly and being specific about what is not working. Double check for understanding by asking the employee to speak back what he or she has understood. Collaborate to set measurable performance standards and agree where possible on what should be done. Keep private records regarding the discussion. Communicate and provide feedback regularly—deliver improvement-oriented feedback in private and achievement-oriented feedback in public.

If these tactics still don't improve performance, then the leader should take decisive action. Where possible, try putting the employee in a role he or she is better suited for. Both the team and the employee need reorganization and/or release to keep productivity going.

Re-thinking the Hiring Decision

Managers should note that while these two issues are situated with the employee in question, they are also reflective of the supervisor who hired that employee. The employee is not the mistake; rather, their place in that role is the mistake. Somehow, the hiring did not sufficiently assess the then-candidate's motivation, compatibility, or competence. Maybe the decision was made too hastily. Maybe the decision was insufficiently vetted over multiple interviews. Maybe some information surfaced later that had a negative impact. Whatever the ultimate reason, managers can gain long-term return on investment by analyzing the specific scenarios that motivate letting go of employees to avoid repeating similar mistakes in the future.

Techniques for Firing: When It's Time to Let Go

While hiring takes a great deal of energy and preparation, so does firing. When firing appears inevitable, managers should do their homework and prepare sufficient documentation about the situation to support the decision. If it is your role, design in advance a severance package that would suit both the employee and the organization. Such packages are designed to provide a financial cushion between jobs and might include continued health benefits for a time, as well as private outplacement counseling.

Even leaders with a great deal of experience in firing would do well to envision the 'firing interview' scenario and perhaps even role play it with another person in advance. This is a situation that is sensitive and delicate, and leaders will benefit from giving it sufficient emotional attention. Being prepared will help fortify your resolve so that you can carry through quickly and compassionately with what must be done. Know that while firing is stressful, it's essential to the organization's growth—and generally to the employee's growth as well. When the fit isn't right, it isn't right for either the organization or the employee.

Brian Tracy offers several tips leaders can implement when firing:[101]
- <u>Timing</u>: Consider having the firing interview in the morning early in the week—Monday, Tuesday, or Wednesday.
- <u>Location</u>: Pick a non-personal spot, like an empty office or meeting room.
- <u>Method</u>: Tell the person clearly that you're letting the person go because the job is not right for him or her. Speak with kindness: indicate that the person is good and has done good things, but that this is no longer a good fit.
- <u>Manner</u>: Be kind, gentle, empathetic, and firm. Don't hold out false hope. Then leave the room. You could offer the use of an office, desk, or telephone if the separation is amicable, as well as a cover story to protect the person's self-esteem. If the separation is not amicable, insist that the employee leave immediately.

Brian Tracy's tips here correspond with traditional firing methodologies and are especially applicable to problem situations.

However, there is a new process coming into vogue with companies—it's called transparent separation.

Transparent Separation

Harvard Business Review offers an alternative firing procedure called transparent separation,[102] which applies to many termination scenarios (other than large-scale layoffs or where keeping the employee around hurts the organization). It involves having an interview with underperforming employees and encouraging them to look for a new job ASAP because they are going to be let go soon. This approach motivates employees to make the transition on their timing and terms, and it can be a positive conversation rather than a negative one.

Using the transparent separation technique, leaders should avoid ambiguity and clarify that the decision is final. However, you don't need to set a strict departure deadline at first unless employees are lingering, unproductive, or negative. Give them flexibility to leave work during office hours for interviews but remind them that productivity is not allowed to slip during this transition time. Ideally, departing employees should complete their last day around the time that their replacements are recruited.

Why bother with transparent separation? This approach benefits departing employees because it's easier to find a job if they're already employed. Also, it preserves dignity and reputation. This approach benefits managers by improving relationships and bolstering their reputation as compassionate leaders. It also helps smooth out transitions and reduce the legal risk of backlash.

Finally, transparent separation benefits the rest of the employees in the company by reducing overall anxiety. Employees who see colleagues suddenly "disappear" one day often feel higher levels of stress, wondering whether they might also be blindsided by a layoff. Such employees might deliberately avoid even productive types of disagreement with managers and stifle innovation because failure feels risky. However, because transparent separation helps employees feel safe from the threat of unexpected termination, they are "happier, more creative, and less likely to preemptively leave."[103]

Career Patterns

If you need a little more reassurance about firing an employee or assigning them to a different role in the company, consider how new technology developments have an impact on the education and work relationship. Heather McGowan, a future-of-work strategist, notes: "The old model of work was three life blocks: Get an education. Use that education for 40 years. And then retire. We then made the faulty assumption that the next new model should be: Get an education. Use it for 20 years. Then get retrained. Then use that for 20 more years and then retire."[104]

However, now and in the near future, the more successful model will be one of continuous lifelong learning because the pace of change, technology, and business is rapidly accelerating. In fact, "the fastest-growing companies and most resilient workers will be those who learn faster than their competition."[105]

How does this concept apply to firing? While a departing employee may not have been the right fit for his/her role or team, the employee may not be the problem; rather, the hiring selection or specific placement may be the problem. As the employee moves on to learn new skills or moves into different responsibilities, that person will have new chances to flourish. This is consistent with the model of continuous lifelong learning and growth in a career. In short, it's often better for an employee to leave a team or role that doesn't fit well and take time to pursue new training or education. This may open new options that may be a far better fit for his or her capabilities well into the future.

Key Takeaways

Richard Branson of Virgin Atlantic teaches: "Clients do not come first. Employees come first. If you take care of your employees, they will take care of the clients."[106] The military has a similar mantra: "Take care of your people and they will take care of you and the mission."[107] This certainly showed up in Captain Swenson's dedication to his team.

The best and most productive employees invariably feel cared for, respected, rewarded, and secure. Employees work with the highest energy and diligence for managers who have their best interests at heart—who are dedicated to the employee's advancement and development. Conversely, when employees feel that management doesn't sufficiently "have their backs," their loyalty quickly wanes. Forbes advises: "If as a manager you're more concerned with building your empire than with those who are helping you build it, safe to say it will be noticed. Self-interest being a powerful motivator, employees are understandably focused on their careers. After all, as the saying goes, it's the station WIFM (What's In it For Me) that everyone's tuned to, all day every day."[108]

Mindfulness in management builds strong teams—mindful managers invest in employees and reap the benefits of their great work. Your success as a leader will be determined by your ability to elicit extraordinary performance from people, and by your ability to build a winning team by motivating others to give their best toward the achievement of the goals of the organization. Sometimes your team's success will ride on you letting go of certain people at certain times. To the degree to which you are successful at all these tasks, you will be given ever-greater responsibilities and larger organizations to manage and to lead.

In sum: "Leadership is a choice. It is not a rank," says Simon Sinek. "I know many people who are at the bottoms of organizations who have no authority and they are absolutely leaders, and this is because they have chosen to look after the person to the left of them, and . . . to the right of them. This is what a leader is."[109]

4

Inspiring Responsibility

Consider this metaphor: in business, employees spend their days driving a car owned by someone else toward a destination defined by someone else. When employees feel empowered about their jobs, they perceive that they're in the driver's seat for their role—they can push the gas pedal or hit the brakes depending on what they're facing. They actively evaluate the road, choosing one lane over another on the way toward their destination. And as they achieve goals like reaching the destination set out for them, they feel empowered.

Unfortunately, some employees behave as though they are simply passengers in the car—they don't feel they have control over where they are headed. Maybe they don't fully understand the company vision or they don't passionately believe that what they do contributes to the bigger picture. At the end of the day, it's 9-to-5 and a paycheck . . . and that is that. Employees who see themselves in the passenger seat may point fingers to escape negative outcomes. Blaming is a means of shifting responsibility away from themselves; blame puts people further in victim mode and disempowers their ability to act.

Sometimes blaming takes the form of complaining. Wayne Dyer taught: "All blame is a waste of time. No matter how much fault you find with another, and regardless of how much you blame him, it will not change you."[110] Owen Young wrote: "There is a single reason why 99 out of 100 average business [people] never become leaders. That is their unwillingness to pay the price of responsibility . . . the hard driving, continual work . . . the courage to make decisions . . . the scourging honesty of never fooling yourself about yourself."[111]

Taking responsibility is the critical difference between employees who see themselves metaphorically as passengers versus those who see themselves in the driver's seat. Put simply, employees in the driver's seat take ownership of their role and see its importance in the overall company outcomes. As employees embody an attitude of responsibility, they shift themselves to a more powerful energetic position because they are in a space of creation rather than a space of reaction.

Instead of looking for some other person or situation to blame when something goes wrong, employees who see themselves in the driver's seat search for a lesson, possibility, or solution. From the lens of introspection, they ask themselves what role they have played in the challenge and what they can learn. Sir Josiah Stamp said: "It is easy to dodge our responsibilities, but we cannot dodge the consequences of dodging our responsibilities."[112] Seeking growth is a form of self-empowerment, and it doesn't come from blaming others.

Taking responsibility "puts [employees] at cause and not at effect," says Dina Marais, meaning that they realize that they are *creating* and not merely *reacting to* circumstances. Taking responsibility enables employees to "appreciate that things happen *for* [them] and not *to* [them]. Taking responsibility puts [them] at choice and that allows [them] to choose how to respond to life's challenges."[113]

How Leaders Can Help Employees Step into the Driver's Seat

Sometimes employees can spontaneously make this transition into the driver's seat, but sometimes they need a leader's support and example. A story from military history shows how leaders can empower those they lead to take the driver's seat—or the gunner's position, in this case. Years ago, a squad that hadn't encountered much action was carefully clearing a section of buildings.

Suddenly, they came under fire and people scrambled for cover. Immediately, the leader directed the machine gunners to suppress an enemy position in an adjacent building, but one gunner did not engage. The leader again gave the order, and again, the gunner did not engage. Instead of threatening this gunner or removing him, the leader "calmly moved to the gunner's position, took the machine gun, and fired a burst."[114] Then, the leader handed the weapon back and gave the instruction again—and this time, the gunner did not hesitate.

In this high-pressure situation, the leader helped his subordinate step out of victim mode (being fired upon) and into the metaphorical driver's seat (by returning fire as ordered). In the world of business, leaders can support and empower employees who freeze under pressure or who are perhaps unsure how to step into the driver's seat for their roles. This might involve showing the way or providing scaffolding and mentoring as they learn to engage with their tasks as assigned.

One way that leaders can empower employees to take on organizational goals is to provide latitude wherever possible for self-determination. That is consistent with the adage that "involvement leads to commitment." Woodrow Wilson said, "I feel the responsibility of the occasion. Responsibility is proportionate to opportunity."[115]

For example, Robert Kistner suggests that leaders might let employees and teams set their own budgets toward key performance indicators. An advantage of this approach is that it elicits involvement and commitment from employees: if they articulate what they can and will achieve if they receive a certain budget, then they are much more likely to achieve those things. Leaders can utilize self-determination with budgets to build accountability. Enabling employees to propose their budgets puts them in the driver's seat and removes excuses like: 'the company didn't give us enough funding,' or 'the company doesn't have any idea what budget we need to accomplish the key performance areas they are requiring.'

In addition, when employees are one-hundred percent responsible for their budgets regarding key result areas, Robert Kistner suggests leaders can leverage this by saying, essentially, "You told me you could and would achieve these goals with this amount of funding. I provided the funding. How are you doing on the goals?" This approach activates ownership of both budgets and organizational goals. It empowers employees to feel the power of choice and reduces the chance of blaming by removing excuses and justifications.

In other words, empowerment improves attitude because it inspires employees to take the job on themselves. Robert Kistner reiterates the mindset of empowerment: "I have a lot of assets around me to achieve my goals; I just have to implement them properly to achieve my goals."[116] Those attitudes give personal life and accountability to the goals of the organization.

Stephen Covey advised: "Look at the word responsibility—'response-ability'—the ability to choose your response. Highly proactive people . . . do not blame circumstances, conditions, or conditioning for their behavior. Their behavior is a product of conscious choice, based on values, rather than a product of their conditions, based on feeling."[117] Robert Kistner describes how employees who get things done have an attitude of responsibility, such as: "You can rely on me. You can rely on me to help achieve company budgets and to be responsible with company funds. You can rely on me to hit the numbers and targets. I don't spend time justifying why I can't reach those numbers. If there's some external force blocking one route, I'll find another route and keep going."[118]

"Employees with this attitude use organizational goals as a platform to launch into an 'I am responsible' mentality. I must go out and do the job. These are the numbers I must hit and I'm going to hit them no matter what. It's up to me to make it happen. I'm not dependent on people, places, and things to achieve my goals."[119]

There's always going to be stuff going on around you in the hospitality industry, notes Kistner, but successful employees "are not deterred by that stuff. You can't be deterred by outside influences. You've got to commit to 'this is what I'm going to do.'"[120] With that commitment, employees can look around and see what's in their realm of influence. Harland Svare noted: "In your area of responsibility, if you do not control events, you are at the mercy of events."[121] In sum, leaders can help employees step into the driver's seat by coaching them via questions: What tools do you have? What resources do you need? Where can you get that support, or where can you improvise to work with what you've got in the parameters of achieving what you've been assigned?

One solution, Harvard Business Review explains, is all about focus: "To motivate an employee to work toward your goals, you need to take a Judo-like approach: find the person's locus of energy and leverage it to achieve your ends."[122] In Judo, instead of stepping in the way of an attack and receiving its force directly, participants actively harness their opponents' strength, energy, and force to their advantage. Similarly, instead of pushing solutions on employees, leaders can tap into the employee's energy and ingenuity to "pull solutions out of them."[123] Helping an employee step into the driver's seat "gets employees' attention at the very least; ideally, it prompts them to clear the obstacles impeding their motivation."[124]

Chapter Roadmap

In this chapter, we will begin by discussing briefly how leaders translate their organizational goals and vision into reality. We'll look at a high-level overview of how implementation sometimes becomes stuck because of both external and internal influences.

Next, we will discuss four strategies that leaders can use to help employees take a personal stake in achieving organizational goals.

1. First, leaders who clarify the logical rationale behind goals help employees understand why their efforts make a critical difference in the larger picture.
2. Second, leaders foster employees' emotional buy-in by attaching positive personal outcomes to accomplishing organizational goals. Employees who are emotionally invested will launch their creativity, innovation, and care into achieving those goals.
3. Third, leaders blaze trails when showing the way by example. Through cultivating strong relationships, leaders step forward and invite others to follow.
4. Finally, leaders boost employees' empowerment by helping them cultivate mental agility.

The key takeaway from this chapter is the commitment: "I am responsible." At the end of the day, that attitude inspires the persistence, drive, and dedication employees and leaders need to assess and surmount obstacles. With the strategies in this chapter, leaders can help each person in the organization move into personal accountability for the success of the company's goals. "Good business leaders create a vision, articulate the vision, passionately own the vision, and relentlessly drive it to completion,"[125] said Welch.

Leaders Translate Vision into Reality

Winston Churchill taught: "The price of greatness is responsibility."[126] One of a leader's key responsibilities is generating a vision for the organization. In the business world broadly, and in the hospitality industry specifically, organizational growth depends on achieving goals at all levels of leadership. At the outset of each year or period, the company's top minds come together to focus on strategy. They analyze data, outline trends and patterns, and define targets for the coming year—in short, these leaders strategically define the big-picture, visionary decisions that steer the course of the company. Jack Welch wrote: "A leader's job is to look into the future and see the organization not as it is, but as it should be."[127]

Translating these high-level strategic decisions from theory into practice requires the careful orchestration of many moving parts where the rubber meets the road. In other words, transforming vision into reality means launching systematic, goal-oriented organizational action. Leaders identify who should do what at what level to achieve the desired outcomes. Then, they collaborate to define priorities and schedules, set checkpoints and deadlines, allocate resources, and assign key roles to various teams and layers of management.

At that point, leaders communicate their vision to employees and teams by delivering informative, motivational spoken or digital messages. To generate collective enthusiasm, leaders hold kick-off meetings regarding updates, expansions, and new projects. By extolling the growth of technology, the frontiers yet to conquer, and the power of change, leaders instill excitement in employees and elicit their commitment to achieving organizational goals. To promote accountability, leaders communicate specific key performance indicators and checkpoints. After articulating their vision and setting parameters for achieving that vision, leaders send employees off to get it done.

Importance of Individual Ownership

Steve Jobs taught: "If you are working on something exciting that you really care about, you don't have to be pushed. The vision pulls you."[128] Why is it, then, that enthusiasm for the company's fresh, roaring goals often tends to evaporate? Where does the vision get lost in the humdrum of day-to-day paperwork, meetings, and reports?

When initiatives struggle, it's common for leaders to wonder: how can we more effectively help employees take responsibility for fulfilling their roles in achieving organizational goals? The process of transforming vision into reality requires each employee to be fully on board and committed—when one person or department gets out of sync, the entire company feels out of sync. In other words, unless each employee takes responsibility for his or her role, the organization will struggle to achieve its desired outcomes.

Analyzing Patterns of Breakdown

When real-time performance is out of sync with desired outcomes, there are two main areas of potential breakdown—external and internal. As a comparison, when mountain climbers fail to reach the summit of Everest, they point to external breakdowns, such as problems with the weather, their gear, oxygen tanks, or guides. In addition, they reveal internal breakdowns, such as failures of their resolve, mindset, or conditioning. Reaching Everest's summit requires successful coordination and execution of both external and internal factors. This metaphor applies to companies that are working to implement goals that might feel as large to employees as climbing Everest feels to the climbers. Let's look a little more closely at several external and internal factors that inhibit employees from taking responsibility for their roles in achieving organizational goals.

External Factors

Employees may fail to achieve their assigned goals because external factors come into play, such as when a global or local economic recession reduces the amount of discretionary funding that consumers must invest. In the hospitality industry, extreme weather like hurricanes, or political/social unrest might deter potential purchasers from visiting resorts and thereby reduce the number of sales.

An accumulation of external factors can impact employees' abilities to achieve defined sales targets and can create a domino psychological effect. For example, some may rationalize: "Well, the other teams didn't achieve their goals, so *we* don't have to achieve ours." Others may cite external events as limitations: "It wasn't our fault: conditions didn't end up being what the leaders expected when they set those goals for the year." Some may justify missing targets by pointing fingers: "How can they expect us to hit our numbers when we needed a larger budget than we were given?"

With a touch of insightful humor, Louis Nizer said: "When a man points a finger at someone else, he should remember that four of his fingers are pointing at himself."[129] In short, external challenges need not halt progress; rather, they signal the need for innovation along on the road to achieving the organizational goals.

Internal Factors

While external factors can impact the way things get done, they cannot deter people who are fully committed to achieving the vision by any route possible. Often, internal factors play a bigger role when employees fail to achieve assigned goals. Even when leaders do their jobs well in orchestrating all the external support systems, employees may struggle to take a personal stake in goals that were set by upper management. However, that is precisely what employees are hired to do: to chase defined targets with enthusiasm and dedicate their time and effort to helping the organization achieve its vision.

Experienced leaders have seen that employees who take high levels of responsibility for organizational success are more enthusiastic overall about their jobs. As employees accept accountability for achieving assigned goals, they feel a sense of mission that sparks individual creativity, ingenuity, and even bravery.

This decision to take responsibility begins in the mind, says Marianne Williamson: "You may believe that you are responsible for what you do, but not for what you think. The truth is that you are responsible for what you think because it is only at this level that you can exercise choice. What you do comes from what you think."[130] Jim Rohn echoed this sentiment: "You must take personal responsibility. You cannot change the circumstances, the seasons, or the wind, but you can change yourself."[131]

With the right internal mindset and external support, however, it is possible to achieve organizational goals that are as lofty as summiting Mount Everest—even if reaching them will tax each person's resolve and talent.

Four Strategies for Motivating Responsibility

1. Harness Logic: Clarify the Rationale

In 1983, seatbelts were almost like decorations in automobiles—only 14 percent of people in the USA wore seatbelts.[132] Why would someone voluntarily wear something uncomfortable when the road seemed safe enough? To inspire behavioral change, safety proponents decided to focus on the rationale: research shows that you're 45 percent more likely to survive an auto crash if you're wearing a seatbelt in the front seat than if you're not wearing one.[133] Seatbelt compliance went up after public safety announcements on TV began showing crash test dummies wearing and not wearing seatbelts during simulated collisions. In large measure due to that public education, seatbelt use rates in the USA climbed from 14 percent in 1983 to 90 percent in 2016.[134] Now, it's far more commonplace for people to buckle up because they understand the reason why this action serves them.

As a comparison, when leaders explain the rationale behind the organizational goals, employees are more likely to change their behavior or take on new endeavors. In other words, influential leaders explain *why* a challenging action must be done and they provide context wherever possible.[135] Employees who understand why they are doing something difficult can discern a higher purpose that rises above self-interest. They are more likely to comply with new norms and practices even when leaders are not directing every step because behavior changes in accordance with understanding.

To provide effective direction and scaffold rationale-based changes in behavior, leaders should over-communicate the reasoning behind the company vision. Explain why the goal matters and what it will accomplish. Explain how it will work and how it fits into the larger vision of the company. Reiterate how achieving this goal is likely to positively impact employees' specific job function this year and in years to come. Prioritize tasks accordingly, and enthusiastically support employees in performing to new standards—including helping with patience when employees need to recover from mistakes. In sum, as leaders show employees the *why* behind the organizational goals, employees are more likely to catch the bigger vision and buy in at a personal level.

2. *Harness Emotion: Generate Belief in the Cause*

Even though research has shown that sugar is unhealthy and addictive for our physical chemistry, how many of us will decide to skip our sodas and desserts based on that information? Look at rising obesity rates in North America and you've got your answer: giving people logical reasons and more information hasn't motivated behavioral change. Instead, people who voluntarily reduce sugar intake do it either because they are essentially *forced* to do it, such as by illnesses, or because they feel emotionally tied to the outcomes and they *choose* to do it.

Attempting to force employees to take responsibility for organizational goals using pressure—like attaching punitive measures to failure to achieve—can damage morale. It's the 'stick' approach, rather than the 'carrot' approach, so to speak. While a stick approach may enforce compliance, it will never inspire enthusiasm. Rather, leaders can ignite enthusiastic compliance by building employees' positive emotional connections with organizational goals.

Building such a connection is perhaps less difficult than it sounds. At a fundamental level, pathos is persuasive—in this case, it's about linking a positive emotion to achieving the goals and vision set forth by company leaders. In the hospitality industry, for example, if a salesperson truly believes that a buyer's quality of life will improve after he purchases a timeshare because he'll be able to take his family on vacation every year and build key relationships that will sustain them through their lifetimes, that salesperson is much more likely to pursue the sale enthusiastically than might a salesperson who is just trying to meet an assigned target number of sales.

3. Correlate Organizational Goals with Concrete Positive Outcomes

Similarly, if employees believe that doing their part in helping the organization achieve its vision will generate concrete positive outcomes, then they are much more likely to contribute. Such outcomes might be correlated to company vision, such as: "If we achieve our goals of building this next resort property, the local community will receive three thousand jobs throughout the project and an infusion of funding and support." That could certainly be motivating for local employees who care about employment in the community and want to make a difference.

As another idea, the positive outcomes could be not specifically correlated to company vision but artificially attached—such as: "If you do your part to help the resort build its next property by this deadline, then we will donate a certain amount of money to your local community." Different artificially attached outcomes may motivate different people. For example, environmentally inclined employees might be motivated by knowing that the resort will plant 1000 trees on the new property by the time it is completed. Other employees might be more motivated by incentives attached to performance—if they passionately desire to achieve the incentives, they are more likely to passionately pursue the associated work. George Lucas advised: "Always remember: your focus determines your reality."[136]

Brian Tracy suggests a unique way for managers to get the best out of each person who reports to them: "The answer is simple: Make them feel happy. . . . Throughout the centuries, wise men, researchers, and scientists of all kinds have sought a 'unified field theory,' a single umbrella-like principle that explains all other principles. In the area of management and motivation, 'make them feel happy' is the unified theory."[137] The challenge is not that leaders don't know how to help employees feel happy, but rather that they forget to do this because they're distracted or they don't understand the importance of helping employees feel happy. By building relationships and showing a genuine interest in employees, leaders help them "feel valuable, respected, and important. They'll feel good inside and want to please [the leaders] by doing a good job."[138]

The possibilities are endless, but the principles are basic: the more that leaders can emotionally connect employees with achieving organizational goals, the more employees are likely to take responsibility for those goals. Leaders can build such connections via actual positive outcomes—good things that naturally occur when employees achieve assigned goals—or artificially-attached positive outcomes, like incentives. "Motivation is the will and initiative to do what is necessary to accomplish a mission. While motivation comes from within, others' actions and words affect it. A leader's role in motivation is at times to understand others' needs and desires, to align and elevate individual desires into team goals, and to inspire others to accomplish those larger goals."[139]

4. Harness Example: Lead the Way

In addition to providing logical reasons for and emotional connections with goals, leaders can inspire employees to achieve by leading the way. History shows how men and women have followed great leaders into battle time and again, knowing that the likely outcome could involve sacrificing their lives. Why did the soldiers not simply turn and run?

One example from World War II highlights the influence of personal leadership. In December 1941, the Japanese invaded the Philippines and U.S. General Jonathan Wainwright assumed command on Corregidor Island. Over 90 days, the Japanese grip tightened on the island and Wainwright directed his defenses with limited available resources. He made "frequent visits outside the tunnels to check on his men and inspire them personally."[140] As a fearless leader and "tenacious warrior, he saw men next to him die and personally returned fire . . . He was a unique frontline commander—a fighting general who earned the loyalty of his troops by sharing their hardships."[141]

On May 6, 1942, Wainwright finally surrendered after holding an unsupported position for a full six months with no outside help. During his three years of captivity as the highest-ranking and oldest American prisoner of war in World War II, "Wainwright kept faith and loyalty with his fellow prisoners suffering deprivation, humiliation, abuse, and torture."[142] He received a hero's welcome home and a Medal of Honor in 1945.

Leadership skills in the army can inform leadership skills in business endeavors. The military defines leadership as "the activity of influencing people by providing purpose, direction, and motivation to accomplish the mission and improve the organization."[143] As a role model, an ideal leader utilizes his or her strong intellect, competence, and moral character to inspire trust and confidence. All these characteristics are critical when the leader needs to harness the support of his or her colleagues in taking decisive action in the organization's best interests.

Military leaders learn that to "inspire Soldiers to risk their lives requires professional leaders capable of providing purpose, direction, and motivation."[144] To develop this level of influence, leaders must do more than simply give orders. Rather, they must persuade people to do what is necessary. "Through words and personal example, leaders inspire purpose, provide direction, and … motivation."[145]

Power to Influence Resides in Relationships

Like troops, employees will rally around a great leader with whom they feel a relationship. Put another way, people will do hard things because someone they respect asked them to do it. When Martin Luther King, Jr. said, "I have a dream," people throughout the United States rallied to support his cause despite personal losses, violence, and the day-to-day effort of swimming upstream against overwhelming tides. A similar principle applies in organizations: when a respected leader articulates a vision and sets goals, employees down through the ranks are more likely to buy in and carry their weight. The people who worked for and with Dr. King bought into his dream, owned it, and dedicated their resources to bringing it into reality. When employees, managers, office workers, and teams can buy into a leader's vision for the company because they respect that leader so much, the organization has a much higher chance of achieving its goals.

We could fill pages describing what it takes for a leader to earn colleagues' respect and dedication, but we will just touch on high points here. For example, leaders should demonstrate attributes of competence, solid character, discipline, humility, confidence, resilience, mental agility, and expertise. These attributes support competencies of communication, leading by example, creating a positive environment, and achieving results. To achieve positive results, successful leaders anticipate concerns and integrate the necessary tasks, roles, and resources to take advantage of the opportunities. In the process, strong leaders provide feedback, execute designed plans, and adapt as needed.[146]

Further, respected leaders have a fundamental understanding of their abilities—their strengths and weaknesses—and they internalize the roles, responsibilities, and actions associated with leadership. Having this understanding of self enables leaders to act and lead with confidence, which is what inspires employees to follow them and buy into their vision. Throughout an organization, influential leaders may be found leading a small team, managing a department, or sitting in the C-Suite. In less-formal capacities outside of rank or position, employees exercise leadership by demonstrating initiative, experience, or technical know-how to take responsibility and contribute to team success.

Influence is an essential component of leadership and it depends on the positive rapport between leaders and those whom they lead. Leaders can build empathy, camaraderie, and mutual trust by showing genuine interest in the employees' well-being. Brian Tracy reminds: "The leader sets the tone by the way he talks, behaves, responds to others, and treats people every day. People tend to 'follow the leader' in that they imitate or mimic the behavior of the leader."[147] In short, be someone whom the people you lead can respect. Strengthen both your character and your connection with your colleagues. Exercise sound judgment and take time to build relationships. Never be shy to offer praise and sincere gratitude for a job well done. Then, when you ask for their help, your employees will respect your influence enough to show up for your vision.

Cultivate Mental Agility as an Expression of Empowerment

In addition to being someone worth following, respected leaders cultivate mental agility as an expression of empowerment in their employees as a means of motivating them to take ownership of organizational goals.

Mental agility is the ability to think flexibly and it helps leaders and employees react effectively to change. Along the path toward tracking and achieving organizational goals, change is the only constant. Dynamic situations can bring on problems and challenges. In terms of taking responsibility for achieving goals, employees and leaders who are intellectually agile will stop fixating on challenges and instead pivot to try new approaches and achieve desired results.

This adaptability relies on curiosity and critical reasoning. "Inquisitive or intellectually curious leaders are eager to understand a broad range of topics and keep an open mind to multiple possibilities before reaching decisions. Critical thinking is purposeful and helps find facts, challenge assumptions, solve problems and make decisions."[148] Mentally agile leaders can work through challenges to find the basis for understanding. They tap into their personal innovation and imagination to reflect and learn continually.

As leaders implement new processes and systems to achieve organizational goals, they rely on intuition, experience, knowledge, and input from their teams. Taking responsibility involves examining problems in depth and from multiple points of view to find solutions. With mental agility, leaders have an easier time isolating the main issues and identifying solutions that work. Mental agility also involves a balance between confidence and humility—leaders need the confidence to believe in their ability to make sound decisions and be responsible, but they also need sufficient humility to change course as needed and anchor themselves to reality.

In sum, by cultivating mental agility and an attitude of empowerment, employees and leaders will be able to take responsibility for organizational goals and shift into the driver's seat within their roles. Leaders can be mindful of employees who may need a little extra support and take time to show them the way.

Key Takeaways

Over the course of a career, leaders practice effectively motivating the people they manage to take ownership of their roles and of organizational goals. As leaders, we cannot do our jobs without the full support of those who work under us. We know that our employees are the hands and feet and eyes of the company; we need to harness employee commitment fully for the company to make any progress toward the vision we set for it. Success is more of a journey than a destination and it doesn't happen overnight. Robert Collier noted: "Success is the sum of small efforts, repeated day-in and day-out."[149]

As this chapter has outlined, leaders have many tools available to help generate motivation, enthusiasm, and compliance in achieving company goals. Four strategies we have discussed include harnessing logic, emotion, example, and personal empowerment. The more effort leaders make to communicate the *why* behind the *what*, the more employees will understand logically what leaders are trying to create and ultimately why it matters in the organizational vision. By showing how achieving company goals will make a tangible difference in employees' lives—in the workplace and in the local communities—leaders can forge employees' emotional connections with positive outcomes and inspire them to dedicate themselves to achieving the outcomes.

As leaders cultivate their character and relationships with colleagues, they develop the emotional pull that great influencers are known for—the pull that generates a committed response to a simple request. Be a leader who can articulate dreams that others around you will own and work to achieve. Finally, leaders empower employees to take on organizational goals by helping them shift into the driver's seat. Provide latitude wherever possible for self-determination, such as allowing employees to set their own budgets toward key performance indicators. This will empower them to feel the power of choice and reduce the chance of blaming or justification.

These four actions will help employees build an attitude of "I am responsible." Such an attitude is the driving force for successful organizational outcomes—each person involved needs to own the process and demonstrate un-stop-ability in the face of resistance. This attitude is the core of resilience and it fuels grit in the face of challenge. This attitude has us laughing in the face of obstacles, and instantly looking for new routes when old routes close. It is the stuff of creativity, ingenuity, and even of hope.

Sailors crossing the oceans and mapping the globe would have gotten nowhere without this attitude of responsibility. Each person on the ship had to be on board with their assigned tasks: hoisting sails, preparing food, or navigating the seas.

Thomas Carlyle said: "A man without a goal is like a ship without a rudder."[150] Employees' daily tasks are small goals that help give direction to the course of the ship. Each time the ship ended up off course, an attitude of "I am responsible" for achieving the designed outcomes is what motivated sailors to re-route the ship toward the desired destination.

For our companies—sailing like ships through the global economy, navigating recessions and literal hurricanes—our goals are our 'promised land' and our employees and colleagues are our sailors doing the day-to-day work of swabbing the deck and handling the rigging.

As leaders who want to inspire collaboration and not mutiny, we must keep employees informed, tap into the reasons behind the actions, and be someone worth following. Harness your words and actions to build vision and create opportunities for personal empowerment. Only then will each person in the organization take on the attitude of responsibility and truly get the job done. Robert Kistner concludes: "It is really very simple: actions speak louder than words. 'I am responsible' is not a fancy slogan. It is our actions that most inspire those around us."[151]

5

Fifteen Master Negotiation Strategies

As a business leader, you're no stranger to negotiation. You've already been through countless negotiation interactions with your family, school, and work thus far. In fact, you likely encounter some type of negotiation—formal or informal—every day as you interact with your colleagues, make sales, communicate with outside vendors, and resolve problems.

Many of you are already highly successful negotiators, and you might wonder if this chapter is too elementary for a person of your capabilities. Our goal is to add to what you know already and provide specific strategies that illuminate what you may do naturally by instinct. Understanding why you are an amazing negotiator will help you improve. You will also be more able to teach others—such as those who work under your leadership or who may be less experienced—the skills of top negotiators.

You have already discovered that negotiation is a skill. It helps you bridge the gap between what you need and what others need—it is a means of collaboration, problem solving, and solution building. Leaders who focus on improving their negotiation skills often see tangible results, such as:

- Higher revenues and profits
- Better salaries, benefits, bonuses, etc.
- Lasting relationships and partnerships
- Strong reputation

The ability to negotiate is valuable to business managers because it develops critical thinking aptitudes and effective communication skills. Those who negotiate well practice listening, understanding, and creatively seeking common ground to arrive at solutions that satisfy all parties involved. They become adept at giving and taking strategically to build a space of agreement amid differing viewpoints.

The best negotiators also develop strong relationships. They become trusted partners and advisors. By cultivating and maintaining positive rapport with all parties, good negotiators establish themselves as top-ranking businesspeople and gain greater opportunities in the future.

Why does strategy matter?

Let's tap into a sports analogy as we think through why it might be helpful to have a strategy for negotiation. Imagine you are the captain of a soccer team preparing to take on a strong opponent in a championship game.

- Before the game, you and your team spend time training, running drills, and visualizing your desired outcomes. You assess your opponent in detail—what they're good at and where they're weak. You come up with tactics and plans that could tip the odds in your favor.

- Then, on game day, as you head out onto the field, you size up the other team and begin to track their patterns. You must control your emotions and stay focused on the outcome you want to achieve.

- After the game, you greet the other team with respect (and maybe a high five). You may replay in your mind some of the key moments and note places where you could improve for next season. You might feel disappointment at the times when you fumbled, but overall, you can come away with positives from your team's performance.

Now, negotiation is obviously different from a soccer game in many ways—most notably in that no one party walks out as the sole winner. In a successful negotiation, both parties give and take to achieve a mutually desirable outcome. Instead of trampling the opposing party, a good negotiator listens and cooperates to create solutions. Since neither party holds all the aces, strategy is key to enabling both parties to achieve positive outcomes.

But, here's why a soccer game is a useful metaphor for a negotiation session: both are intense events that require significant skill. Both require preparation beforehand, solid game-day tactics, and post-game analysis. You can play better as you identify and become adept with successful strategies.

Chapter Roadmap

The remainder of this chapter describes 15 strategies that business leaders can use before, during, and after a negotiation session. The topics are sectioned into three aspects of strategy described above. Here's a brief overview:

- Pre-Game Prep: In terms of 'pre-game prep,' we'll discuss defining your position, researching the other party, anticipating tactics and emotions, and diffusing anxiety.
- Game Day: Successful 'game-day' tactics that we'll cover include establishing a relationship of trust, listening well, giving and taking, using time to your advantage, understanding the role of anger, embodying respect, mitigating disappointment, and knowing where to draw the line.
- Post-Game: After the negotiation, good negotiators do some 'post-game analysis,' including saying thank you to the other party, taking next steps, and reflecting to generate improvement.

Pre-Game Preparation

The four strategies outlined in this section will improve your odds significantly: defining your position, researching the other party, anticipating emotions and tactics, and diffusing anxiety.

1. Define Your Position

It is critical to understand what you want before you ever set foot in a negotiation session. That way, you'll know when to push forward and when to stop. Articulate your needs and priorities to yourself. Verify numbers for accuracy. Know the worth of what you want and understand clearly what you bring to the table. Carol Frohlinger noted: "Don't bargain yourself down before you get to the table."[152]

Designate your absolute musts—where you must walk away if they are not met. Make sure that you are clear on your long-term goals and what you're trying to achieve from the negotiation. This will help you keep the larger picture in mind. Choose areas where you have leeway and can make concessions later.

When working to understand the deal dynamics, consider the following questions:

- Who has the leverage in the negotiation? If the other side is expecting a payment from you, leverage tends to be on your side.
- Who wants the deal more?
- What timing constraints is the other side under? Is time on your side or the other's side?
- Does the other side have many alternatives?
- What is standard in the market? What do similar deals include?

2. Research the Other Party

Do your homework. Find out as much as possible about the people sitting across the table. Find out about other deals they have made. Understand if they prefer to do business with a handshake or with a long contract and prepare yourself accordingly. What are their strengths and weaknesses? This information can help you position yourself favorably. Is there a real or perceived difference in the balance of power between the parties? How can you use this to your advantage?

Now think from the other party's perspective—what are their needs? Where could they be flexible? Come up with a potential solution or two that you could offer that incorporates some of what they need and some of what you need, giving wherever possible.

While we live in a 'politically correct' society, leaders should also consider other sensitive but critical characteristics. While treating everyone with respect, good negotiators carefully evaluate how age, gender, race, religion, health, disability, education, class, wealth, culture, nationality, and other personal characteristics may factor into both sides of the negotiation. Use those characteristics to your advantage and don't neglect them to your peril.

What you learn about the other party may inform your communication tactics. If you are engaging in protracted negotiations, evaluate the most effective ways to convey your messages to this specific party. While written communications have their place, they are more effective in establishing and confirming positions and possibly dealing with easy deal points than in moving negotiations forward on the most difficult issues. Whoever is willing to initiate a call or set an in-person meeting has the power.

3. Anticipate Tactics and Emotions

If you can imagine what the other party will ask and how you will feel in that moment, you'll be able to prepare yourself for potentially uncomfortable ideas or emotions in advance. You will be more in control during the meeting and better prepared for success. Harvard Business Review notes that over the past decade, "researchers have begun examining how specific emotions—anger, sadness, disappointment, anxiety, envy, excitement, and regret—can affect the behavior of negotiators. They've studied the differences between what happens when people simply feel these emotions and what happens when they also express them to the other party through words or actions."[153]

This research helps negotiators improve their skills by attending to emotions. For example, anxiety shows up before or early in the process; anger or excitement tends to manifest in the heat of discussion; and disappointment or sadness may be felt in the aftermath of the event. There is value in "controlling the emotions we feel and especially those we reveal. In other words, good negotiators need to develop a poker face—not one that remains expressionless, always hiding true feelings, but one that displays the right emotions at the right times."[154]

For example, consider the array of effective (and less effective) emotions illustrated in this true story. One businessman who had negotiated billion-dollar transactions on Wall Street recalls meeting the master negotiator. The businessman was walking on a dirt road through a thatch-hut market outside of Saigon. Young men tried to sell him everything—rice, tires . . . anything money can buy. The man was not swayed. Then an old Vietnamese woman dressed in black approached with a single item inventory: a beaded necklace. Although the businessman may not have been her target demographic, she was a master of negotiation through emotion.

She began with friendly interaction, smiling with teeth stained red from betel nut juice. But the man was not swayed. Then she pulled at his heartstrings with tears and a sad story of needing food for her children and money for the doctor. The man softened but still held his ground.

Finally, she grabbed his forearm and pressed her nails into the flesh deep enough to get his full attention but not to puncture the skin. She angrily challenged his manhood and said that if he was honorable, he would certainly spare a few dong. He was a bit shaken but kept walking. She persisted and the man finally bought the necklace, not daring to even negotiate the price. The old woman's fingers released her grip on his arm and closed around the tattered bills. She hobbled away, victorious.[155]

4. Diffuse Personal Anxiety

The mindset we take into our negotiations can dramatically impact the results. Just as an athlete needs to be "in the zone" before the championship game, so negotiators need to be in a solid place. Some people feel distress and a desire to escape from situations that have the potential for undesirable outcomes. Anxious negotiators often make weaker first offers, exit early, and achieve lower outcomes than more confident negotiators.

To counteract anxiety, practice patience and persistence—stay in the scene rather than wishing to escape. Rehearse in advance and become familiar with the situation. Over time, negotiations will feel more routine. Overall, the more prepared you are, the better you'll play on game day. It's been said that luck happens when preparation crosses opportunity. John F. Kennedy advised: "Let us never negotiate out of fear. But let us never fear to negotiate."[156]

Game Day: Negotiation Event

From opening moves and observations, through give and take, how you play the game will have a lot to do with the outcomes you achieve. Here are eight strategies you can use on the field for a successful negotiation session. Note that the numbering here will pick up from the prior section and add toward the fifteen total strategies.

5. *Establish a Relationship of Trust*

Set a positive tone by welcoming the other party with enthusiasm and respect. Be open and sincere. Honesty, integrity, and dignity are palpable qualities, and the foundation upon which constructive negotiations are built. "You are best positioned to negotiate when the other party respects you, not only as a businessperson, but as a human being. Trust, which is gained through that respect, is the key to successful negotiation."[157]

One way to enhance trust and lay the groundwork for a successful resolution—especially if there is any kind of dispute—is to use what could be called the 'teapot steam strategy.' Start the negotiation by encouraging the other side to tell their story, and to unload, if necessary. You don't have to agree with everything that is said, but you can acknowledge that you hear want is being said. Take all the verbal punches they want to throw and learn from each swing. This is like the hot steam streaming and screaming out a teapot. After a person has had the chance to air concerns and feel understood, the temperature will drop, and that person will be more likely to listen and explore options.

Negotiation guru Christopher Voss offers helpful wisdom: "If your first objective in the negotiation, instead of making your argument, is to hear the other side out, that's the only way you can quiet the voice in the other guy's mind. But most people don't do that."[158]

6. *Listen Well*

Most of the time we are so busy making sure that the other party hears what we say that we forget to listen. But, it has been said that "the best negotiators are detectives. They ask probing questions and then stop talking. The other negotiator will tell you most things you need to know—all you must do is listen. Many conflicts can be resolved easily if we learn how to listen. You can become an effective listener by allowing the other person to do most of the talking. Follow the 80/20 Rule: listen 80 percent of the time and talk only 20 percent of the time."[159]

Try asking questions that are simply worded, pre-planned, open-ended, and clarifying. Then listen without interrupting the responses. Make eye contact and take notes where appropriate.

One researcher describes listening with "four ears."[160] In other words, skilled negotiators listen for these four components:

a. What is clearly being said—gain insight into the other party's thoughts, needs, and feelings via their words
b. What is not being said—recognize what speech conceals and silence reveals
c. What the other person wants to say but does not—hear the essence of things in the other party's logic and emotion
d. What you are saying to yourself—pick up on your perceptions and inner voice and allow your informed intuition to act as a coach

Articulate aloud what you hear, saying something such as: "What I'm hearing is that you would like to achieve this, and you have some flexibility on these other two issues. I think we can find some common ground here." Understanding what all parties need and working for all concerned is vital. Creativity is essential to good negotiation; seeing the situation in only black and white (win-lose) creates limited thinking. When you achieve your goals, be considerate of the other party by masking excitement so that they don't feel they have lost.

Don't be afraid to allow silence. Give yourself and others the time and space to reflect on what has been said. Work with the rhythm of the conversation and allow space. Lance Morrow noted: "Never forget the power of silence. That massively disconcerting pause which goes on and on and may last induce an opponent to babble and backtrack nervously."[161]

One way to use a calculated silence to your advantage is to simply count to ten silently. Bill Coleman counsels: "This is a classic negotiation technique. It's a gentle, soft indication of your disapproval and a great way to keep negotiating. Count to ten. By then, the other person usually will start talking and may very well make a higher offer."[162] Robert Court agreed: "It's a well-known proposition that you know who's going to win a negotiation; it's he [or she] who pauses the longest."[163]

7. Give and Take

Ask for what you want. As you share your needs, speak from the perspective of how they work to the advantage of the deal and favor the other party as well.

Forbes outlines several questions you can ask to clarify where you might be able to give and take in negotiation: [164]

- Is this the best pricing or offer you can give me?
- What assurances do I get that your product or solution will work for me?
- Who are your competitors? How do their products compare?
- What else can you throw into the deal without cost to us?
- What is your desired timing for the deal?
- How does our deal benefit you?

Plan to make concessions. Always have in mind a few things that you can give up later. Note that if you wait to share your concessions until after you have shared your needs, the other party may feel like you are moving toward their goal and they may be more collaborative. Separate "deal points" from "discretionary points." Be reasonable. If everything is a deal point, then you will probably not succeed in the negotiation because you have nothing to give. If you get all your key deal points in return for giving on the discretionary points, then there is more chance of success.

8. Use Time to Your Advantage

Experienced negotiators determine in every negotiation session whether time is on their side or the other side. Time is on your side if the other party is under constraints or schedules for completion. If they are hurting to get things done, then they may be more willing to come toward your objectives. Move slowly, but keep in mind that delaying too much could create annoyance or cost you the deal, so find the right balance. Timing and momentum go together. It is helpful when time is on your side.

Also, feel free to take time before making final decisions; don't be pressured to sign quickly. Be patient and spend enough time to craft a good deal.

9.   Understand the Role of Anger in Negotiation

Negotiation can be a space where tempers flare. Those who use anger believe that it will help them win a larger share of the pie. This view stems from what researchers call the "fixed-pie bias" wherein people assume that negotiation is a zero-sum game in which their interests conflict directly with their counterpart's interests. In this worldview, angry negotiators assume that they seem stronger, more powerful, and better able to succeed in the grab for value.[165]

Unfortunately, anger reduces joint gains, cooperation, and even accuracy. To diffuse anger, frame solutions cooperatively, actively build rapport, and apologize when needed to reduce hostility. A creative coping strategy is to reframe anger as sadness, which can lead to cooperative concession making rather than impasse. If all else fails, bring in a third party or hit pause and reschedule for another time.

Take care never to threaten or shout unless strategically planned—negotiation is not about winning or dominating the other side. Most deals are only possible if both people feel they're getting something out of it. If the other party feels attacked or doesn't like you, they are less likely to make a deal. The reality is that if you seal the deal, you're going to keep working with the people you're negotiating with. It doesn't help to yell or say something you don't mean in the heat of the moment, especially in negotiations that involve parties in long-term relationships.

With the foregoing in mind, an occasional strategic display of emotion can be effective. For example, an attorney known for always remaining calm and collected recounted one negotiation where the "level" approach was not getting anywhere.[166] In fact, it almost seemed to provide the broker on the other side with a perceived license to stomp around and be abusive.

Assessing the situation, the attorney calculated the right moment and then deliberately and knowingly went full-on ballistic. The drastic change from the calm and collected approach to strategic fury completely shocked and quieted the broker, and then allowed the negotiations to proceed on a solid basis to a successful resolution. It was like the attorney was suddenly speaking the broker's emotional language and using anger to communicate where calm had failed.

In cases like this, strategic expression of anger and other emotions can be effective, but they should only be rarely used. The attorney in the foregoing example noted he only had to use the "nuclear option" in about three negotiations in over 40 years. But if you need it, then use it.

If tensions rise, cope with your emotions first. It's surprising to watch even high-level business deals break down because someone involved starts thinking or acting childishly. When this happens, everything goes out of balance. Negotiating is often extremely stressful for both parties, and that's why having a sense of humor goes a long way.

You may be able to help the other party think through and cope with their emotions. Do what you can to diffuse tension—take a break, speak calmly, and invite third-party assistance such as mediation. A successful negotiator acts as the stable anchor—the respectful adult at the table who focuses on understanding. Practice using inclusive language like "we" and "us" rather than "I" or "you." This can help build bridges and demonstrate mutual benefit.

10. Distinguish Key Points: Easy vs. Hard, and Now vs. Later

Expert negotiators are skilled at categorizing components that need to be addressed. Strategically, it makes sense to separate easy elements from more difficult-to-agree-on elements. For example, as you approach your next negotiation, separate what seem to be "easy points" from "hard points."

Create a feeling of cooperation and progressive momentum by helping the parties agree on as many easy or common points as possible. Yes, yes, yes often leads to more yes. If a point becomes a stumbling block, don't let it bog down the negotiations. Simply acknowledge the point and set it aside on a list of matters to be addressed later and then get back to the business of "yes, yes, and more yes" on other points. After creating that "can do" environment, return to the outstanding hard points and note that they are often much more manageable—it may feel like they shrank from mountains to speed bumps.

Expert negotiators also strategically separate "now points" from "later points." Suppose some of the points are too unknown or hard to decide during the negotiations. Consider agreeing upon all the points that can be decided and then addressing the outstanding points at another time. For example, in a lease negotiation, imagine that a landlord and tenant could not agree on what the rent should be five years down the road. Rather than letting that disagreement hold up negotiations on the other terms, the parties simply agreed to defer that decision for five years and then have an appraisal mechanism in place to resolve the issue if the parties could not later agree.

11. Mitigate Post-Game Disappointment and Regret

Most complex negotiations will end with each side having achieved some of its goals and not others—it's a mix of wins and losses, not a binary outcome. Still, it's natural to look at the negotiated agreement afterward and notice emotions of disappointment or regret. We may wonder: Should I have pushed harder? Was there anything else I could have achieved?

To reduce regret and disappointment, here are two strategies from the Harvard Business Review. First, during the event itself, consider slowing down the process so that each side has ample time to consider outcomes before making a final decision. Be sure to raise any questions or fears you have so that they can be addressed during the negotiation.

Second, after an agreement has been made and tension is released, consider saying: "We have terms we can all live with. But now that we know we've reached an agreement, let's spend a few more minutes chatting to see if we can find anything that sweetens it for both sides."[167] This is not an attempt to renegotiate; rather, it is a way to help both sides feel even more satisfied and stave off regret.

12. Know Where to Draw the Line

Don't be afraid to walk away. If the other party wants your business, they will call you back. John F. Kennedy said: "We cannot negotiate with those who say, 'What's mine is mine and what's yours is negotiable.'"[168] As you show respect and deal fairly, you can expect the other party to do so as well. If they don't, you might choose to find another means of reaching your goals. Some of the best deals we do are the deals we don't do. It is good to know when to walk away from a transaction rather than enter a deal for the sake of making a deal or out of pride even if the arrangement is harmful.

Remember that whoever can walk away from the deal has the ultimate power. A businessman saw this principle in action with his five-year-old son. They walked through a street market in Mexico and the boy showed interest in a comb that flipped in and out of a case like a switchblade. The vendor immediately picked up on that interest and offered to sell the comb normally priced at $20 for a dramatically discounted $10.

Without a word, the boy turned and started slowly walking away. The salesman smiled and said, "Ok, Ok just $8." The boy inspected the comb again and stepped out of the stall not speaking. The man called out, "OK, only $5." This process went on several more times. A group of other vendors gathered to watch the negotiation heckling their colleague to make the sale whatever the cost. Game on.

Finally, the price was down to one dollar. The young boy inspected the comb one last time and then walked away. The vendors shook their heads. One even offered a similar comb for free, but it was game over. None of us had ever seen a negotiation like that before. One side didn't say a word and was simply willing to walk from the deal. Even though the boy ultimately decided not to buy the comb, he would have gotten it for an amazingly discounted price if he had chosen to buy it.[169]

In sum, every negotiation involves strategic opening moves, push and pull toward differing objectives, and a final agreement (if one can be reached). Managing your emotions along the way will help you keep the big picture in sight.

Post-Game Analysis

Negotiation of the basic terms may be complete, but now the transaction is in progress or the project is prepping for kickoff. Here are three short strategies for wrapping up the negotiation well: say thank you, take next steps, and seek ongoing improvement. We have also included a few resources you might read for more info.

13. Say "Thank You"

After the negotiation is complete, take time to thank the other party for their time and effort in creating a solution. Show respect. If appropriate, send an email or a note acknowledging them. While this may be less pivotal in a single-transaction negotiation, it can make quite a difference in a long-term relationship. By showing gratitude, you will feel more complete with the process, and the other party will likely also feel more committed to making the deal work smoothly.

14. Take Next Steps

Follow up on the things you agreed to do. If you laid the groundwork in your negotiation session for a contract or deal, begin drafting. Involve your teams and lawyers—you know the process that's right for your business. If you are working with a contract, note that you may have ongoing negotiations and rounds of comments as all parties come to a final product. As these communications occur, you'll be glad that you kept any anger or difficult emotions in check during the initial session. Your efforts to follow up on your end of the bargain help the other party trust you more in this and future deals.

15. Seek Ongoing Improvement

Every athlete gets coaching—even the best of the best work with mentors who can spot patterns and point out areas for improvement. As you think back on your negotiation game day, consider what went well and what you may want to improve for next time. If your colleagues or leaders were present, consider inviting their input and implementing their suggestions. As you know, business involves a series of negotiations, and it's a skill worth cultivating. By reflecting on your missteps and your successes, you'll become more adept over time.

Keep improving your skills by learning from the gurus of negotiation. Although we cannot endorse any particular author or philosophy, here are some books that many people have found helpful:

- *Getting to Yes: Negotiating Agreement Without Giving In* by Roger Fisher, William L. Ury, and Bruce Patton
- *Getting More: How You Can Negotiate to Succeed in Work and Life* by Stuart Diamond
- *Crucial Conversations: Tools for Talking When Stakes are High* by Kerry Patterson, Joseph Grenny, Ron McMillan, and Al Switzler
- *Influence: The Psychology of Persuasion* by Robert B. Cialdini
- *Bargaining for Advantage: Negotiation Strategies for Reasonable People* by G. Richard Shell
- *Never Split the Difference: Negotiating as if Your Life Depended on it* by Chris Voss and Tahl Raz
- *Kiss, Bow, or Shake Hands: The Bestselling Guide to Doing Business in More Than 60 Countries* by Terri Morrison and Wayne A. Conaway

Key Takeaways

The ability to negotiate successfully in today's evolving business climate can make the difference between success and failure. It is a skill worth mastering. The strategies we've discussed in this chapter can be a good addition to the negotiation strengths you already possess as a business leader.

Don't worry about taking on everything at once—just pick one or two strategies that stood out to you as you were reading, and start there. You've probably already thought of a way to implement some of these ideas. If you can dedicate only five minutes, try these ideas:

- Next time you are going to negotiate with a client, spend five minutes reading about them online before they arrive. Even a quick glance can help you know better who they are or what they've done recently so you can speak to them in a personal manner.
- If you feel anxious, try spending five minutes during the day or an hour before the negotiation thinking through your

questions and imagining the other party's responses. Maybe you could role play with a colleague for a minute to test drive your ideas live. This will help you feel calmer and iron out kinks.

- If you feel angry or frustrated as tensions rise in the room, set a timer on your watch or phone and commit to speaking calmly for five minutes before you jump into the heat. Take a breath and notice the difference.

- If you don't normally follow up after the event, try investing five minutes drafting a quick email that says something like: "Thanks for your time talking with us yesterday. We are looking forward to working with you. Let us know how we can help—you've got my number."

Soon, it'll become second nature for you to prepare carefully before you ever walk into the negotiation session. You'll get good at defining your position, understanding the other side, and prepping your emotions. Then, when you walk into the room, you'll be able to skillfully establish a relationship of trust, listen for spoken and unspoken cues, and use time to your advantage. You won't get sidetracked by anger; instead, you'll tune into humor and patience. Finally, you'll strengthen your reputation as you follow through on the negotiation's next steps and offer an expression of thanks.

If you keep these strategies in mind each time you step into a negotiation scenario, you will be well on your way to making better deals, reducing frustration, and having more satisfying business relationships. You'll also be able to share them when the time is right with your trainees or teams as your career grows.

6

Defining Creativity in the Workplace

Creativity and innovation have always been at the heart of every successful organization. In fact, IBM surveyed more than 1,500 chief executive officers and found that they repeatedly ranked creativity as the number one factor for business success—valuing creativity even above management discipline, integrity, and vision.[170] While it's easy to envision entrepreneurship as a hotbed of creation—launching fresh concepts and methods—creativity is also a driver of day-to-day business leadership in established companies.

Brian Tracy observes: "There seems to be a direct relationship between the quantity of new ideas that you generate in your work and the level of success that you achieve. One new idea or insight can be sufficient to change the direction of an entire company."[171] Although creativity has always been at the heart of business, supporting creativity hasn't been at the top of the management agenda. In other words, business leaders have plenty of opportunities for growth in terms of nurturing creativity in their teams and employees.

In today's innovation-driven economy, creativity can fuel decision making and research that becomes the bedrock of new, successful methods. Your company's profitability, income, and prospects depend on creative contribution and implementation. Business leaders do well to encourage suggestions and ideas from each employee because each person can suggest improvements within their line of sight.

Chapter Roadmap for Part One of the Series

This chapter is the first in a two-part series providing strategies for business leaders in managing for creativity. In this chapter, we'll take a deep look at what exactly creativity is in the workplace. How do business leaders define it? How does it support the goals and work of the organization as a whole? Then, we will provide the first five strategies that business leaders can use to cultivate creativity in the teams and employees they manage.

As a preview for the next chapter, Part Two of this series will cover five more strategies leaders can use to set the stage for creative problem solving and invite the organization's best ideas. In Part Two, we will also turn the lens inward and discuss several ways that business leaders can nurture their creativity, both on and off the clock.

What is Creativity in the Workplace?

Most of us can name people we think are creative, like Einstein, Edison, Da Vinci, etc., and most of us can name tangible results of creative thinking, like novels, inventions, or theories, but most of us struggle to define the actual concept of creativity. Go ahead. What's your definition of creativity? Is your definition about a way of being or about an identity?

Defining Creativity

As a nuanced phenomenon, creativity could be simply "the ability to transcend traditional ways of thinking or acting, and to develop new and original ideas, methods, or objects."[172] Let's look at three relevant components of that definition.

1. *DOING.* First, creativity is an 'ability.' It's a skill specific to an individual, like the skill of running five miles, or doing quadratic equations, or writing poetry. For some people, certain skills come naturally whereas other people must work to acquire those same skills. Maybe you're a whiz at calculus but you struggle to cook a casserole. The good news is that skills—like creativity, calculus, flexibility, poetry, etc.—are acquirable with enough effort and dedication.

2. *TRANSCENDING.* Second, creativity is about 'transcending' traditional ways of thinking or acting. That means going above and beyond, or around, over and through. Creativity is about improving upon what exists. It means thinking differently by recognizing the limitations of what already exists and trying to resolve them. This concept is encapsulated in the US Marine mantra "Improvise, Adapt, and Overcome."[173] Some creative people don't have to try hard to 'think outside the box'; rather, they may have to try harder to fit within acceptable boxes and labels given by society and the workplace. Many creative individuals manifest independence and a willingness to be different.

3. *DEVELOPING.* Third, for creativity to develop new and original things, it must go beyond imagination and into actual development. People with creative ideas should do the research to prove those ideas. People who create processes must also develop tests to ensure that those processes function as intended. People who successfully create objects or products take the time to build them. Sometimes, the people who create can network to get their ideas and objects within their optimal markets. Other times, the people who create ideas are not the optimal people to scale products into marketability—that's where managers and leaders can translate ideas into actual revenue or efficiencies and cost savings to move the baton across the finish line.

Creativity in Problem Solving

For managers, creativity has a lot to do with problem solving. Brian Tracy indicates that the average manager spends 50 percent or more of his/her time solving problems, either alone or with others. Thus, a leader's "ability to deal with difficulties and solve problems will, more than anything else, determine everything that happens in [his or her] career. In fact, it is safe to say that an individual with poor creative-thinking skills will be relegated to working for those with developed creative-thinking skills."[174]

That is an observation, not a criticism. Creative people are not better or more valuable than implementers because both are essential to success. For example, where would a creative idea be without the people who handle logistics, development, marketing, shipping, ordering, and the more 'mundane' aspects of transforming a creative idea into an actual revenue-generating item on the organizational balance sheet? The key is for leaders to recognize where the individuals they manage are most talented and to draw the best out of everyone to contribute to the success of the company.

Creativity is a skill that allows you to draw understanding from the world around you, connect those observations to your existing knowledge reservoirs, and imagine new applications of your knowledge on the world."[175] It's a tendency to generate or recognize ideas, alternatives, or possibilities that may be useful in solving problems and communicating with others.

Creativity is the process of creating something unique and new. It's as simple as seeing what others are not seeing, and putting together systems, processes, and products in a new way to create new synergies. And even where several people may see the issue and solution, the person who acts and implements the solution is more likely to succeed. How many people throughout history saw the need to bind papers together before the Norwegian, Johan Vaaler, invented the paperclip?

For something to be creative, it is not enough for it to be new; it must also have value or meet the demands of a specific situation. It doesn't have to be huge or groundbreaking (e.g., the paperclip). Sometimes subtle shifts in what we do or how we do it can be sufficiently creative to be the stuff of innovation. Putting your sales crew in a different location, entering a yet-unserved niche, and building demand among markets or demographics where it didn't exist previously can all be innovative.

Creativity in Personalities

How can leaders recognize creativity in their team members and employees? Research shows that creative personalities may exhibit a combination of playfulness and discipline, humility and pride, and introversion and extroversion. Highly creative people are often seen as exceptionally bright, insightful, fresh, and passionate. Some creative team members are rebellious and independent. Many are passionate about their work yet can be objective about it as well. Many creative individuals are highly sensitive, which can lead to heightened suffering at times, but also heightened enjoyment at other times.[176] Those sensitive types sometimes notice details that others may miss and thus see connections beyond what is apparent.

Tests for creativity measure not only the number of alternatives that people generate but also how unique each of those alternatives is. Creativity is linked to fundamental qualities of thinking, such as flexibility, tolerance of ambiguity or unpredictability, and enjoyment of things heretofore unknown.[177] Brian Tracy summarizes: "Creativity is a natural, spontaneous characteristic of positive individuals with high self-esteem."[178]

Some studies show that men and women who evidence "genius" have three habits in common[179]—and these characteristics are completely learnable and replicable for those who want to develop them:

1. The ability to concentrate single-mindedly on one thing without becoming distracted. Sometimes writing down the details enhances the ability to focus 100% on solving a problem.

2. The ability to see the big picture by remaining open-minded, flexible, and even childlike in examining possible solutions to a problem. They suspend judgment and criticism and avoid becoming attached to their ideas.

3. The ability to take a systematic, orderly approach to problem solving. While some solutions show up from the subconscious or aha moments, many solutions come from simply running the checklist of questions: Why? Why not? How? Could there be another option?

Five Strategies Leaders Can Use to Inspire Creativity in Teams and Employees

"If there is a bottleneck in organizational creativity," asks Scott Cook in Harvard Business Review, "might it be at the top of the bottle?"[180] The role of business leaders in nurturing the creative process is this:

"One doesn't manage creativity. One manages *for* creativity."[181] Until recently, the responsibility of innovating new ideas and products was left to research and development teams. Managing creativity was something of an enigma. How do you manage something so abstract as innovation? Today, essential elements in team leadership roles include the ability to creatively manage teams and inspire diversity.[182]

"How do we encourage creativity in the modern-day organization? And what are the foundations that propel us to great innovation? There are lots of ways we can innovate in the workplace and make our workplaces more stimulating for creativity to flow. We just have to give our teams the freedom and confidence to explore ways of doing what they do better."[183] This section provides five strategies that leaders can use when managing for creativity. They support leaders in nurturing and inspiring creativity in their teams and employees.

1. Harness Organizational Creativity: All Minds on Deck

Leaders can set the stage for creative work by gathering the right people at the right times in the right environments to handle the right amount of creative work. Re-cast the roles of employees to invite them to contribute imagination. Cook notes: "Traditional management prioritizes projects and assigns people to them. But increasingly, managers are not the source of the idea."[184] When ideas are born from the ranks and owned by the teams who conceived them, managers play a support function in guiding those ideas to fruition.

For example, Harvard Business Review describes how Philip Rosedale, founder and chairman of Linden Lab, leads by giving workers wide-ranging autonomy, and "the greatest success comes from the workers' own initiatives."[185] Of course, there must be a balance about initiatives—and many must be driven from above—but when employees generate the plan, they are perhaps more passionate, more engaged, and more informed about how to make those ideas work well.

Know the Big Picture

You don't have to be a creative genius, but you need to know what the teams are trying to accomplish so you can evaluate their work and provide meaningful, specific feedback. You can identify weaknesses in the ideas and help the team compensate for them. Your guidance inspires trust and keeps the team on track toward their designated end goal. While some might believe that removing all limits enhances creativity, research shows that creative people "typically work best when they have clear direction and understanding of the goals."[186] Norman Barry said: "Give me the freedom of a tight strategy."[187]

Ask Innovative Questions

As a leader, you can bring 'all minds on deck' using deliberate, innovation-savvy thought processes and questioning techniques, such as:

- Invite the group to scrutinize an unexpected failure, success, or outside event for new business opportunities. For example, when the prices of oil skyrocketed in the 1970s, companies began to innovate smaller cars, solar panels, and alternative fuel sources.

- Analyze changes in market demographics (like aging consumers or Millennial buyers), societal values (like emphasis on eco-friendliness or fitness), or knowledge (like scientific or economic trends) for impact on the organization and sales trends.

- Compare the reality of what is with what should be, and look for any inconsistencies or niche problems to solve. How could we use this product or service to accomplish other things? How could we combine our products/services in a new way to match the desires of the emerging demographic? How could we make our product stronger? What should we add or remove from it?

- Ask specific, goal-grounded, fill-in-the-blank-style questions like, "We could cut our costs by 20 percent if . . .?" Or, "We could double our sales if . . .?" What you unearth as you listen may surprise you.

2. Collect and Nurture Diverse Groups

As a leader, it's your role to bring together diverse groups, build enough trust and credibility to unite them, and make the discussion safe for unique perspectives. Collect people across gender, race, ethnicity, age, life experiences, skill sets, educational backgrounds, and more. As you bring in people from various disciplines and backgrounds, you can invite them to apply their thinking to an assigned topic in a new way. For example, invite your team to apply one field's methods or habits of mind to another field's problems to produce breakthroughs. By enabling teams to connect ideas from different contexts, you set the stage for innovation.

How can you gather the right mix of people? Building a diverse and cross-functional team may be easier when leaders allow team members to recruit new team members. This responsibility allows them to "pick candidates who fit in with the team culture and share similar values," and thereby have a better chance of meshing with the group to produce great results.[188]

One way to enhance diverse thinking is by bringing together people who have multiple social identities. Research by Henri Tajfel defined social identity as a "person's sense of who they are based on their group membership(s)."[189] Such group membership could involve anything from social class to family of origin to favorite football team, etc. It might involve changeable characteristics—like hair color, college affiliation, and avocation—as well as generally non-changeable characteristics like race, ethnicity, and gender. The group that we 'belong to' connects us with certain perspectives and insights, such as beliefs, worldviews, cognitive awareness, and social categorization. Because social identities endow individuals with specific, identity-related knowledge, leaders can tap into those identities to combine knowledge sets productively.

Although social identities can construct the sense of 'in-groups' and 'out-groups'—potentially having a lowering diverse people's willingness to collaborate with people they perceive as 'other'—leaders can capitalize on having a variety of social identities on their teams to positively enhance the outcome of a project. How?

For example, a study at the University of Michigan asked female engineers to imagine new features for a cell phone for women.[190] One unique aspect of this experiment that informs management strategies is this: if people are required to suppress certain parts of their identity to fit in, the company may lose out on a valuable source of creativity.

Looking a little deeper into a leader's role in drawing out information from social identities, consider the importance of policing potential discrimination by in-groups against out-groups. For example, a female engineer in a predominantly male work environment may not naturally voice female-oriented insights about cell phone (or other product) design. Perhaps she may feel a need to conform, or she may not want to stand out as 'different' because she doesn't trust she will be heard and validated—regardless of whether the final design bears her suggestions or not. Thus, when managers can identify multiple social identities, they can actively and deliberately create a safe space to allow those voices to be heard. In doing so, leaders can tap into a potentially rich (and often otherwise unheard) source of creativity.

Beyond gender identity, social identity shows up in country or place of origin, heritage, religion, languages, education, life experiences, family, and more. An ex-Marine might have valuable input on the psychological aspects of sales. A computer scientist and father of two children might have unique insight into computer programs geared toward children. Even subtle cues that stem from social identities can be valuable in nurturing organizational creativity.

3. Neutralize Rank

Because most companies are structured hierarchically, differences in status among collaborators can impede the exchange of ideas. For example, if a manager speaks, the team is trained to listen and accept, but if a new hire voices an idea, people may be less willing to engage with the idea simply because the new hire presented it. Or, a new person might feel less comfortable speaking in the room with higher-ups in case the idea is rejected.

How can leaders remedy this concern? Remind teams that salary doesn't determine sway in creative collaboration. Reward people who help others succeed regardless of rank. Sometimes, Harvard Business Review notes that managers need to figure out a strategy for how to simply get certain people to "shut up" at certain times.[191]

When you connect teams so they can explore new ideas and concepts, you're cultivating a networked organization. Networked organizations are structured on the belief, that every individual can collaborate, innovate, and solve the problems of an organization.[192]

Forbes recommends that leaders coach teams—including members of all ranks—through five steps in the creative process:[193]

- Doubt everything and challenge current perspective.
- Probe the possible and explore options.
- Diverge: generate new and exciting ideas, even if they seem absurd.
- Converge: evaluate and select ideas to drive breakthrough results.
- Re-evaluate relentlessly to keep pace with changing times.

By putting teams with members from all ranks in the organization through these five steps, leaders will take advantage of multiple vantage points and foster ideas that break outside of rigid thinking.

4. Don't Write Off the 'Loonshots'

As industries evolve, business goals and priorities will need to keep pace. Eight in ten CEOs surveyed by IBM indicated that they expected their industry to "become significantly more complex;" however, only 49 percent were confident that their organizations were "equipped to deal with the transformation."[194] Global dynamics and changes in technology are the reasons to consider 'loonshots'—a term coined by researcher and physicist Safi Bahcall. He defines 'loonshots' as widely-dismissed ideas or projects whose champions are written off as crazy but that lead to pivotal breakthroughs.

For example, when President John F. Kennedy announced to Congress in 1961 his goal of putting a man on the moon, he received grand applause. However, four decades earlier, when a scientist named Robert Goddard described the principles that might get us to the moon—including liquid-fueled jet propulsion and rocket flight—he was ridiculed as clueless about physics. Goddard had done the experiments and written up the results, yet he couldn't gain support for his game-changing invention.

The New York Times wrote that Goddard "seem[ed] to lack the physics knowledge ladled out daily in high schools," which was that

Newton's law on action and reaction made rocket flight in space impossible. Fourteen years after Goddard's death, the Apollo 11 rocket was successfully launched to the moon. The following day, the New York Times printed a (sheepish) retraction acknowledging that apparently "rockets did not, in fact, violate the laws of physics" and "the Times regrets the error."[195]

Safi Bahcall says of this: "Kennedy's speech marked the original moonshot. Goddard's idea was a classic loonshot. A moonshot is a destination. Nurturing loonshots is how we get there." In addition to jet-rocket moon flight, this category could include many currently well-known pharmaceutical drugs that were shot down repeatedly but were finally accepted and went on to revolutionize the health industry. It could apply to essentially any idea that was underestimated, blocked, or mocked at the time it was conceived, but that went on to do the great things for which it was destined.

What is the business leader's role in nurturing loonshots? Bahcall counsels: "Rather than champion any individual loonshot, [leaders] create an outstanding structure for nurturing many loonshots. Rather than visionary innovators, [leaders] are careful gardeners. They ensure that both loonshots and franchises are tended well, that neither side dominates the other, and that each side nurtures and supports the other."[196] Business leader Robert Kistner advises: "Striving for the impossible is the only way to succeed in the possible."[197]

5. Foster Creative Collaboration for Best Outcomes

History is littered with stories that illustrate the success of the "lone inventor," who comes up with a new idea and changes the world. Johannes Gutenberg is known for inventing the printing press, and Thomas Edison is known for creating the first practical light bulb. Some inventors share a single claim to fame: Wilbur and Orville Wright made human flight possible in 1903. Steve Jobs and Steve Wozniak created Apple and revolutionized the way society experiences modern computers. These innovators were often more motivated by the technical challenges and romance of the quest than they were for personal gain.

While a lone inventor may spark an idea, solve a specific piece of the puzzle, and dedicate extraordinary interest to a problem, widely successful inventions are more often the work of teams. Edison collected a group of engineers to help him refine his invention. Steve Jobs contributed ideas, business savvy, and design and Steve Wozniak brought the engineering know-how.

None of this is news for business leaders but the rubber-meets-the-road management question becomes: how can we support both the creativity of an individual who has an outside-the-box idea and facilitate collaborative creative processes for group innovation? At some level, the two contradict each other: one person with an idea is likely to be stifled by a group or may not share the idea, conforming instead to groupthink. On the other hand, a group with the right chemistry can layer brainpower and solve complex problems that no individual within the group knew how to solve alone.

To support the individual with an idea, start by listening. Take the person seriously. Vet the idea with peers and, if it seems like a "go," allow that innovator to drive the process as much as possible. Understand that he or she might be motivated by the challenge and quest even more than by a hope of credit or financial reward—and tap into this wellspring of human energy.

If the person becomes too rigid or myopic along the way, a good business leader will engage to bring greater perspective to the project. Now, if push comes to shove, the leader's view must prevail. But usually, innovative individuals are incentivized to collaborate because they want to see their ideas come to fruition, and that almost always requires the work of many players in an organization.

Key Takeaways

In sum, your role as a business leader in managing for creativity is to first recognize what creativity is and how it shows up in the employees and workplace you support. Notice the relationship between the number of new ideas that you and your teams generate and the level of success you achieve. Then, deliberately implement strategies for drawing out more creativity from your teams.

In this chapter, we have covered five time-tested tactics that leaders use to harness organizational creative thinking. In terms of key takeaways, consider: What can you do in the workplace today to continue nurturing diverse voices within your teams' collaborative processes? What is one step you can take to ignite the inspirational intersections in the various social identities that make up your teams?

Further, consider what 'loonshots' are in your stewardship: are there seemingly crazy ideas that your teams are currently kicking around? Are these the sorts of ideas that, with the right support, might transform your process or industry? What would it take for you and your team to move those ideas one step further toward fruition? Not each one of them will take off, but if just one does, it might take your company 'to the moon' in terms of success.

Finally, as you foster creative collaboration, take time to reward creative innovations. Feel free to structure rewards in any way that suits your organization but know that rewards function as both carrots and validation for employees. Companies that reward creativity show that they value it, thereby inspiring people within the organization to pursue untested theories and concepts.[198]

Brian Tracy reminds leaders: "Companies that create positive corporate environments receive a steady flow of ideas from everyone on the staff."[199] Because happy, valued employees and executives are more creative, do what you can to reward, recognize, and reinforce your staff. This will encourage risk-taking regarding suggesting new ideas and processes. Because creativity can be stimulated by desirable goals, don't overlook the power of providing rewards for solving pressing problems in the organization.

Now that you've finished reading Part One, we invite you to read Part Two of this series, which provides five more strategies that leaders can use in fostering creativity among teams and employees. Perhaps even more interesting, Part Two also offers several insights for nurturing your creativity as a leader.

Most business leaders have tight schedules and are juggling resources and logistics just to keep everything on track toward defined goals. When you're accountable to higher management and shareholders, it's hard to take time to nurture your creativity. Yet, chances are, when you entered your field, you had ideas you hoped to bring to fruition. Maybe you've checked some of those off your list at this point, but maybe there are others still calling for your attention. In Part Two, we will provide several specific insights for re-enlivening your creativity as a leader of your teams and in your career. Read on!

7

Building Creativity in Leaders and Teams

"The desire to create is one of the deepest yearnings of the human soul."[200] In business as well as in life, Maya Angelou's words apply: "You can't use up creativity. The more you use, the more you have."[201] In today's innovation-driven economy, creativity can fuel decision making and research that becomes the bedrock of new, successful methods.

Albert Einstein summarized: "Creativity is intelligence having fun."[202] Your company's profitability, income, and prospects depend on creative contribution and implementation. As we noted in Part One of this series, business leaders do well to encourage suggestions and ideas from each employee because each person can suggest improvements within their line of sight. "Creativity involves breaking out of established patterns in order to look at things in a different way."[203] As a skill that leaders and employees alike can cultivate, creativity is "the ability to transcend traditional ways of thinking or acting, and to develop new and original ideas, methods, or objects."[204] It shows up in big-picture ideas, out-of-the-box possibilities, and perspective-shifted actions. It's a tendency to generate or recognize ideas, alternatives, or possibilities that may be useful in solving problems.

Chapter Roadmap

This chapter is the second in a two-part series providing strategies for business leaders in managing for creativity. Here, we provide five additional strategies that business leaders can use with the teams and individuals they manage to set the stage for creative problem solving and invite the organization's best ideas.

Then, we turn our lens inward and discuss several ways that business leaders can nurture their creativity, both on and off the clock. Because leaders set the tone and tenor, it is wise for them to invest in their creativity and career. In this section, we provide specific tips and justification for the importance of each leader owning and cultivating creativity in himself or herself.

In case you haven't yet read Part One, we invite you to look there for insights about what exactly creativity is in the workplace. How do business leaders define it? How does it support the goals and work of the organization as a whole? We provide details in answer to these questions as well as the first five strategies that business leaders can use to cultivate creativity in the teams and employees they manage. Part One is a great pre-cursor and complement to Part Two; they go hand in hand in supporting business leaders in managing for creativity.

Five Strategies Leaders Can Use to Inspire Creativity in Their Teams and Employees

In Part One, we provided the first five strategies that leaders can use to spark creative thinking and problem solving in the teams and employees they manage. Now, those strategies don't necessarily precede the strategies presented here. Rather, the ten tactics cumulatively form a toolbox from which leaders can select the most applicable solution for each situation. In any case, the role of the business leader remains one of nurturing the creative process: "One doesn't manage creativity. One manages *for* creativity."[205]

Thus, here in Part Two, we will provide five more insights for sparking creativity by intentionally designing space for innovation, coordinating innovation and technology, scaling creativity via careful process, supporting two critical metaphorical roles—artists and soldiers—and paying attention to soft skills in management. These five strategies encourage and support creativity and innovation in modern organizations. They bring both stimulation and freedom into the workplace, thereby giving teams confidence to explore.

1. Intentionally Design the Space for Innovation

Forbes contends: "Just about everybody agrees that in the modern competitive world of business, creativity is essential to success. Yet, so many leaders of organizations hinder original thinking by not giving their teams the room they need to be truly creative."[206] Successful leaders develop the capacity for radical originality, and they create space for their teams to re-imagine and re-invent the status quo in totally unexpected ways. Thereby, they generate a culture that is open to creative risk-taking—one where failure is an accepted part of the creative process.

Often, leaders will be responsible for creating the space for groups to collaborate and create. This may involve logistics such as carving out time and designating a room. Other strategies include:

- Try collecting people at higher-energy times of day like mid-morning, rather than, say, right after lunch when our bodies divert energy from our brains toward digestion.
- Some sources suggest utilizing relatively small groups, such as four to seven people, for ideal brainstorming.
- Pick a room with natural light where possible because sunlight is a natural energizer. Avoid dark spaces or spaces with harsh fluorescent lighting as they diminish brainpower.
- Organize the task into manageable chunks, or deliver the task to the group and let them chunk it into pieces they will tackle.
- Consider offering one specific question per session, such as "How can we reduce costs on [a process] by ten percent over the next three months?"
- Set a timeframe in advance, such as between 15 and 45 minutes. Put away cell phones and laptops where feasible.
- Take breaks. Offer light snacks and coffee where appropriate.
- Set the emotional terms in advance to reward participation and mitigate instant criticism.
- Focus on quantity of ideas rather than quality and suspend judgment or evaluation while the group is collecting ideas. Praise participation, even if the quality of ideas is low.
- Keep a record of ideas and revisit that after the session.

Sometimes these spaces will happen in a virtual setting: creation online in private or collaborative workrooms. Take advantage of technology. Even in today's highly networked world, organizations often "fail to take full advantage of internet technologies to tap into the creativity of many smart people working on the same problem."[207]

Some leaders strategically apply time pressure in a healthy way to stimulate the creative process. Deadlines are a natural motivator. For example, consider NASA's Apollo 13 mission to the moon. When the spacecraft experienced unexpected problems, a life-threatening situation required immediate action. NASA leaders quickly assembled a team to brainstorm solutions for saving the crew while using only the items that were available on the spacecraft. Responding to this time crunch, the team designed a pinch-hit solution that was good enough to protect the lives of the Apollo 13 crew members until they could return to Earth.

While creativity can flourish in a pressure-cooker approach, where teams have limited time to solve specific problems, leaders should also consider the value of removing time pressure for 'finished' products. For example, it takes time to come up with solid, refined ideas. Creativity often involves kicking around countless possibilities, following leads, doing initial testing, and then circling back to the drawing board to tweak the idea or begin afresh.

As a leader, you must prioritize time for creation. Unjam the schedule; push off meetings. In an open-floor office, provide a venue for quiet thinking. In a walled-in office, create space for collaboration. Facilitate a mix of solo effort and team effort to produce the most successful ideas.

2. Deliberately Coordinate Innovation and Technology

A study from the University of Oxford's Business School looked at how leaders can achieve collaboration for creating radical innovations.[208] When no obvious antecedent exists, it's difficult for a vision to be shared effectively. In other words, when leaders need to encourage teams to solve a problem that has never been solved before, or break new ground, what can they do to help team members develop shared vision?

The study found that the answer lies in merging prototypes, metaphors, analogies, and even stories to coordinate team members' thinking.[209] When enough minds can arrive 'on the same page,' they can link up to experiment with new, creative pathways.

- Technology can support this process through mock-ups and sketches.
- Stories can connect people with the key elements of the issue they are facing.
- Metaphors help people think in comparisons, blurring the direct links enough that there is room for imagination.
- Analogies help collaborators mentally overlay solutions from other problems or industries on what they are trying to solve.

Some of the most creative innovations in one industry are merely importing and adapting solutions from another industry to solve unique problems.

As one idea, consider how technology and artificial intelligence that is already prevalent in everyday life can differentiate competitors in the hospitality industry. What if the hospitality industry creatively integrated even more digital components into the experience of purchasers and vacationers? Some competitors are already leading this frontier by introducing novel means of automatization and artificial intelligence to launch the hospitality experience of tomorrow.

For example, customers who regularly order products online or ask "Alexa" or another artificial intelligence device for information may seek those similar things in their hotels or resorts. Hotels may improve efficiency by enabling guests to order room service, spa treatments, transportation, entertainment, or other services on a tablet device. Making a call to room service or the towel desk is already a thing of the past. If clicking or tapping is too much effort, guests might prefer simply asking "Alexa" or AI for what they want: "Alexa: put in my order for a cheeseburger, coke, and fries. Also send me some fresh towels." Done. With a knock on the door, food and fresh towels arrive. "Alexa: send up a bottle of champagne with ice and a vase of flowers by 6 PM tonight." That is the hotel of the future . . . for now.

As another idea, aggregator business models use digital technology to revolutionize the way customers book and experience their vacations in the travel and hospitality industry. Successful companies may own no tangible assets; rather, they take on the networking role. Popular websites like Expedia or Trip Advisor don't own the properties; rather, they bring the owners and consumers together in a trusted and convenient space for transactions and become a one-stop shop for consumers. This model allows a company to collect information about a particular good and service provider, make the provider their partner, and sell services under their own brand. Future-focused resorts and hotels can capitalize on this successful model to introduce more services in-house for guests on property, and in pre-arrival stages.

Overall, "The best single definition of creativity is 'improvement.' Every single idea that improves the way we live and work, in large or small ways, is an act of creativity."[210] Creativity shows up in implementing innovative ways of managing, harnessing strategies to outpace the competition, and marketing established products to new demographics. The hotel or resort of the future is always evolving, and creative teams and managers can keep abreast of innovation by adopting technology, adjusting business models, and coordinating innovative thinking across industries.

3. Scale Creativity Via Careful Process

When a creative idea takes off, smart leaders want to scale it into a company-wide benefit. Unfortunately, sometimes adding more layers—management, bureaucracy, processes, infrastructure, etc.—can weigh down what was working about the small idea. This added weight may make people less inclined to take risks because mistakes have too great of an impact. Kim Scott of Google asks: "How do you get lift out of adding layers, instead of weight?"[211] She suggests investing in infrastructure—high or low tech—that makes collaboration easier.

On one hand, implementing a process can scale an individual idea into a company-wide methodology. What benefits one team can benefit the entire organization . . . right? This looks like standardizing "the way we do it" and relying on processes to streamline. On the other hand, relying on process means that new thought is not part of the plan. When organizations focus on process improvements, they often hamper innovation. Some companies might avidly focus on getting better and better at "the way we do it" but they're doing something that the market has rendered obsolete (think of Kodak or Blockbuster). In creative work, problems are best tackled from many angles, rather than from an efficient, standardized process.

A leader's role is to manage up and laterally: you must sell the creative idea to the investors and the organizational entities it needs to succeed. You must secure the resources, but also achieve the buy-in and support of other departments and stakeholders. The idea may sell itself to a degree, but leaders must build a niche for the idea in house and out in the market.

4. Separate Soldiers from Artists and Support Both

Safi Bahcall differentiated two roles that are critical for generating creative concepts and then taking them across the finish line in development: artists and soldiers.

Artists

The 'artist' role in a business organization is one of creation. The team member artists are comfortable with ambiguity and are more about generating possibilities than about making all the possibilities efficient or workable. Thus, artistic ideas naturally have a high failure rate—and that is desirable for this role because it means that their output is high. Ask them: what are the loonshots? What are our embedded beliefs about our customers, our competitors, and the nature of our markets? What if our current beliefs are wrong? Let's suspend disbelief and judgment. How might a creative person get around the current limitations? Talk through all the loonshots out there and ask how we can use those ideas to outperform our competitors.

When dealing with artists, leaders must give them space and license to think and protect artists from the people whose roles are different because artists may limit ideas when they fear someone criticizing: "How do you expect to sell that?" or "How could that ever work?" Free the artists to throw thousands of ideas against the wall and anticipate that one or two might stick. The artist's role is vibrant but also mentally tiresome, so be patient. Give them room. "On the creative side, inventors/artists often believe that their work should speak for itself. Most find any kind of promotion distasteful."[212] That's why you have the soldier role.

Soldiers

'Soldiers' in the business organization are those who move an idea from point A to point B and across the finish line. They are responsible for promotion, efficiency, and operational excellence—getting things done on time, on budget, and on spec. When dealing with soldiers, leaders should create metrics. You want a low-failure rate as the troops marshal the idea across the goal line. This is not the time to follow multiple ideas; this is the time to mitigate concerns and deliver a high success rate.

Those in 'soldier' roles may lack patience for those in 'artist' roles, even though the artists may have generated the very ideas that the soldiers are bringing to fruition. "On the business side, line managers/soldiers don't see the need for someone who doesn't make or sell stuff—for someone whose job is simply to promote an idea."[213]

Business leaders, then, "take on the role of project champions: they are bilingual specialists, fluent in both artist-speak and soldier-speak, who can bring the two sides together."[214]

Note that soldiers and artists are not necessarily strict roles. Some people—especially in smaller companies—may wear both hats, but not at the same time. For example, a team may be tasked with inventing ideas and brainstorming one day, and then evaluating and developing a work schedule for those ideas the next day. The point is that leaders should make separate space for the different activities of creation and production.

5. Remember Your Soft Skills in Management

"Business innovation is nothing without great ideas, but creativity is difficult to spark on a schedule. It requires a steady hand to manage the creative process and move it forward in a productive way."[215] Managers who succeed in this role demonstrate an ability to handle different types of innovation projects, from radical, one-time innovation to continuous-ongoing evolution. They support technical problem solving to generate novel solutions, and they are grounded in understanding how innovation works at a core level. They also manifest the soft skills and leadership capabilities for successful innovation.

The importance of soft skills cannot be overstated. For example, if you've heard much about Steve Jobs—co-founder of Apple, Inc.—you likely have heard about two things: his brilliance, and his inability to work well with others. He often acted from pure genius, but he had an abrasive, narcissistic personality and struggled to sustain good working relationships.[216] Business Insider notes: "His mammoth personality could inspire those around him just as easily as it could tear them down."[217] Jobs was known for storming into or out of meetings, shouting insults, and emotionally wounding those closest to him.

In the early 1980s, after Apple had grown large enough that Jobs could not control every aspect of it, Jobs noticed that the popular Apple II had essentially run its course and he wanted to build a prototype with a mouse and desktop icons. Jobs was a brilliant innovator; however, he couldn't get the top management at Apple to agree to the project. So, he "simply hijacked a team working on another project, took the best ideas from Xerox and elsewhere, and added some. The result was a renegade team at Apple, hidden away in a building off the main campus, that was tasked with creating the first Macintosh."[218]

Jobs assigned the team a simple task: "Build the coolest machine you can." Because this technology had never existed in this form before, the team struggled to get things right—disk drives, software, and hardware all took several iterations. Jobs would often callously but directly tell people on the team who presented their work, "That sucks," and send them back to the drawing board.

Further, Jobs required that the team members defend their ideas—if they could, they earned his respect; if they couldn't, he would blow them out of the water. Jobs did not have the most effective management style, to say the least, and by age 30, he was fired from Apple.[219] (Note: we will pick up this story in the Conclusion and let you know what happened next to Jobs, so read on . . .)

The key takeaway from this story is that effectively managing creative teams requires solid team-management skills, but also requires technical expertise and an understanding of the creative employees' work. Managing creative teams has a lot to do with ensuring that the surrounding workplace culture is designed to foster and nurture creativity, especially given that creation often involves spouting hundreds of ideas for a single one to stick. If people perceive risks and criticism in their environment, they may be unable to—or refuse to—create. Personal brilliance is not enough; a drop of kindness will go a long way. Where helpful critique is required, business leader Robert Kistner advises: "Be careful that your criticisms are not actually throwing boomerangs that it will come back to hurt you."[220]

How Business Leaders Cultivate Their Creativity

We've dedicated most of this chapter to discussing strategies for nurturing creativity in the employees and teams you manage. Here, we'd like to shift gears and talk about nurturing creativity in yourself as a business leader. Some of the same concepts apply—for example, you need to carve out time for yourself to think and process. You need a safe, enlivening environment with times for collaboration and times for quiet thought. You will become more creative as you engage with diverse groups whether at work or in other venues.

Most business leaders have tight schedules, juggling resources and logistics just to keep everything on track toward defined goals. When you're accountable to higher management and shareholders, it's hard to take time for yourself or your projects. But chances are, when you entered your field, you came with ideas and skills—things you hoped to bring to fruition. Maybe you've checked some of those off your list at this point, but maybe there are others still calling for your attention. From your vantage point in ascending leadership, you have a unique perspective on your company and your industry. You are beginning to see more clearly the connections—and limitations—that you weren't aware of when you entered the field.

The best suggestion we can offer here is this: get in touch with what you love about your work. If you've lost sight of that vision in the busy-ness of schedules, meetings, lunches, deadlines, sales numbers, and more, take a moment to reconnect. Touch base with what enlivened you as you entered the profession. What did you hope then to create? How have you managed (or set aside) those goals?

Earlier in this chapter, we referred to Steve Jobs when discussing the importance of soft skills when managing creative teams. Now let's circle back and see how Jobs recaptured his creativity after a career setback. To a graduating class at Stanford University, Jobs described how disoriented he felt when he was fired from Apple at age 30. He had helped grow that business from two people in a garage to a $2 billion-dollar company with over 4,000 employees. Apple had recently released its best creation—the Macintosh—which he helped create.

Then, when his vision of the future diverged with the managers he had hired, he was fired. At that point, he felt like a public failure, and like he had let down "the previous generation of entrepreneurs" because he had dropped the baton just as it was being passed to him.[221]

However, Jobs realized one critical thing: he still loved what he did. "The turn of events at Apple had not changed that one bit. I had been rejected, but I was still in love. And so, I decided to start over."[222] He couldn't see it at the time, but later he said that getting fired from Apple was the best thing that could have happened to him. Why? Because it liberated him from the heaviness of being 'successful' and infused him with the lightness of being a beginner again. Being fired "freed [him] to enter one of the most creative periods of [his] life," he recalled.[223]

In the five years after he was fired, Jobs started two new companies— NeXT and Pixar—and married an amazing woman. Pixar studio created "Toy Story" and went on to become a global leader in animated films. Soon, Apple bought NeXT and Jobs helped develop some of the products that fueled Apple's renaissance after the Macintosh.

About this transition from frustration into creativity, Jobs highlighted the importance of loving your work:

> Your work is going to fill a large part of your life, and the only way to be truly satisfied is to do what you believe is great work. And the only way to do great work is to love what you do. If you haven't found it yet, keep looking. Don't settle. As with all matters of the heart, you'll know when you find it. And, like any great relationship, it just gets better and better as the years roll on.[224]

While we are not suggesting that you get fired from your job to kickstart your creativity as business leaders, we are recommending that you take stock and ask yourself what you love most about your work.

What drew you to the hospitality field in the beginning? What motivated you to create the career you currently have? Are there ways to harness the things you love about your work into a new epoch of creativity as a business leader?

Only you know the answers to these questions. Even if you don't feel ready to, say, start the most successful animation company in the world, there are things you can create with your work and life. These flashes of creativity don't need to be monumental, but they can enliven your career. Maybe you find new ways to interact with your teams, or new solutions for meeting sales goals. Maybe you connect products and services into a new package. Maybe you shift your management tactics slightly and notice a positive effect downstream.

Maybe you embark on a new project for yourself outside of work that lights you up and thereby infuses your work with more meaning. Kurt Vonnegut noted: "To practice any art, no matter how well or badly, is a way to make your soul grow. So, do it."[225] You've probably seen what happens when an executive finally makes good on a personal goal that he or she has had but has been putting off—it's like the person comes alive. Find ten minutes a day to begin writing the novel you've wanted to write. Find an hour to begin training for that triathlon you've been contemplating. Take some extra time to nurture your relationships at home. All these things feed you as a business leader. They rejuvenate you and free up personal bandwidth for creation at work and in your life.

Brian Tracy claims that the great majority of people do little or no creative thinking at all, and it's time for leaders to begin a whole new way of looking at the world. "Everything that you are or ever will be will come because of the way you use your mind. If you improve the quality of your thinking, you will improve the quality of your life."[226]

To prime the pump of ideas, ask yourself: what are my top goals right now? What are the main obstacles between me and my goals and how could I remove one of them? What are my most pressing problems? What are my ideal outcomes? What would I dare to attempt if I knew I couldn't fail? These sorts of focused questions tap into the conscious mind and the subconscious mind. The conscious mind is objective, analytical, rational, critical, and pragmatic. It is responsible for analysis and decision making. However, the subconscious mind is the storehouse of retention, which recalls data, houses memories, and combines existing information into new forms and patterns. Together, these two modes of thinking combine to produce 'superconscious' inspiration, intuition, insights, and imagination.[227]

Key Takeaways

"Your time is limited," counseled Jobs, who passed away in 2011, "so don't waste it living someone else's life. . . Don't let the noise of others' opinions drown out your own inner voice. And most important, have the courage to follow your heart and intuition. They somehow already know what you truly want to become."[228]

In sum, investing your energy consciously into what you love—both on the clock and off the clock—will have a tangible impact on your career over time. You'll be better able to inspire creativity in your teams and you'll see subtle shifts in your work that help you fuel your passion for your career.

8

Thirteen Strategies for Business Innovation

Remember in the 'old days' when we had to pack a paper map for a road trip? Now we simply Google directions. To listen to music, we used to haul around a Walkman and clunky cassette tapes. Now, we carry thousands of songs in a single device. When was the last time you rented a movie from the video store?

Marching to the tune of innovation, Google Maps replaced Atlas, iTunes took out Sony Discman, and Netflix supplanted Blockbuster. Wonder what we will be using a few years from now to accomplish our day-to-day activities. Soon, we may reminisce: "We used to have these silly old things called smartphones . . ."

This narrative of user-friendly technological progress is really one of business innovation—time and again businesses evolve, pivot, invent, and create to keep pace with changing times and with new methodologies.

Leadership and Innovation

Leaders drive and facilitate innovation in business. According to the Center for Creative Leadership, "Studies have shown that 20 to 67 percent of the variance on measures of the climate for creativity in organizations is directly attributable to leadership behavior. What this means is that leaders must act in ways that promote and support organizational innovation."[229]

In general, innovation refers to creating newer, more effective processes, products, and ideas.[230] Innovation is drawn forth in response to market thirst, external regulation shifts, and internal company vision. For businesses—and particularly those in the timeshare industry—innovation often involves implementing fresh ideas, streamlining processes, creating dynamic products, or improving existing services. Leaders who actively support innovation increase the likelihood of their companies successfully tapping into emerging markets and demographics.

Savvy leaders look at innovation and creativity from many angles and ask meaningful questions. They experiment with both group brainstorming and solo idea generation. They examine the point where process standardization begins to limit freeform expansion. Leaders also scrutinize the success of top-down initiatives compared with ideas that come up through the ranks.

Where Innovation Gets Stuck

Despite all the hype about innovation and the fact that now more than ever businesses are craving the agility to pivot, leaders often find that successful ideas can be hard to come by. Maybe it's difficult to foresee what ideas will be most successful in the evolving markets. Sometimes budgets and busyness limit a company's ability to fund and facilitate innovation. Some ideas lack potency and others get strangled in red tape.

Research indicates that while organizational tendencies like routine, tradition, and homogeneity can initially streamline processes, they can also create invisible boundaries or limits. For example, established businesses stream revenue by replicating a successful product or process and scaling it up. These standardizations and procedures become "the way we do it." They buttress rapid expansion . . . but not necessarily innovation. In fact, some research shows that layers of management thicken the bureaucracy—dampening entrepreneurial spirit and risk taking.

Kim Scott, Director of Online Sales and Operations for Google, asks: "How do you get *lift* out of adding layers instead of *weight?*"[231] She believes that creativity within an organization depends on vibrant, ongoing collaboration and free idea flow—which often dry up as a business adds people and projects. One solution she suggests leaders try is investing more in infrastructure, whether high-tech or low-tech, that makes collaboration easier.

Chapter Roadmap

Diving into this and other solutions, the remainder of this chapter focuses on 13 actionable, present-moment strategies that business leaders can use to spark greater innovation among their employees and teams. Smart leaders will see tools here that they can import directly or modify to suit their unique environments.

Thirteen Leadership Strategies for Sparking Innovation

1. Leaders Provide Intellectual Challenge and Independence

Intrinsic motivation goes a long way toward innovation. When leaders provide autonomy and ownership for jobs, projects, or tasks, employees are motivated by the freedom to do things their way.

Think of jazz improvisation: each musician is familiar with her instrument and with musical chord structures. Put another way, she has mastered the fundamentals of personal contribution (instrument) and shared language (chords). Then musicians with these skills come together and improvise freely within a jazz standard. They put the song together fresh each time they play it, experimenting with note sequences and rhythms and harmonies. And it works.

In business, leaders bring together teams made of diverse individuals who have unique skill sets. With some basics in place like an employee's personal strengths and training, teams can improvise inside of a shared effort or project. This allows businesses to customize fresh and innovative solutions for specific needs and clients.

As a leader, you know your teams. You collect people with solid groundwork understanding of both the critical issues surrounding a project and the company's capability. What if you try turning them loose on an idea and see what happens? Allow people to bring their passions to bear. It's your privilege to provide intellectual challenge and independence.

2. Leaders Open the Floodgates of Ideas

If you've long been struggling with a particular issue in your business, gaining fresh perspectives could provide a breakthrough. Invite your teams to help solve chronic problems. You might kick off a brainstorming session by asking employees to answer this question: what would you start, stop, or keep if you were the sole owner of this company? You might hear a revolutionary idea. Go with it and give the innovator full credit. Leaders like Ronald Regan and Bob Woodruff, CEO of Coca-Cola, believed: "There is no limit to what a man can do or where he can go if he doesn't mind who gets the credit."[232]

Welcome ideas from all levels of the organization. Don't punish people for "bad" ideas. Also avoid criticizing or penalizing employees for coming up with ideas that don't pan out. As a leader, you have authority in the room to calm the naysayers. Openly consider the merits of each idea: what would be gained by implementation? Is the idea feasible? If not, let the employee know why so he can up-level his thought process.

In addition to opening the floodgates of ideas about company-level problems and solutions, smart leaders zoom in. Consider giving employees the authority to try new ways to do their jobs. They know the daily ins and outs of their work better than anyone else in the company because they deal with present-moment problems that evolve. They are positioned to optimize.

As a leader, you might take your hands off the wheel a bit and encourage individuals to innovate. Help them seek support by sharing problems and ideas for solutions with maintenance, co-workers, and managers.

Forbes recommends that leaders encourage key people to spend at least 15 percent of their time exploring and prototyping new ideas.[233] This invitation can yield small insights that create lofty results over time.

3. Leaders Invite Diverse Perspectives

Frans Johansson, author of *The Medici Effect*, interviewed people doing highly creative work in many fields and discovered that innovation is more likely when people of different disciplines, backgrounds, and areas of expertise share their thinking.

Sometimes the complexity of a problem demands diversity of insight. For example, it took a team of mathematicians, medical doctors, neuroscientists, and computer scientists at Brown University's brain science program to create a system in which a monkey could move a computer cursor with only its thoughts. [234]

Leaders see new ideas form when people integrate information from unique knowledge sets. For example, consider that people who exist inside of multiple social identities such as "Asian and American" or "woman and engineer" can often generate and integrate ideas from those unique knowledge sets. For example, leaders in a tech company may solicit ideas from female engineers about tailoring a tech device specifically for a female market. As a leader, you might consider your employees' unique knowledge sets and find ways for them to bring those to bear. Take the lid off conformity and tap into insight.

In another framing of diversity as a resource, leaders can support the application of one field's methods or habits of mind to another field's problem to produce a breakthrough. What if you help your marketing teams tackle a project using the scientific method? It might not yield a perfect solution, but this creative analytical overlay is guaranteed to get them thinking in fresh ways.

4. Leaders Take Risks

Leaders see value in taking calculated risk. The Wright brothers took risks testing out their flying device—they resolved that the chances were worth the payoff.

Dave Berkus describes several risks that business leaders face in terms of market, product, finance, competition, and execution. [235] You don't know what the market will do and whether it will latch onto your product. You don't know exactly how funding and finances will run. A competitor might show up suddenly and do what Netflix did to

Blockbuster stores. You might face challenges in teams and execution. In short, doing business has inherent negative risks, but smart leaders take calculated positive risks to solve—and help their teams solve—key problems.

Looking at the big picture, leaders can ensure that behaviors, systems, and processes are not barriers to constructive risk taking and experimentation. Strong leaders dare to accelerate through near-term failure by building momentum and speed through new learning for long-term results. You might deliberately encourage your employees to try even those ideas that they feel are a little risky. Help your teams make it through roadblocks, twists, and turns by staying open, agile, and curious.

5. *Leaders Create an Environment for Growth*

The image above shows an innovative take on a city-center forest: man-made "trees" in Singapore gather rainwater, shelter animals, and delight visitors. As a leader, you oversee establishing an environment for growth. Rearrange the furniture if that's what it takes. Something as simple as changing where people sit can transform how teams interact and how innovative ideas are generated.

Invest in training your teams because innovation is a skill that can be strengthened over time. Bolster their abilities in associating, questioning, observing, networking, and experimenting. Send people to conferences and networking events to get exposed to new people and new ideas. Take the time to connect with, coach, mentor, and develop your people.

Constructively challenge their thinking, strategy, and behavior through the lens of innovation. Stretch people to create, innovate, and envision alternative futures. In sum: growing your people helps grow a culture of innovation.

6. *Leaders Fan the Flames of Creativity*

Innovative leaders ask good questions like:
- What do you really want to happen?
- What do you think is stopping us?
- What has been successful so far?
- What have you already tried?

- Who else might be able to help?
- What'd happen if you did nothing?
- What one small step could you take now?
- On a scale of one to ten, how motivated are you?[236]

As your teams open up to you, recognize that they may be feeling vulnerable and validate them along the way. Be patient and appreciative—take time to deliver meaningful recognition when things work, and support when things don't work out as well. Always acknowledge ideas and let employees know the status of proposals. Prevent burnout with a good work-life balance and distributed workloads. Allow people to play.

7. Leaders Map the Phases of Creative Work

A leader has the vantage point to map out the stages of innovation and recognize the different processes, skill sets, and technology support that each requires. From where you sit, you can see the bigger picture and guide your teams through the process of developing ideas, refining, and all the steps along the way until those ideas begin generating revenue.

Visionary leaders are aware of what activities fit in which phases of development. For instance, efficiency-minded management "has no place in the discovery phase," says Mark Fishman. Because it's impossible to know in advance what the next breakthrough will be, "you must accept that the discovery phase in . . . innovation is inherently muddleheaded."[237]

In mapping the phases of creative work, leaders must do several things:
- Know where you are in the process.
- Appreciate the different creative types among your people and realize that some are better at certain phases than others.
- Be tolerant of the subversive—out of "rebellious" thinking great ideas are born.
- Bring together people with complementary skills and support them in innovating in harmony.

While the exact details of brainstorming strategies and idea development are vast topics, suffice it to say that leaders can best nurture innovation by giving each phase its due time. For example, when your team is brainstorming, teach them to save criticism for later. After ideas are on the board, then invite an analytical constructive review. Patiently walk your team through refining ideas, fusing concepts, and ultimately creating an innovative, workable solution that will deliver results. One step at a time.

8. Leaders Shepherd Innovative Ideas Through Commercialization

Survey data about product innovation in the EU between 2012–14 shows that leaders are responsible not only for facilitating idea generation, but also for shepherding great ideas to market.[238]

Experienced leaders know that they need different types of employees to handle this transition. Few people have equal capabilities in idea generation and idea commercialization; that's why large corporations normally separate the two functions. Eventually, an idea is developed to a point where it is best served by people who know how to take it to market.

Unfortunately, projects can lose steam at the handoff since the passion for an idea is highest among its originators. Leaders can keep fanning the momentum by adeptly handling timing and supporting the transition. In your organization, you may address this issue by choosing to round out individual skill sets for creative thinkers so that they can steer the entire process. Or, you may simply allow them to run with their unique strengths and then pair them with complementary resources.[239]

9. Leaders Untangle Bureaucracy to Nurture Ideas

While innovative ideas invariably must be sculpted to fit a company, managers should recognize that this process can dull good ideas as one component gets shaved off and another gets tacked on to appease an agenda. After a few key changes, the original innovative idea loses freshness and potency, and it no longer serves the purpose it was created to serve.

Some leaders decide to contain the negative components of this revision process by going flat. A "flat" management structure doesn't have long approval cycles and disjointed lines of communication that impede innovation. In organizations where flat management is not feasible, leaders can achieve similar results by empowering workers to act independently.[240]

10. Leaders Embrace Failure as Part of The Process

It's worthwhile to decide that failure is part of the learning process. A single value-creating idea might require hundreds of dud ideas. Innovative leaders embrace the certainty of failure. But, they also go one step further and quell employees' fear.

One reason employees may not express their ideas is that they don't want to rock the boat. They don't want to be perceived as a failure if what they share doesn't work out. Leaders can actively create a sense of psychological safety where open and honest communication can prevail by patiently tolerating mistakes and rewarding lessons learned. Ideas don't always work the first time, yet teams that seek innovation will be crippled if they fear mistakes. Russell Lundstrom, founder of Simple Smart Science, notes: "People are taught from an early age that mistakes are bad. We make great efforts to remove the fear of making mistakes in our company."[241] It is a fine balance because mistakes can carry a cost, but leaders should enable teams to reach beyond their comfort zones.

In the best environments, failure can be the ultimate learning experience. Wherever feasible, tell your employees: "I want you to feel free to fail and try again." Regularly analyzing mistakes can help team members untangle what didn't work and recognize similar patterns sooner in the future. Such discussions help transform fear and foster a creative, adventurous culture.

11. Leaders Set the Example

As a leader, you are the model for your entire team. The Center for Creative Leadership found that leadership behavior contributes between 20 to 67 percent to the climate for creativity in an organization. Further, they argue that "*leadership* is the most important factor needed to foster creativity and fuel innovation at the individual, team, and organizational levels."[242]

Think creatively about your work. Minimize your stress so you can be at your best—take a walk when you need to recharge and don't skip your lunch break. Be curious, confident, courageous, and collaborative. Be authentic.

The innovation potential of teams or organizations will be directly proportional to your innovation embodiment. Make sure your behaviors are not unintentionally limiting an innovation around you. You might ask, "How could I encourage even more innovation here?" Visionary leaders behave as the collaborative innovator they wish to see in their organizations.

12. Leaders Keep Their Doors Open

Your work keeps you running from place to place but do what you can to keep yourself open so that employees feel free to offer ideas. Even if a suggestion comes at a time when you're too busy to listen, don't brush it off. Instead, let that person know, "I'm putting out fires here, but I'm interested—send me an e-mail, and I'll get back to you ASAP." Then follow through promptly. Forgetting to get back to people is one of the surest ways to discourage the flow of ideas. Keep the office door open as much as possible.[243]

Let teams know that you welcome ideas at any time in any form: in the suggestion box; by e-mail, voicemail, or memo; at staff meetings, or during hallway conversations. This encourages people to share their thoughts in the first flush of enthusiasm so that good ideas don't end up on the back burner where they may be forgotten. When you're receiving suggestions, it can help to remember how many of your best ideas succeeded despite the lack of guarantees. One of your best skills as a leader is the ability to listen.

13. Leaders Reflect and Synthesize

Set aside time regularly for integration and synthesis. Because innovation is often a cyclical adventure, it's easy for both leaders and teams to get somewhat lost in the process. As the one in charge, your role is to keep focused and keep marching.

Throughout your successful path into management, you have developed personal strategies for reflection. Forbes reported that one

CFO sets aside every Sunday evening to mind map his most complex or strategic issues. He lays out all the pieces and then links them up by associating the divergent parts into an integrated whole.[244]

Identify your best way(s) to cut through clutter and gain clarity and new possibility and do those things daily or weekly. When a project is gaining momentum, you may need to reflect and synthesize more often than when it is well established. Reflection is also useful for teams because it keeps the big picture in mind for all participants. Good leaders create clarity out of chaos.

Key Takeaways

In short, leaders invariably have a great impact on innovation in their companies—for better or for worse. Some leaders function as a nozzle, stifling innovative ideas, while others serve as an amplifier. Where does your leadership style fit on the spectrum? What shifts can you make today?

Working with your teams to transform business processes and create better products takes time and patience. If you are open and enthusiastic about the cycles of generation, testing, and development, then your employees will join you and step forward bravely to participate.

One military leader summed it up this way: "Key drivers of innovation are providing vision and motivation, giving credit where due, and banishing fear and judgment."[245]

Regardless of which leadership strategies you find most effective to spark innovation with your teams, the key takeaway is this: do more of what gets your employees thinking. Be open and supportive. Then sit back and be amazed at the results.

9

Understanding the Power of Business Culture

The Link Between Culture and Strategy

Harvard Business Review asserts that "strategy and culture are among the primary levers at top leaders' disposal in their never-ending quest to maintain organizational viability and effectiveness."[246] On one hand, "strategy offers a formal logic for the company's goals and orients people around them."[247] On the other hand, "culture expresses goals through values and beliefs and guides activity through shared assumptions and group norms."[248] In some ways, strategy is the organizational mind whereas culture is the heartbeat. And as much as logic influences leadership, the heartbeat is often louder and more persuasive. John Doerr puts it this way: "Culture, as the saying goes, eats strategy for breakfast. It's our stake in the ground; it's what makes meaning of work."[249]

Illustration: WWII Military Culture

To illustrate the power and importance of culture in a military context, historian Richard Overy asserts that culture was even more significant than atomic weapons in empowering the Allies to win World War II. Overy explains that the Axis nations "did not properly stress administration, logistics, and organization because of their more martial military cultures," which "prepared their militaries to focus on the fighting of battles and campaigns, not the managing of overall war efforts."[250] However, the Allied nations' military culture excelled at managing overall war efforts and ultimately prevailed in the conflict.

For example, by mid-1944, Ford's Willow Run plant was producing one B-24 Liberator bomber airplane every 63 minutes. Sheathed in 4,200 square feet of bonded aluminum, the Liberators were both rugged and versatile. They served in every theater of the war with 15 Allied air forces, delivering critical fuel and supplies, dropping special agents behind enemy lines, and stalking submarines in the Atlantic. In short, the Allied culture of harnessing efficient manufacturing to create machinery and organize initiatives that supported soldiers was even more powerful than primarily training excellent soldiers.

Overlooking Culture is a Leadership Mistake

Because culture is not highly visible and is not captured on financial sheets, some leaders hesitate to take it seriously, preferring instead to focus on more visible, measurable things like revenues and sales. However, research shows that ignoring culture is a mistake with long-reaching consequences. Why? As a metaphor, consider the role that ocean currents play in a surfer's ability to ride waves. Although currents themselves are not always visible, they are powerful and they influence other visible things, like wave size, quality, direction, and rhythm. Ignoring currents means that surfers are more likely to be caught in dangerous rip tides and less likely to fulfill their goals of catching waves. Yet, by learning to feel the underlying currents and tides, surfers can move into position, sense rising and falling wave rhythms, and catch show-stopping rides.

Like ocean currents, organizational culture is both subsurface and powerful. Much of culture is grounded in unspoken and unwritten norms. For example, culture often lives within the beliefs and behaviors of managers and employees, and it generates social patterns that become predictable (like waves) to the extent that leaders are aware of culture. When leaders take time to understand the complexities of existing organizational culture, they can assess both its intended and unintended effects. By tapping into employees' views of culture, leaders can identify subcultures that can affect performance, as well as how aligned strategy is with culture. "Whereas strategy is typically determined by the C-suite, culture can fluidly blend the intentions of top leaders with the knowledge and experiences of frontline employees."[251] In this way, leaders can harness both culture and strategy to produce results.

Chapter Roadmap

This is the first in our three-part series regarding the power of culture in organizations. This installment is designed to help leaders look more closely at current culture by noticing unwritten norms that inform behavior patterns. We discuss the link between culture and behavior, particularly in terms of what constitutes an intelligent corporate citizen. We also provide several examples of companies nationwide that are hitting a home run with their cultures. In sum, this chapter enables leaders to pull culture out of the shadows, see what makes it tick, and understand why it is powerful.

Seeing culture is the first step in harnessing its power in service of desired objectives. This information forms the springboard for the upcoming chapters, which provide tips for leaders who want to spark evolution within organizational culture to align it more closely with values. As culture and strategy come into sync, leaders see better results and employees feel more connected with their work.

A Working Definition of Organizational Culture

Culture is the medium in which business goals can be achieved, according to *Measure What Matters*. Goals and culture are interdependent: they provide a blueprint for aligning teams toward common objectives. "Culture is the tacit social order of an organization: It shapes attitudes and behaviors in wide-ranging and durable ways. Cultural norms define what is encouraged, discouraged, accepted, or rejected within a group."[252] In short, culture equates with the unwritten rules of a group.

One of the key things to note is that organizational culture is all about the beliefs of a collective. Although each employee's methods and opinions will necessarily differ, culture is the common language that unites all employees' performance and behavior. "An important and often overlooked aspect of culture is that despite its subliminal nature, people are effectively hardwired to recognize and respond to it instinctively. It acts as a kind of silent language."[253] In addition to offering vision and an ethical rubric for operations, culture influences the tempo and mood of the entire company. Regardless of whether business culture arises spontaneously over time or is shaped deliberately, it forms "the core of a company's ideology and practice."[254]

Out of the Shadows: Seeing Current Culture

Where is culture evident? It shows up in everything from the company's philosophy, office design, remote workplace options, dress code, business hours, logo design, branding, etc. For example, consider the way that the following categories evidence culture:

- Workday Pacing: Imagine a typical workday at a gilded financial firm on Wall Street and a workday at a tech startup in California. What is the tone of the office environment and the expected workday length for employees? How do these elements affect employee satisfaction and public perception of the company? Those things are part of culture.

- Dress Code: Are employees expected to wear suits/skirts or jeans at the office? One dress code is not inherently better than another, but their differences affect the cultural experience of the office for both employees and clients.

- Office Design: Where do people sit at work? Alone or with others? Consider whether closed office spaces may reflect a hierarchical, individualistic culture, whereas open offices reflect a more horizontal, collaborative culture. Each configuration of offices affects the culture.

- Origin Story: How was the company founded? Consider also how a company's origin story—such as Apple's founding by Steve Jobs and Steve Wozniak—also evidences and influences culture. If the origin narrative is one of industrial disruption and innovation, that provides a unique culture right off the bat, which differs from a company with an origin narrative rooted in tradition and status quo.

- Place in Industry: Is the company fighting for entry or protecting its turf? In addition to company size, its place in the industry affects everyday culture. If it is a smaller company struggling to gain a foothold, it may naturally have a more innovative, competitive, risk-taking strategy because the company has less to lose. If it is a larger company with an assured product and sales pipeline, it may have a maintenance strategy with less risk tolerance.

- Leadership Values: How approachable and open are the company's leaders? The culture of an organization holds clues for how its leaders feel about transparency, accountability, vulnerability, engagement, and innovation.[255] Some leaders are more agile and inviting, while others are more traditional and authoritative. No leadership style is correct, but each style affects the culture.

- Products and Services: What products or services is the company providing? Are those products intended for wealthier people or for more economical use? Do they appeal to a younger or older demographic? A company's culture is established by its offerings, services, and business model, as well as by the personalities and priorities of its clients.

- Location: Where is the office headquartered? Bustling city or sprawling suburb . . . or completely online? Corporate culture is also informed by the surrounding local culture: consider how daily business operations likely occur differently on the West Coast than they do on the East Coast. Contrast the formal bowing greeting one might experience regularly in a Tokyo office with the informal-sounding Southern drawl and handshake greeting one might experience in a Houston office. Even regionally, cultural norms affect how colleagues address each other in the office, and how they interact with clients.

- Age: Is the company newer or quite established? It's normal for a company's culture to evolve as it grows and pivots over time: newer startups are nimbler than are established, larger companies. Note that culture is not set in stone; it will evolve as the company matures. Left unchecked, these evolutions may or may not be productive. So, leaders would do well to keep tabs on status quo as well as shifts in culture.

- Organizational Hierarchy: How many layers of management are there within the organization? How do those layers support or impede communication and growth? Companies with flatter org charts may have more incentive for employees to collaborate across departments, whereas companies with more developed hierarchies could value conformity over innovation.

Illustration: Southwest Airlines' Employee-Centric Culture

Recently, two brothers, who are adult children of a military/commercial pilot, decided to follow their father's example into the airline industry. After looking at many possibilities and consulting with their father, both brothers decided to join Southwest Airlines' pilot training program—largely because that company's culture makes it one of the best companies to work for in the United States. In 1971, Southwest Airlines began flying with just three planes, and it has since expanded to employ more than 60,000 people. In addition to providing great service, Southwest's culture is "one of its most celebrated assets."[256]

For example, as the company grows, rather than simply focusing on resumes, managers "are encouraged to hire for attitude and train for skill."[257] The idea is that specific skills can be taught but a positive attitude is inherent to personality and is critical for success—pick a person with the right attitude and they'll learn the necessary skills. "Founder Herb Kelleher is credited with instilling the idea that happy employees create happy customers, and profitability follows. With core values of a 'Warrior Spirit,' 'Servant's Heart' and 'Fun-LUVing Attitude,' Southwest asks employees to embody hard work, perseverance, proactive customer service and lighthearted fun in everything they do."[258]

That attitude is apparent on any flight where flight crews and pilots exhibit humor and fun in their announcements, which are normally delivered stiffly and formally on other airlines. Finally, Southwest focuses on rewarding employees as its "culture of service thrives on appreciation, recognition and celebration."[259] Putting its money where its mouth is, Southwest provides loans for new pilots to complete its flight school, and this program benefitted the two brothers immensely. Who wouldn't want to join a company like that?

Culture Informs Behavior

The deepest strength of culture is its ability to motivate or constrain behavior—to educate everyone in the organization about what is acceptable and unacceptable. The culture of an entity is synonymous with "the beliefs and behaviors that determine how a company's employees and management interact and handle outside business transactions."[260] When leaders begin to proactively assess the current culture in their organization—as influenced by the factors above as well as by many other things—they can begin to harness the power that culture carries. By driving the organization's unspoken assumptions and worldviews, culture creates action. "When properly aligned with personal values, drives, and needs, culture can unleash tremendous amounts of energy toward a shared purpose and foster an organization's capacity to thrive."[261] Consider how culture fuels accountability, corporate citizenship, and scaling and growth.

Accountability

How are an organization's cultural values transmitted and enforced? Generally, cultural elements become a company's way of doing business because they spring from the behaviors and values of the founders and early managers. It's a sense of 'this is the way we do things around here.' Thus, culture becomes implied more than expressly defined, and new hires can pick up on it as they integrate into the company. Colleagues and peers know they can count on each other and nobody wants to be the weak link. In a healthy and productive culture, everyone on the team moves the work forward because of the social contract as well as because of company goals. "Peak performance is the product of collaboration and accountability."[262] In short, culture creates an unwritten system of responsibility.

Corporate Citizenship

By describing and codifying the values of "an intelligent corporate citizen," culture helps people behave consistently according to a "common set of values, objectives, and methods."[263] With a set of corporate values, organizations can self-govern in ways as shared principles become louder than rules, and as purpose becomes louder than incentives. In an evolving business environment, "we're asking people to *do the next right thing*. A rulebook can tell me what I can or can't do. I need culture to tell me what I *should* do."[264] When employees and teams are able to do the next right things consistently and make decisions that are in line with company culture, that enables the organization to scale values such as productivity, compassion, and creativity. An organization with a clear and embedded culture inspires trust in employees, which boosts innovation, productive risk-taking, and ultimate performance.

Behavioral consistency serves to both reduce inefficiency and increase trust among all players. How? When clients know that they can receive excellent service from any person in a company under any similar set of circumstances, they will be more confident in creating lasting business relationships. Similarly, when employees know what they can expect from their managers and leaders, they can feel more secure in their daily work. This trust goes both ways in the sense that managers will feel more comfortable trusting employees with more freedom when they know that their employees will behave according to an acceptable set of company cultural norms.

As an example, "Florida-based grocery chain Publix Super Markets is the largest employee-owned grocery chain in the United States, employing over 225,000 employees, whom they call associates."[265] In addition to being one of the ten largest-volume national supermarket chains, Publix "has earned a spot on Fortune's 100 Best Companies to Work For list for the last 23 consecutive years."[266]

So how has Publix accomplished this? It has an employee-centric approach to culture, wherein associates are eligible to buy shares in the company, which incentivizes hard work and provides a sense of company pride. By providing company ownership, Publix motivates behavioral excellence from each employee. Further, Publix helps employees chart their career paths by offering a career site with relevant resources and job opportunities. This helps employees grow over time, gain training to be promoted over time, and rise within the company over the long term. This builds loyalty and retains talent.

Scaling and Growth

As companies grow and scale, culture creates behavioral coherence and efficiency because culture is "a manual for quicker, more reliable decisions."[267] By codifying values and behaviors inherent in an organization, culture teaches employees how to act and teaches customers what to expect. Thus, corporate culture provides a training shortcut of sorts—it teaches employees to think and respond consistently so that leaders don't have to micro-manage decision making.

This streamlines company performance and frees up leaders to use their strengths to lead as employees "work in unison for the common objective and [are] proud of their results."[268] Research indicates that "even more than wage dissatisfaction, corporate culture is a more reliable predictor of attrition."[269] So, by focusing on culture, leaders will retain more employees who can help scale and grow the company over time—imagine just the cost and time savings from not having to hire and train people in the wake of attrition.

Finally, by influencing behavior, culture gives organizations a leg up on their competitors. "In our open-sourced, hyperconnected world, behavior defines a company more meaningfully than product lines or market share."[270] Consistent input and strong relationships go a long way in boosting sales. Put another way: "When companies 'out-behave' their competition, they also tend to outperform their competition."[271]

Illustration: Adobe's Culture of Inclusion and Creativity

We see this power of culture in the software giant, Adobe, which promotes a culture that values "quality, creativity, and opportunity."[272] For the past 20 years, Adobe has been on Fortune's 100 Best Companies to Work. "Adobe generates a strong culture by offering highly competitive benefits to its employee and building diversity, inclusion and fairness into the workplace."[273] It also provides bi-annual breaks so that employees can step away from the hustle and recharge, returning to their desks with their heads clear.

To show its commitment to diversity, Adobe encourages employees to bring their unique insights to the table and show appreciation to others for speaking up. Investing "time and energy into promoting pay parity and opportunity parity across the organization,"[274] Adobe is committed to fairness and employee recognition. Key takeaways: hire people for the value they bring to the culture and help everyone feel like they belong.

Key Takeaways

We'll offer one final illustration here of a company with a strong culture of social responsibility. Business Leadership Today recently reported that NDIVIA, a tech company headquartered in Santa Clara, California, had the best company culture in the United States.[275] Particularly as employees are navigating the shift from remote and hybrid work environments back to in-person work environments, NVIDIA focuses on social responsibility by making their people their top priority. This reflects the values of the company's culture, which include: "agility, collaboration, innovation, integrity, and performance."[276]

Along those lines, NVIDIA employees indicate that their work feels both "challenging and meaningful, with great compensation and a democratic culture."[277] There's a prevailing sense that the company is authentic and its "leaders walk the talk with culture and values."[278] Those sentiments point to an effective cultural mix of leadership values and caring.

In conclusion, as you can see from the examples and detailed information offered in this chapter, culture has an unmistakable effect on an organization's ability to achieve its goals. Culture's invisible currents show up in a company's age, location, origin, industry, workplace environment, and more. Because culture creates unwritten but predictable behavior patterns, leaders can capitalize upon culture to produce desired outcomes. As leaders invest in creating an optimal company culture, they strengthen the values that drive internal decision making, external client relationships, and, ultimately, the bottom line.

10

Sparking Cultural Evolution

Culture Informs Strategy

When health insurance giant Aetna merged with lower-cost U.S. Healthcare in 1996, the two entrenched company cultures clashed so loudly that reverberations threatened the well-being of the entire combined organization. By the early 2000s, Aetna's rapport had eroded steeply with customers and physicians, and it was being sued repeatedly. Although its surface revenues remained steady, it was losing roughly one million dollars per day because of labyrinthine processes, hefty overhead, and some ill-fated acquisitions.

Interestingly, Harvard Business Review notes that many of the "problems Aetna faced were attributed to its culture—especially its reverence for the company's 150-year history."[279] Why? Isn't reverence for the past a good thing in terms of building tradition? Well, not always.

In this case, venerating the past encouraged employees to be wary of risk and more comfortable with stasis than with growth. Further, the culture created a crew of Aetna 'insiders,' who were with the company before the merger and who did not appreciate U.S. Healthcare's more aggressive business style. "Culture is like the wind. It is invisible, yet its effect can be seen and felt. When it is blowing in your direction, it makes for smooth sailing. When it is blowing against you, everything is more difficult."[280] When the weight of cultural stalemate had nearly drowned the company, a new CEO came on board—the fourth CEO in five years. To say that employees were majorly skeptical of yet another 'transformation' initiative would be an understatement.

But this CEO took a different tactic: he invested time in the trenches, so to speak, and listened to employees' viewpoints at all levels. He asked for their insights and involved them in strategic planning. From these conversations, he was able to pinpoint a key concern in the way the company was managing medical expenses, which was spurring the company's loss of rapport with physicians and patients. After addressing that concern, eliminating 5,000 jobs, and challenging long-standing assumptions, he and his colleagues slowly implemented a new culture and way of doing business that reinfused the company with respect and pride. Within a few years, "employees felt reinvigorated, enthusiastic, and genuinely proud of the company. And Aetna's financial performance reflected that. By the mid-2000s, the company was earning close to $5 million a day"[281] and its stock price was rising steadily.

As we see with the example from Aetna, when culture is working against strategy, it's hard to ask employees and managers to consistently perform new, desired behaviors in familiar situations. It's the business equivalent of the adage that you can't teach an old dog new tricks. But this change makes the difference between strategy that fails and strategy that works. This chapter focuses on empowering business leaders to create sustainable cultural change that supports their organization's strategy. When leaders realize that culture is working against their strategy, they have their work cut out for them because implementing necessary culture change is often the most challenging part of implementing any initiative.

Chapter Roadmap

This is the second part in our three-part series designed to help leaders harness the power of business culture. By way of review, in the first part, we defined organizational culture as the beliefs and unspoken assumptions held by leaders and employees. We showed how culture is rooted in everything from the company's origin story and physical location to its office design, dress code, and workday pacing. And we clarified that culture's power lies in its ability to influence social patterns and collective norms.

In this part, we will provide five tactics for leaders who want to spark evolution within their current organizational or team culture to align it more closely with their desired strategy. These tactics include tapping into emotional and social dynamics, beginning with an apology, tuning up feedback systems, trying pulsing as a means of present-moment awareness, and playing the long game patiently.

By way of preview, in our upcoming chapter, we will discuss the critical importance of rooting culture in values. Including research from a study published in Harvard Business Review, we describe eight values that should inform functional culture for working groups at any level: from teams to regional groups to the organizational level. As culture and strategy come into sync, leaders see better results and employees feel more connected with their work.

Why is Culture Hard to Change?

Corporate culture often becomes entrenched. Culture is remarkably enduring because of social reinforcement of patterns so that people who "fit in" to it are drawn to the organization. Over time, culture can become like a homogenous echo chamber, resistant to change. Keith Cunningham, author of *The Road Less Stupid* asserts, "The reason companies lose relevance, go broke, or fade into the sunset is because they continue to grow, but fail to evolve."[282] Leaders have plenty of practice with sparking necessary evolution in products, sales procedures, market positioning, hiring, management tactics, and more.

But sparking evolution in culture can be tricky because lasting and sustainable shifts can't merely happen through mandates from the top. Rather, change must emerge within the habits and perceptions of people who drive "how things are done around here"[283] from the ground up. Put another way, leaders can mandate compliance, but they can never successfully mandate trust, heart, or talent—the things that make an organization succeed.

As leaders look more closely at current culture by noticing unwritten norms that inform behavior patterns, they can unearth the often-invisible links among culture, behavior, and values. This information is essential for productive change when culture is less than ideal. As you consider your team's current culture, you might realize that it could use a bit of a tune-up.

Does the existing culture hamper the achievement of goals? The saying, "culture eats strategy for breakfast,"[284] implies that culture and strategy are somehow at odds, and that culture is more powerful than strategy because culture can 'chew up' strategy for breakfast and then go on with its day. However, this imbalance is neither necessary nor helpful. Rather, it occurs primarily when there's a lack of alignment between culture and strategy. Brian Tracy advises: "If what you are doing is not moving you toward your goals, then it's moving you away from your goals."[285]

Here's an everyday example to illustrate the point about alignment between culture and strategy. Imagine that you set a dietary goal to lose ten pounds (that's your objective). You come up with a strategy to help you achieve that goal: eat three low-calorie meals per day without snacks. However, if your behavior pattern (culture) over the past two years involves grabbing a sweet latte and donuts for breakfast, you can see right away that there is a lack of alignment between entrenched behavior (culture) and the implementation of your strategy of eating low-calorie meals.

It's easy to see that behavior must conform to objectives or there's no hope of success. Put another way, until you evolve your entrenched cultural beliefs about breakfast, your goal will stay out of reach. This behavioral change will likely seem unpleasant because who wants to replace donuts with, say, oatmeal? Similarly, businesses can have all the beautiful strategic objectives in the world, but until culture is such that the implicit biases and behaviors support the new objectives, the objectives won't get off the ground.

Five Tips Leaders Can Use to Spark Cultural Evolution

When the existing organizational culture is not conducive to current objectives, leaders can proactively launch a cultural evolution. Leaders are responsible for shaping culture through accountability, consistency, trust, and solid communication. Here are five tips for leaders who want to spark cultural evolution: 1) tap into emotional and social dynamics; 2) begin with an apology; 3) tune up the feedback systems; 4) try pulsing as a means of present-moment assessment; and 5) don't worry if it takes time.

1. Tap Into Emotional and Social Dynamics

First, take time to understand the current culture, and assess the specific ways that it differs from the desired culture. To get an accurate feel for current culture, connect with people at all levels. Ask questions. Watch how employees move through the workday and what they accomplish. What are the social dynamics of teams? Do team members understand their roles clearly? Do all team members feel psychologically safe with each other so that they can tolerate risk and innovation? Sit in on meetings to see how people connect (or disconnect) on an interpersonal level, and how those connections affect fluidity of performance. How connected do people feel to the company's mission overall? Do they find meaning in their work? Notice places of inefficiency and inverse productivity at all levels of the organization.

Quiz managers on their views of what is working well and where the points of friction arise. How can we support any weak links to help improve functionality? Check in with partners and board members about their views. In short, do your homework to see what culture is present and how that culture is supporting or detracting from desired goals. This step is key because many employees don't directly think about the unwritten, established cultural norms; rather, they live those norms without thinking that things that could (or should) be different.

After you've done your homework, settle into a vision process. In this context, it's less about external factors like market positioning, and more about internal factors related to culture. Dream big—what would high-functioning teams look like? What would it take for each person to feel connected to the company's mission? Since employees are the main asset of any company, how can we bolster their needs and enable them to enjoy top-notch performance?

This can and should happen at the team level, manager level, or top leadership. The main question is: given what our current culture is, how can we get to where we want to be? Be clear with all involved

about what must change and why. When we stop "dancing around setbacks," we remove the shame around trying hard and failing.[286]
By establishing cultural methodology for the company, leaders help employees work in unison according to shared priorities. "Culture can also evolve flexibly and autonomously in response to changing opportunities and demands."[287]

With deft leadership, culture can adapt to new inputs and needs, particularly when those changes are implemented in ways that account for existing cultural values. The architecture of changing culture is particularly helpful when leaders want to create new growth—they must persistently reinforce transformation from legacy culture into the desired new culture.

Similarly, Harvard Business Review advises that "unlike developing and executing a business plan, changing a company's culture is inextricable from the emotional and social dynamics of people in the organization."[288] Thus, to kick off cultural evolution, leaders must clarify their aspirations by articulating the high-level principles that guide the organization and by connecting those aspirations to emotional and social dynamics.

2. Begin with an Apology

In *The Road Less Stupid*, Cunningham doesn't pull any punches: "The lousy culture you have now was created by you. It is a perfect reflection of what you have tolerated and therefore is your fault."[289] Ouch. He suggests that we initiate cultural change with an apology that owns our role in the current environment. If we as leaders had built a better culture, then that would be what is present. But . . . the culture we have now is one we want to change, not relish. So, own it. Maybe we were afraid to have the tough, essential conversations because we wanted to keep the peace. Maybe we missed key indicators.

Whatever the reason that culture has gone south, Cunningham suggests that we candidly articulate the problem, and then state what we will do about it. Try something like:

> "I admire and respect you, but I have let my admiration for you cloud my judgment and my willingness to say what needs to be said. Candidly, I have probably . . . elevated being liked over

being successful."[290] I lost sight of our outcomes because I was busy not rocking the boat. But it doesn't matter if we have the world's best vision statement or mission. "The truth of the matter is we can have the best vision and mission statement in the world, but if no one has a clue how that translates to [results], then we have no shot at accomplishing that mission or delivering on those values."[291] That's on me as a leader. But now I am asking you for help identifying what has gotten in our way and designing the go-forward plan to help us accomplish our priorities. I commit to leading with courage and holding everyone accountable—including myself—so that we can all succeed together.

Along these lines, business leader Robert Kistner says, "If I have an employee who is far out in left field – that's on me."[292] Granted, leaders aren't responsible for employees' misbehavior or mediocrity. However, when leaders become aware that an employee is 'far out of field' and they do nothing to teach, motivate and correct the employee, then the leaders become complicit in the behavior, and they signal to other employees that such behavior is acceptable. In short, there's real power for change and growth when leaders own their responsibility in proactively creating or passively allowing the acceptable status quo in the work environment.

3. Tune Up the Feedback Systems

Third, to monitor the progress and effectiveness of ongoing cultural evolution, leaders should harness the company's systems of evaluation and feedback. Tap into pre-existing surveys, training sessions, conferences, and more to help everyone learn the *what* and *why* of the desired cultural shifts. Doing so will integrate desired cultural transformation into performance management and will build buy-in over time. "Vision-based leadership beats command-and-control. . . . When performance management is a networked, two-way street, individuals grow into greatness."[293]

Corporate cultures that produce high levels of motivation often include two elements: support for work-specific tasks, and support for interpersonal needs. Just supporting one of these without the other tends to drain productivity. For example, if leaders mostly support work tasks by providing resources, time, and shared analysis, teams will do decent work. But if leaders also take time to provide attendant feedback, encouragement, and recognition, teams will grow faster. John Doerr notes: "Where people have authentic conversations and get constructive feedback and recognition for superior accomplishment, enthusiasm becomes infectious."[294]

4. Try Pulsing as a Present-Moment Assessment

One method of offering regular feedback is by taking the pulse of workplace culture. It's asking essentially: "What's here right now?" In this moment, how is morale? What are the expressions on people's faces? Is the tone in the office happy or somber? Walk through the halls and peek at people. Do you see any smiles? Do you notice productivity that's not fabricated just because you're watching? Leaders might survey team members about whether they have recently had a conversation about goals with their managers and whether they have clarity about their career opportunities. Does anyone seem confused or frustrated? You can tell by looking at people how they are feeling about their work that day.

In pulsing, leaders might go one step further and inquire about team members' health, motivation, and energy. How often are they feeling 'in the zone'?[295] Do people seem like they've had enough sleep, generally? What wins are occurring at 9 AM? And at 10 AM? And at 1 PM? Are there moments to celebrate today? By taking the pulse of company culture, leaders can pick up on subtle signals of distress and keep on top of issues as they arise rather than waiting for them to hit a breaking point. "Pulsing gauges the organization's real-time health— body and soul, work and culture."[296] This information helps leaders understand what culture is present, and that information is key anytime leaders are trying to create a sustainable change.

After pulsing, it's time to communicate. As with any feedback method, culture controls communication methods that make an organization more functional . . . or less functional. Many times, group conversations about culture—such as town halls or annual kickoffs— can generate enthusiasm and lay the foundation for shared expectations. Then, leaders can follow up with individuals in one-on-one meetings, such as performance reviews and coaching sessions. "By reiterating and rewarding desirable culture in both group and private conversations, leaders can ensure that cultural change is effective on both individual and collective levels throughout the organization,"[297] Cunningham continues. In any plan for cultural evolution, leaders must consider effective methods of communication and feedback, including short-term pulse information and longer-term guidance.

5. Don't Worry if it Takes Time

Finally, take heart: rebuilding culture is like "your first scuba dive, when you go thirty-five feet down and you're scared out of your wits. But when you come back up, you're exhilarated. You have a new insight into how things work beneath the surface."[298] All changes take time to gain traction, but each cultural shift toward your desired aspirations will help the organization sync up culture and strategy for maximum efficiency. Make an effort to demonstrate the desired cultural shift so that everyone can see that leaders walk the talk. Tap into networks to reinforce common purpose and safe havens. As time passes, be sure to celebrate wins and small steps along the way to the goal.

Although it's easier for leaders to avoid the friction involved with sparking organizational change, remember that friction can help demonstrate traction—it shows that things are changing, and it also highlights what elements need more support. Ultimately, Cunningham reminds us, "the key to a great culture is creating and fostering never ending conversations about the rules of the game so everyone knows how to act how to communicate and how to treat each other."[299] The long road to cultural change happens one conversation at a time.

Key Takeaways

A word here about timing and mindful preparation for change. Why might leaders elect not to initiate cultural change at this point even if they know it needs to be done? The project takes time. Some experts put it bluntly: don't bother starting the process if you're not willing to stick with it day in and day out because little dabs don't do it. Giving periodic lectures or buying more break room snacks will not work. Leaders need grit and persistence because implementing cultural change is neither fast nor easy.

If you're considering kicking off cultural change but the process seems overwhelming, you can start with preparation. Preparation comes before the apology, should you choose to go that route. Start gathering information about where you are and where you want to go. Strengthen or re-write your company values because those form the basis of your target culture. Ask for insight. Survey your teams to see what is working and what isn't.

Finally, from the lens of mindfulness, consider your life: do you have the time and energy to pour your heart into this process? Are things stable in your home life? How is your health and well-being? Do you have the strength for the long haul in guiding cultural change? Further, how are your relationships in the C-suite? Is everyone informed of the current status and on board with the next steps? Because transparent leadership is key to cultural change, do the work on yourself first so that you are living the desired culture fully before you ask the employees to live it as well. They will look to your example for both accountability and motivation.

As you put in the initial thought and preparation, you'll be able to launch and sustain the process of cultural change over the long term. Doerr reminds leaders why the effort is worthwhile: culture is "our stake in the ground; it's what makes meaning of work."[300] When it comes to achieving goals, leaders find that culture is often the secret ingredient that "can fluidly blend the intentions of top leaders with the knowledge and experiences of frontline employees."[301] Leaders who understand the power of culture can shift the social norms that drive organizational behavior. Sparking cultural evolution as needed is worth doing because a healthy business culture can attract and retain talent, streamline day-to-day operations, and boost the bottom line.

11

Anchoring Culture in Values

How Value-based Culture Averts a Crisis

Having a company culture rooted in values helped American Red Cross leaders find their way out of an embarrassing situation. In 2011, one of the employees in charge of handling social media sent out the following tweet on the American Red Cross's official Twitter page: "Ryan found two more 4 bottle packs of Dogfish Head's Midas Touch beer. . . . when we drink we do it right #gettngslizzerd"[302] [sic]. That post was meant for the person's private account, and she didn't realize that she had posted publicly. Although the social media director found and removed the post an hour later, it had already gone viral.

What should leaders do in this situation to salvage the company's reputation? What would leaders at your company do? Well, the American Red Cross turned to its cultural values for a solution: compassion, collaboration, creativity, credibility, and commitment. Certainly, a tweet like this on the official page could damage the credibility of the entire organization as readers wondered what was going on behind the scenes. Some companies would have terminated the employee and required a public apology.

However, instead of firing the employee, the American Red Cross social media director simply replaced the tweet with a dose of honest, creative humor that showed compassion for the employee's mistake and re-established the company's credibility. She wrote: "We've deleted the rogue tweet but rest assured the Red Cross is sober and we've confiscated the keys."[303] Since nothing can fully be deleted from the internet, Red Cross took ownership and acknowledged the mistake in a way that engaged authentically with the public.

Going one step further, the Red Cross creatively turned this blunder to its advantage for fundraising and donation of blood. The Dogfish Beer Company reposted the tweet along with a message inviting people to support the Red Cross. For several weeks after that incident, the two companies linked up for a creative, spontaneous partnership of sorts that encouraged many donations (and many beer sales).

In fact, some people began to tweet things like, "After I drop off a pint of blood to the @RedCross, I'm replacing it with a pint of @dogfishbeer #getngslizzerd."[304] Tapping into the value of collaboration, the Red Cross and Dogfish Beer transformed the mistake into a mutually beneficial situation.

Although the situation could have gone differently in a company with a more rigid culture and leaders could have fired the employee for this offense, the Red Cross chose a route consistent with its cultural value of compassion. About this incident, the social media director blogged: "We found so many of you to be sympathetic and understanding. While we're a 130 year old [sic] humanitarian organization, we're also made up of human beings. Thanks for not only getting that but for turning our faux pas into something good."[305] In short, the Red Cross's value-based culture turned a moment of reputational crisis into something that benefited public relations and blood donations. That's culture done right.

Chapter Roadmap

This is the final part in our three-part series designed to help leaders harness the power of business culture. By way of review, we have defined organizational culture as the beliefs and unspoken assumptions held by leaders and employees. Rooted in everything from the company's origin story and physical location to its office design, dress code, and workday pacing, culture has a powerful influence on social patterns and collective norms.

In this part, we discuss the power of anchoring culture in values and leadership transparency. Guided by research from a Harvard Business

Review study, we describe eight values that inform functional culture for working groups at any level, from local teams to global leadership. As culture and strategy come into sync, leaders will see better results and employees will feel more connected with their work. Finally, we outline how cultural values help leaders get the right people on the bus, thereby improving hiring and retention. Since people are the root of culture, attracting and keeping the right people will help improve organizational success.

A Culture of Transparency Improves Collaboration

Consider the forces that link goal setting, culture, and transparency within the organization. Transparency "is about accountability, measuring and bias for urgency, a focus on solutions, calling it tight and saying what needs to be said, being kind and generous, acknowledging one another and expressing appreciation."[306] John Doerr adds: leaders need to cultivate the right culture—one of "ruthless intellectual honesty, a disregard for self-interest, and deep allegiance to the team."[307]

In research regarding leadership transparency, a parallel term is *vulnerability*, which Brené Brown defines as the "birthplace of innovation, creativity and change."[308] Leaders who are vulnerable at appropriate times can connect departments and teams, both horizontally and vertically. Transparent leaders enable the whole organization to pull toward the desired outcome, and they create a culture of openness and acceptance.

What prevents leaders from getting on board with transparency? Being open in the business realm is sometimes disconcerting for leaders: "Transparency is scary. Admitting your failures—visibly, publicly— can be terrifying."[309] But it is valuable, nonetheless. Leaders who are willing to set a corporate culture of living authentically, voicing concerns, capitalizing on strengths, and supporting teams can draw diverse groups into unified work. In fact, "once you start having honest, vulnerable two-way conversations with your direct reports, you begin to see what makes them tick. You feel their yearning to connect to things bigger than themselves. You hear their need for recognition."[310]

In general, leaders who reinforce a culture of transparency see higher rates of goal achievement. Such a culture encompasses everything from "how we talk to each other, how we treat each other, how we trust each other, [to] how we handle conflicts."[311] Such a culture syncs with strategy and forms the underlying basis of relationships within an organization.

Illustration: Pixar's Focus on Transparency Boosts Originality

You likely know Pixar as a successful, industry-transforming film company based on creative animation. "Pixar's culture is the secret sauce to developing so many box office successes,"[312] and its culture of transparency is designed to reward originality. In the idea-generation phase, Pixar's culture is one of psychological safety, which encourages employees to experiment and innovate. Anyone familiar with brainstorming knows that you leave the table wide open at the start so that all ideas are welcome. Shooting down ideas initially will only limit people's willingness to bring more ideas for fear of ridicule. However, there comes a point when ideas need to be weeded out so that teams can focus their energy on the best ones.

Here, Pixar's culture balances collaboration and creativity. Team members respectfully provide candid feedback on works in progress, and it's not all positive. "Pixar practices radical candor to promote transparent conversations. Colleagues are not meant to judge their peers,"[313] but rather to judge the work. With honesty, people collaborate to help the best ideas succeed.

Values are the Link Between Strategy and Culture

According to Harvard Business Review, the following eight organizational values inform healthy business culture:[314]

- *Caring:* This value prioritizes cultivating interpersonal relationships; developing loyalty and trust; and collaborating in interdependent work environments.
- *Purpose:* This value focuses on incorporating idealism and altruism into the daily, often mundane aspects of professionalism; fostering unity and sustainability; and emphasizing shared goals and a cause greater than self.

- *Learning*: This value is about harnessing exploration and creativity to expand innovation while rewarding curiosity and open-mindedness
- *Enjoyment*: This value encourages leaders to add a pop of fun into the daily grind, and foster playfulness and humor
- *Results*: This value motivates leaders and teams to celebrate achievements and wins of all scales. It rewards laser focus and goal accomplishment.
- *Authority*: This value fosters respect for strength, boldness, and decisiveness. It also rewards confidence and productive competition.
- *Safety*: This value creates reassurance and helps individuals feel secure and protected amid change. It rewards preparation and planning to mitigate risk and boost predictability in the work environment.
- *Order*: This value encourages leaders to create clear structure and shared norms. It rewards cooperation and respect for customs and rules.

As leaders, you can see how these values make goals more achievable. However, you'll also notice that not all goals can incorporate all eight values. For example, leaders should balance the value of *enjoyment* with the value of *order* because healthy work environments can't be all play or all rules. As another example, the value of *authority* will need to be balanced with the value of *safety* because competition and security are both useful in achievement, but they can be at odds with each other philosophically.

As leaders craft goals and strategize around these eight values, teams will feel inspired to innovate and take risks, even as they are rewarded for compliance and results. Team members will feel more anchored to the projects and more connected to each other. A well-defined set of values aids in shaping the company's strategic direction. It helps leaders make decisions that are in harmony with the organization's core principles, which, in turn, leads to more coherent and effective strategies.

These values help solidify the link between culture and strategy so that all engines are firing in sync toward the same organizational objectives.

The following table shows several ways of aligning strategic results and cultural values:

Strategic Result	Cultural Alignment with Result
Delivering outstanding customer service	Emphasizing achievement, caring, problem solving, collaboration, and relationships
Implementing new initiatives	Emphasizing authority, competition, innovation, teamwork, and risk-taking
Managing a product development team	Emphasizing collaboration, innovation, learning, enjoyment, and results
Ramping up to overcome a competitor threat	Emphasizing authority, order, achievement, and purpose
Building morale	Emphasizing enjoyment, collaboration, caring, purpose, and safety

Illustration: Google's Performance Values

As a practical example, Google studied culture within high-performance teams using five value-based questions[315] that highlighted underlying emotional and social dynamics:

- *To understand team structure,* Google asked if members were clear on their roles and on the team's overall objectives and key results.

- *To address concerns around psychological safety,* Google asked whether team members felt comfortable with risk taking, or whether people would feel embarrassed if ideas didn't work. This information helped team leaders make changes in the tone of the work to support innovation and penalty-free appropriate risk-taking.

- *To understand employees' personal connection* to the mission overall, Google asked people to share whether they felt their work was significant. If they received feedback that employees felt their work was routine or empty of value, then Google's leaders were motivated to reassign employees or educate them on their place in the larger goals. To the extent people can work on

156

things that they value, they will bring more life to those projects.

- *To identify any weak links and provide extra support* where needed, Google asked how well team members felt they could depend on each other to deliver quality work on schedule.
- *To understand employees' awareness of larger goals*, Google asked them whether they believed that the work the company was doing fundamentally mattered. This information helped inform company goals and highlight employee concerns.

By clarifying the underlying cultural dynamics on teams who worked well together and achieved their targets, Google leaders were able to shape policies and methods to provide to all teams.

Strong Cultural Values Get the Right People on the Bus

Since employees are the greatest asset for any company, leaders dedicate themselves to getting 'the right people on the bus.' Jim Collins writes in *Good to Great*: "You need to get 'the right people in the right seats.' Only then do you turn the wheel and step on the gas."[316] Employees are the first and ongoing line of defense, and culture is what informs their behavior. As leaders take ownership of curating culture and revising it when needed, they can tackle root problems in the trenches and in hiring. This will help set up a strong line of defense with personnel. Because culture is rooted in the beliefs and behaviors within the organization, "culture is about the people you recruit and the values they bring to bear."[317]

What Type of People Does Your Company Attract?

Thinking of the type of people you hire, consider the importance of traits like "accountability, measuring, a bias for urgency, a focus on solutions, calling it tight—saying what needs to be said—being kind and generous, acknowledging one another, and expressing appreciation."[318] Culture controls which conversations are welcomed, and which are shunned. Do we address problems or avoid them? Do we dress up or dress down? Are all included, or are there cliques of insiders? For example, consider how people with free-thinking tendencies and spontaneous lifestyles might steer clear of employment with rigid dress codes and long hours. Likewise, a company with a 'good old boys' culture might not attract, hire, or retain top female business professionals. Someone who graduated from Berkley might not fit naturally with a company in rural Texas.

We could go on and on, but the point of these examples is that culture affects who gets on the bus in the first place, and it absolutely affects who stays on the bus long term. From the lens of personnel, why should leaders spend time rebooting current culture and investing in change? Not only does great culture make companies more effective, but it is also a magnet for hiring and retaining excellent employees. "Creating and sustaining a world-class culture is an ongoing but immensely rewarding initiative. It lowers turnover, improves efficiency, and makes the business a good place to work."[319]

How Well Are Your Managers Aligned with Your Target Culture?

Leaders must train managers to align fully with the new, desired culture. Such leaders are pivotal in not only demonstrating the cultural changes but also in supporting others in following suit. These managers will listen and teach inside organizational conversations that emphasize the importance of the changes. "The companies that treat their people as valued partners are the ones with the best customer service. They have the best products and strongest sales growth."[320]

Are You Willing to Let People Go When Necessary?

In addition to tenacity and persistence, know that you'll have to be willing to let people go. For example, there's often one or two people on a team who think they're immune to cultural transformation. They think they're special, and they will drain the energy of the team until you let them go. Sometimes, leaders effect cultural revolution by letting go of people who don't buy into the target culture and hiring new people who do. This must be handled empathetically, but it is one of the most direct ways of kick-starting new culture. Cunningham almost taunts: "The reason we hesitate to have the hard conversations is because we don't care enough. If you truly cared enough, you would say what needs to be said."[321]

The flip side of this issue is when managers see employees as fungible and easily replaceable. Employees are not keyboarding widgets. It can take substantial time and investment to move employees into harmony with an organization's culture. As that happens, it may be worth the continued investment it takes to retain those employees who are a solid cultural fit.

Illustration: Xerox Returns from Bankruptcy with Cultural Overhaul

In 2000, Xerox was $18 billion dollars in debt and on the brink of bankruptcy after its stock fell 26 points in a single day. Enter new CEO Anne Mulcahy. When one customer suggested, "You've got to kill the Xerox culture [to survive]," Anne retorted, "I am the culture."[322] With this remark, she showed how, as the new CEO, she was taking ownership personally for mistakes of the past administration to turn the company in a new direction of fiscal functionality. "Mulcahy was a champion of Xerox and its values—including that of corporate responsibility—and she believed in the loyalty of customers and especially employees."[323]

As Anne set about revamping company culture, she focused on keeping the right people on the bus. She met personally with her top 100 executives, informed them of the tough situation, and said they were welcome to stay if they would commit fully to the new culture and new financial plan. All but two of those executives elected to stay, and most of them were still with the company eight years later when Xerox had "paid off its debt and revamped its product offering and business model."[324] With a strong leader and the right people on the bus, Xerox survived.

Key Takeaways

In addition to visionary ideals and mission statements, organizational culture "is functionally about value-driven behaviors that lead to successful relationships among colleagues and clients."[325] As a reminder, the eight values presented by Harvard Business Review include: caring, purpose, learning, enjoyment, results, authority, safety, and order.

The key takeaway for leaders and teams is to proactively consider these cultural values as they craft goals and strategy. This helps people feel more anchored to the initiatives and projects, as well as more connected to each other and the organization. Values play a pivotal role in shaping the culture and strategy of an organization, ultimately driving results in the workplace.

When a company's values align with its culture, employees are more likely to feel connected, motivated, and engaged. The values discussed in this chapter help solidify the marriage between culture and strategy so that all engines are firing in sync toward the same objectives. Values, culture, and strategy become interconnected, creating a powerful synergy that drives positive results, fosters innovation, and enhances the overall well-being of the workplace. As leaders, we must nurture these values because they drive sustained success in the dynamic business environment.

PART TWO.
LEADERSHIP AS
TRANSFORMATION CATALYST

SIMPLE BLUEPRINTS FOR
BOLD LEADERSHIP AS
AN INNER JOURNEY OF GROWTH

12

Leadership as Stewardship

Releasing Micromanagement

Occasionally, leaders find themselves deep in the minutia of micromanaging their employees. Chieh Huang defines this rather humorously as "taking wonderful, imaginative people, and bringing them into an organization and then crushing their souls—by telling them what font size to use and other ultimately unimportant things that limit their ability to innovate freely."[326]

Micromanagement varies by organization and by leader, and while companies do gain credibility from having unified font sizes in their publications, micromanagement generally signals an imbalance. A leader has become too involved in decisions that are better handled by the employees.

Generally, when leaders hover too close to their employees, their intent is positive. They are trying to help employees get things right and overcome challenges that they (the leaders) have already solved in prior roles. They're sharing strategies and suggestions while ensuring company objectives are met. At some level, micromanagement may have to do with retaining control over the work and product. For instance, leaders start at the bottom of an organization doing the work. Then, if they're doing well, they are rewarded with more work and with entry into management. Then, if they're good, they begin managing the managers. At this point, leaders start to lose control over the output of their jobs and may feel they need to micromanage to retain some ownership over the quality of the end product.

Even if it stems from positive intent, however, leadership by micromanagement isn't effective at producing excellent results or happy, problem-solving employees. Worse: it tends to backfire in the long term. At some point in time, effective leaders must hand the work and the day-to-day mission efforts over to the employees.

Leaders who prefer a hands-on approach may worry that if they micromanage less, they will have to clean up more messes from employee failures. What these leaders are missing is that while they will likely see some failures, they will also likely encounter "surprising innovation as smart, capable employees begin to solve problems and deliver solutions"[327] they never imagined, or that are outside the realm of the leaders' training.

For example, a Millennial-age employee may have a different or more innovative take on a company's technology concern or product than a Boomer-age manager may have. If the manager can step back enough to allow the employee to analyze the issue and implement solutions, the manager may be surprised when something works that wasn't evident from his or her vantage point. "That's when having great people around you makes all the difference . . . if you don't crush them via micromanaging."[328]

Trust as the Solution

The best solution—and perhaps the only solution—to micromanagement is trust. To cultivate trust in employees, a leader who tends to micromanage must reframe: learn to celebrate failure as a milestone in the process of growth and success. Bob Burg reiterates: "Give people something good to live up to—something great—and they usually will. In fact, often they'll even exceed those expectations."[329]

Letting go is akin to the process that occurs when a parent is teaching a child to ride a bike. When a father begins teaching his daughter to ride, he may start by holding the seat of the bike and running alongside as she pedals. She is steadied by her father's hand, but she can only ever ride as quickly as dad can run. There's a moment of magic that occurs when he releases the bike for the first time: he holds his breath, watching his daughter begin to steady herself as she pedals free for the first time. She'll wobble a bit and may tip over, but more often, she bursts ahead with confidence in her capability—exhilarated with her new skill.

In a business environment, a caring manager may run alongside a pedaling employee for a time, but this is never the best long-term use of energy for the employee, the manager, or the company. Instead, managers should steady as needed, help employees up if they fall, but most often should stand back and appreciate the employee's skills when she's doing well at the thing she was hired to do. For a micromanaging leader, the ability to release is grounded in the ability to trust.

Trust is the glue that enables people to rely on each other. This is true in all relationships and particularly in the workplace. Business leader Stephen R. Covey teaches: "Trust is the glue of life. It's the most essential ingredient in effective communication. It's the foundational principle that holds all relationships."[330] As a two-way principle, trust involves give and take: leaders must make the effort to trust their employees, and leaders must be people that employees can trust.

Think back over the past few years of your career. What aspects of micromanagement have you witnessed or experienced firsthand? Consider the following prompts if needed:
- Have you felt a manager or colleague exerting undue influence over your work?
- If so, how did that affect your ability to produce?
- In what ways might you have tried to manage your employees' work too closely for them to be effective?

Chapter Roadmap

Through the remainder of this chapter, we will look in depth at these two distinct aspects of trust with the goal of considering leadership as a stewardship of influence.
- First, we'll consider how leaders can show trust to their employees. As a way of releasing micromanaging tendencies, but even more as a way of building a healthy workplace, leaders may try out five recommended strategies for building trust with

employees: having a growth mindset, giving credit, listening, offering support, and looking for inspiration.

- Second, we will turn the lens inward and discuss what it takes to be a leader who is worthy of trust. We'll consider especially three aspects that enable leaders to behave as stewards: identity, income, and influence. Taken together, these three things empower leaders to become people their employees can trust.

How Leaders Show Trust to Employees

It's All About How You Treat Them.

Showing trust to employees is all about what you do. Your trust level for your employees is evident in your actions and in the way you treat them. As discussed above, leadership styles that lean toward micromanagement show low levels of trust for employees. On the other hand, leadership styles that give more room for employee innovation show higher levels of trust for employees.

David Horsager, author of *The Trust Edge: How Top Leaders Gain Faster Results, Deeper Relationships, and a Stronger Bottom Line*, notes: as a leader, you may "have a compelling vision, rock-solid strategy, excellent communication skills, innovative insight, and a skilled team, but if people don't trust you, you will never get the results you want."[331] Without trust, the workplace becomes a place of "skepticism, frustration, low productivity, lost sales, and turnover."[332] However, leaders who build trust with teams "garner better output, morale, retention, innovation, loyalty, and revenue. . ... Trust affects a leader's impact and the company's bottom line more than any other single thing."[333]

A relationship of trust helps employees feel room to grow and experiment and solve problems while knowing that their leaders will support and guide them appropriately. Leaders who trust employees are involved in helping employees expand their vision and avoid potential hiccups. But they also back up and allow for innovation and real growth—even when it means there will be some moments of failure. At those moments, leaders earn further trust from employees by 'having their backs' in essence—acknowledging together what didn't work and helping employees walk forward.

"The very first job of a leader is to inspire trust. Trust is the single most essential element to our ability to deliver extraordinary results in an enduring way. Trust is integral to building high performance because it enables an organization to work as it should; it's the first defense against dysfunction and the first step towards delivering better outcomes."[334] For the most part, business leaders understand the importance of trusting employees and being someone worth trusting, but there is always room for growth. Thus, here are several specific tactics leaders can use to build or enhance trust, and to rebuild it when it has been lost.

Five Methods for Showing Employees That You Trust Them

Trust is tangible, as Stephen M. R. Covey teaches: "Contrary to what most people believe, trust is not some soft, illusive quality that you either have or you don't; rather, trust is a pragmatic, tangible, actionable asset that you can create."[335] Before he passed away, former President George Bush, Sr. provided insight regarding leadership and overcoming challenges, and these suggestions are highly applicable to building trust. [336] Please note that all quotations in the five elements below are from President Bush.

1. *Have a Growth Mindset.* Leaders build trust with employees by showing that they don't sweat the small stuff. Every little bit counts toward creating desirable outcomes, but good leaders embody the idea that "out of adversity comes challenge and often success,"[337] and they help employees not feel too down when work takes a bad turn. Sometimes those rougher moments are the birthplace of innovation.

2. *Give Credit.* Good leaders build trust with employees by fairly managing blame and credit. President Bush advises: "Don't blame others for your setbacks. When things go well, always give credit to others."[338] When an employee does good work and receives credit from a leader, trust grows between them. Employees learn that the leader is not out to shirk blame and hog credit, and employees are willing then to bring forth their

great ideas and trust that the leader will handle the information wisely.

3. *Listen.* "Don't talk all the time. Listen to your [employees] and mentors and learn from them."[339] When you listen as a leader, you may hear things from your employees that you perhaps didn't anticipate. You'll receive insight and show you care. Also, in listening, you make space to understand what your troops think of you. President Bush counsels, "Don't brag about yourself. Let others point out your virtues, your strong points. Nobody likes an overbearing big shot."[340]

4. *Offer Support.* "Give someone else a hand."[341] When an employee is hurting, show that employee you care by offering support. People may be skeptical at first about whether you have their best interests in mind, but leaders who follow the golden rule will build trust over time. This becomes even more critical along the trajectory of your career. "As you succeed, be kind to people. Thank those who help you along the way. Don't be afraid to shed a tear when your heart is broken because a friend [or employee] is hurting."[342] Staying connected to people throughout your career will not only enrich your work, but it will also cultivate long-lasting relationships of trust.

5. *Look Inward.* "Say your prayers!"[343] Regardless of your religion or belief structure, it is relevant for leaders to turn their attention inward. Many leaders, like President Bush, reference prayer. Others reference meditation or mindfulness practices. Any of these efforts helps leaders practice the skills of seeing a bigger picture—recognizing how to free the mind from common pitfalls and patterns of thinking. By connecting with oneself and/or with a higher power, leaders will find the steadiness and vision to support their work and relationships.

In sum, a quotation from Henry L. Stimson articulates the point: "The only way to make a man trustworthy is to trust him."[344] Leaders are uniquely positioned to help employees grow by showing trust.

How Leaders Merit Employees' Trust

It's All About Who You Are.

In addition to giving trust, leaders must be worthy to receive trust from their teams. On one hand, as mentioned above, leaders gain trust at work by how they interact with employees—by providing solid interaction and room to grow, by delivering results, by being dependable, by giving credit where credit is due, and so on. On the other hand, leaders earn trust through their character—by being worthy of employees' trust.

Titles, in and of themselves, do not necessarily equate to trust. For example, giving someone the title of General does not make that person immediately trusted or respected. Trust and respect must be earned; it cannot be bestowed by mandate. Sometimes a Sergeant may be more trusted and respected than her superior officer because she earned that trust and respect. In reality, an individual can be highly trusted and respected without any title at all—he or she has simply earned that respect.

Who you are makes a huge difference in how well you can lead. General Colin Powell shares: "The day soldiers stop bringing you their problems is the day you have stopped leading them. They have either lost confidence that you can help them or concluded that you do not care. Either case is a failure of leadership."[345] A manager who does well at work won't merit quite the level of trust from employees when he has serious unaddressed concerns in his personal life, or when his work and personal lives are inconsistent with bedrock values. Instead, managers who merit the highest levels of trust from employees are those who treat their leadership as stewardship.

Significance Comes from Serving

Leaders in any area—business, politics, sports, art, academics, theater, and so on—don't own that area and any associated title. Rather, they are stewards of it for a time. Significance in life and career ultimately comes not from status or salary, but from serving. In this way, leadership is a stewardship of service and influence.

"At its most basic level, stewardship is acting upon the understanding that leadership is a temporary role which is outlasted by the lifespan of an organization," holds Bekele Geleta, former Secretary General of the International Federation of Red Cross and Red Crescent.[346] At an individual level, stewardship focuses on promoting the well-being of each person within an organization—helping each employee feel valuable and valued. Leaders who are good stewards promote effective team interaction across the organization—providing motivation and supporting conflict resolution.

At a global level, leadership as stewardship involves ensuring that the institution's values and missions are working effectively within the constraints and possibilities of the worldwide business community. Faced with competing responsibilities, global leaders as stewards remain committed to their organization's long-term mission through short-term strategies that stay faithful to the organization's core values.

Steven Nardizzi, CEO of Wounded Warrior Project, maintains that by "creating a culture of stewardship, a successful organizational leader can empower everyone in an organization to be both a leader and a steward, regardless of their position in an organizational hierarchy. Thus, leadership through stewardship should be a fundamental aspect of not just successful organizations, but of our shared culture as citizens of this 21st Century global society."[347]

Three Ways to Frame Your Leadership as a Stewardship of Influence

Rick Warren, successful author and leader, offers a three-part strategy for framing leadership as stewardship: harnessing our identity, income, and influence. To illustrate, Warren describes his invitation to speak to players in the U.S. National Basketball Association (NBA) at an All-Stars game. He asked them rhetorically: "So, what's in your hand?"[348] Then, he elaborated:

> It's a basketball. And that basketball represents your identity, who you are: you're an NBA player. It represents your income: you're making a lot of money off that little ball. And it represents your influence. And even though you're only going to be in the NBA for a few years, you're going to be an NBA

player for the rest of your life. And that gives you enormous influence. So, what are you going to do with what you've been given?[349]

Similarly, business leaders often bear roles of great influence, revered identity, and commensurate income. Look more closely at what's in your hands.

1. Identity

The first element of identity is to recognize that you matter. Warren reiterates: "You matter to history; you matter to this universe."[350] This sense of personal value highlights the difference between survival and significance—a "significance level of living" involves discovering or choosing what we are here on Earth to accomplish. Regardless of our wealth or intelligence, we're all searching for solutions to our problems. We're looking for fulfillment, and for a sense of authenticity so that we're not pretending to be someone.

Worldview determines behavior, and behavior determines what we become in life. Warren explains: "I think that comes down to this issue of meaning, of significance, of purpose."[351] It's about quantifying for yourself what you believe and what you hope to accomplish with your life when everything is said and done. These are some of the most fundamental human issues. Understanding your purpose informs your worldview, which in turn informs your approach to life and leadership.

Brenda Barnes adds: "The most important thing about leadership is your character and the values that guide your life."[352] Sometimes we fail to take time to codify what we believe and why. Maybe we're too busy or too little concerned to figure it out for ourselves. However, according to Warren, "Your worldview determines everything else in your life, because it determines your decisions; it determines your relationships; it determines your level of confidence."[353]

One test of the worldview is how we act and lead through difficult times, not just the good times. Robert Kistner regularly shares his mantra with his teams: "I'm alive, I'm awake . . . I feel great!"[354] In fact, some of the team members acknowledge that this mantra has stayed with them over many years and inspired positivity.

In addition to worldview, the question regarding identity is: what are you going to do with what you've been given? Each of us has unique talents, networks, ideas, freedom, creativity, etc. Warren suggests we inquire of ourselves: "What am I wired to do?" Are we wired to be an undersea explorer? To paint? To lead an organization? Then we should do those things. Oscar Wilde famously advised: "Be yourself. Everyone else is already taken."[355] When you embrace your identity, your unique talents will inform your organizational leadership.

2. Income

Just as NBA players gain income from their work, business leaders acquire affluence. Obviously, income is a reward and exchange metric for time invested in work. It's essential and fulfilling. But, when income or affluence becomes our focus, it tends to blind us to greater aspects of our stewardship. It may be tempting to view salary or material wealth as the tangible manifestation of an effective career; however, good leaders focus more on doing good than on acquiring goods. Warren cautions: "Your net worth is not the same thing as your self-worth. Your value is not based on your valuables."[356]

By nature, humans enjoy material things and often hoard them—we try to get all we can, protect them, and get more. We confuse having a good life with looking good, feeling good, and having more. But wealth and affluence can never deliver happiness—if it could, the wealthiest people would be the happiest, yet statistics prove this is untrue. Thus, Warren advocates giving deliberately: "Every time I give, it breaks the grip of materialism in my life."[357]

Giving is the link between income and service. Author Bob Burg teaches: "Your true worth is determined by how much more you give in value than you take in payment. Your income is determined by how many people you serve and how well you serve them."[358] As a leader, your income can represent how well you have served your clients, employees, colleagues, etc. Your income is a manifestation of your stewardship, and it is at your fingertips to use in service of others as you give.

Sometimes, people have limited preconceptions about giving: we think of 'giving back' by writing checks to charities once we have already done well for ourselves. But that's only one specific facet of giving. Rather, giving is a way of being—a commitment and characteristic that permeates everything we do. Giving can be large or small; it can involve money, time, or simple kindness. It is a way of doing business and a way of living life. Significance in life and leadership does not come from status or salary; rather, it comes from serving and giving.

3. Influence

As a business leader with some stewardship of affluence, you also have a stewardship of influence. The purpose of influence is not to build your ego or your net worth. Rather, leaders can use their influence to speak up for those who have no influence. Burg reiterates: "Your influence is determined by how abundantly you place other people's interests first."[359]

Illustrating the powerful influence that a business leader can have on an employee's career, Paul, a project director in a successful company, shared this story. From the beginning, Paul's boss's positive reputation preceded him. "Shortly after I was hired, I learned that the 'Big Boss' was coming into town to meet with the ranks. The staff buzzed with a sense of excitement and anticipation, and I didn't know what to expect. We were waiting outside when a brand new, red Chevy pickup with 'We Play to Win' written in elegant black letters across the tailgate pulled into the driveway. Out jumped the boss—he walked decisively with presence and confidence and the inspirational meeting he led that day was unlike anything I've experienced. As the boss delivered a clear message with humor. He captured the attention of the room, and I resolved to merit his attention by delivering results. I wanted him to know who I was."[360]

The demeanor of the big boss had a meaningful impact on Paul and helped to motivate results. This leader was someone who had captured the trust of his employees through the way he worked with and supported them. In the coming decades that Paul stayed with the company, he saw firsthand how the boss was willing to trust his employees.

For example, Paul shared: "Whenever the boss and I see something differently—from differing work philosophies to differing opinions regarding a specific area of opportunity—we have valuable interactions about those differences. He will listen to my ideas but I must be prepared to support my arguments. I know I'm dealing with his wealth of knowledge and experience, and if I haven't done my homework or due diligence analysis, he's gonna call me on it. When I illustrate the reasons why I believe in a particular effort or direction I think we should take, he will often back my plan even if his initial reaction had been otherwise."[361] This leader is willing to listen to and trust Paul and the other employees. He's willing to invest in their views and provide space for them to do their jobs the way they see fit without micromanaging.

The relationship of trust between Paul and his mentor has spanned more than two decades at this point. Paul shares that the supervisor's leadership "continues to have a significant positive impact on me and my career. He regularly shares articles, books, wisdom, experience, and tools he believes will be useful for me in my endeavors and responsibilities. For example, he taught me that we all continue to evolve if we choose to, and that we improve faster if we focus on the things we're already good at, than if we simply focus on the things we struggle with. I have seen that truth play out in my career. In short, he invites us to be the best version of ourselves."[362]

These words speak for themselves. This leader has a strong and positive professional influence on Paul and the other employees. As a company leader, he doesn't necessarily have to listen to employees, but the fact that he listens supports relationships, trust, and innovation. As a busy leader, the supervisor doesn't have to share specific articles or books that may impact a specific employee—but the fact that he does shows that he cares. That level of care and service is evidence of stewardship and it infuses his leadership with significance.

Another project director in the identical company said of the same boss: he is "a true leader who teaches us how to connect our goals into a personal mission of life accomplishment. Beyond his words is where the real lessons and messages are—he lives and practices what he teaches. He empowers us to feel fulfilled and capable to achieve everything that we want."[363]

If all employees could say this of their supervisors, this chapter would be irrelevant. Of course, this leader isn't perfect. In fact, in describing his growth process through years of sales and into management, the leader shares the importance of moments when his managers showed trust in him. This trust helped him develop confidence as a leader, and it informs the way he has come to influence his teams.

Key Takeaways

In sum, business leaders who view their leadership as stewardship utilize well and fairly the talents of those they lead. Such leaders prioritize the interests of others and are responsible for the consequences of their actions. Further, they ensure that "rewards are distributed in a way that corresponds to contribution rather than power."[364]

As you look at what's in your hand—your identity, your income, and your influence—look for ways that you can use your specific talents, freedom, networks, education, wealth, and creativity to make a difference in the world. Doing this will make you a great leader who is worthy of trust from employees, colleagues, and teams. As you show trust in your employees and step back from any tendencies to micromanage, you'll find your leadership transforming into stewardship and you'll truly be able to call into play your gifts, heart, and personality in service of others.

Trust can't be built overnight; rather, it requires time, effort, diligence, and character. David Horsager compares trust to a forest: "It takes a long time to grow and can burn down with a just touch of carelessness."[365] But, if you focus on the leadership strategies in this chapter, you will build trusting relationships with employees and colleagues, and be worthy of receiving trust in return. Such trust will ultimately drive results that have a positive impact on the organization's bottom line.

13

Success Through Happiness

Dr. Tal Ben-Shahar, former Harvard lecturer, teaches: "There is a common misperception today that success leads to happiness—that the more successful I become, the happier I will become." However, Ben-Shahar explains, success just gives us a temporary high and soon we return to the state we were in before.[366]

In the workplace, we regularly buy into a causal relationship, such that rising levels of success bring rising levels of happiness. For example, succeeding on a project, making a sale, or closing a deal may make us feel happy. These nuggets of success kickstart our sense of external achievement and value. When others praise our work and when we experience rewards like promotions, bonuses, popularity, and more, we naturally feel 'happy' . . . in the moment.

In reality, though, this achievement-based happiness is little more than a dopamine hit. Psychology Today calls dopamine the "reward molecule" because it "is responsible for reward-driven behavior and pleasure seeking. Every type of reward-seeking behavior that has been studied increases the level of dopamine transmission in the brain. If you want to get a hit of dopamine, set a goal, and achieve it."[367] The mistake we make is assuming that the more of these trappings of success we seek and achieve, the happier we will become over time.

In contrast, positive psychology research suggests that if you want to experience longer-term, steady happiness—both on and off the clock—you might try shifting your perspective: instead of thinking that success leads to happiness, consider that businesspeople who seek happiness have greater success. Forbes explains: "Neuroscience and studies of positive psychology prove that happiness is a key driver and precursor of success, with two decades of research backing this up."[368]

Become a Connoisseur of Life

For example, instead of trying to chase happiness through achieving goal after goal, Ben-Shahar proposes that we begin thinking about our lives in a different way: as connoisseurs. Consider how a wine connoisseur slows down, sips, and savors. Similarly, a life connoisseur knows how to slow down and enjoy key experiences and relationships. He or she is present in each moment and interaction. A life connoisseur engages with the things that fuel real happiness by quieting the frenetic pace of life and instead breathing in, recognizing, and experiencing what life has to offer. When we do that, we open ourselves up to heartfelt positivity. This change in the way we experience life brings what Dr. Ben-Shahar calls "the ultimate currency: happiness."[369]

But how can these suggestions gain traction in the world of business? To succeed in the workplace, employees and leaders alike are constantly managing inputs from phone, email, intra-office messaging, and co-worker communications. The sounds of the office are the essence of fast-paced chaos: phones ringing, sales calling, and meeting scheduling. Amid all the sounds and movement—amid all the constant rush of deadlines, meetings, presentations, luncheons, and targets—how can a businessperson consider slowing down as viable?

He or she might wonder: "Doesn't 'slowing down and savoring' mean that important deadlines might come and go? If I slow down, I might not get things done. Someday, when I get my promotion, I'll sit down and savor the moment, but today I have 78 new email messages in my inbox by mid-morning and afternoon meetings from noon to four. I'll just grab more coffee and keep going . . ."

If similar thoughts are on your mind, you are completely right. Perhaps we can find corollaries between the demanding business environment and military combat where one special forces mantra is "Slow is smooth. Smooth is fast."[370]

Nobody would argue that pressing forward continually is a hallmark of productivity. But, consider that slowing down to savor the moment doesn't necessarily equate with laziness or incompetence. Imagine several world-class athletes prepping for a sprint race: amid the crowds cheering and the stress of the moment, they crouch, listening for a single start sound. Their arms pump and their shoes spring off the track, but their internal zone of focus blocks out all external things. In the moment as they are sweating, panting, and sprinting, there may be an internal smile—they are savoring even the burn because that's exactly how it feels to fly down the track at top speed at a world-class event. They are present.

Sure, they don't run that pace all day every day. They slow down, recover, get a massage, catch dinner with friends, celebrate—whatever they do. It's like what life connoisseurs do at work: they ramp up the pace for deadlines, events, and projects. They focus completely and fully on completing the race, and then they relax afterward. There are strategies for getting into the zone of happiness so that even as you're running your own race, you're present and relaxed with the exertion—you're there and enjoying it. That's what this chapter is about.

Chapter Roadmap

This chapter offers five strategies for creating happiness as the foundation for career success. They include trading perfectionism for optimistic realism, being fully present, releasing roadblocks and unproductive fears, introducing new rituals for joy, and turning your attention inward to release what no longer serves you.

Not every strategy outlined here needs to be a perfect fit for you at this moment in your business leadership career, but a few might stand out as relevant. The strategies come in no particular order and you're welcome to mix and match. Sixty percent of workers in significant global economies are "experiencing increased workplace stress" with fears about money and the future topping the U.S. stress stats.[371] These strategies can equip you to be among the less-stressed remainder forty percent. They provide tangible tools, tips, routines, and habits that you can implement to enhance your happiness at work and in your life.

While "success through happiness" is a large topic, we will drill down on a few key concepts including forgiveness, contentment, presence, optimism, and joy. The logic is that as we release ways of being that reinforce negativity, we begin to re-wire our brains to create and experience success and happiness. Pro Tip: Get out your pen and jot some notes down in the margins—why not? Add your thoughts here and personalize your read.

Five Strategies to Build Success Through Happiness

1. Trade Perfectionism for Realistic Optimism

While we'd all love to get perfect scores on our annual review at work, recognizing the downsides of perfectionism can create space for real growth.

Here's the holdback: perfectionism creates dissatisfaction because anything and anyone who is not perfect is 'not good enough.' Dr. Ben-Shahar describes that he had considered himself to be a recovering perfectionist, but he hadn't understood that the plague of perfectionism was so pervasive in society. While striving for improvement and achievement is an ostensibly good thing, perfectionists (unwittingly) take it a step too far: they suffer harmful consequences because of their assumptions that life should be a certain way and work should be a particular way. When those things don't add up perfectly, a perfectionist's way of thinking and being prevents him/her from accepting what is as valid and complete.

What does this mean for happiness and success? Well, when perfectionistic types say that they aren't happy, they might mean that good enough simply isn't good enough for them. Today, they didn't work 14 hours, exercise for two hours, spend three with their families, and get eight hours of sleep; thus, today isn't good enough. They've perhaps bought into the perfect body image, career, family life, and more—and those things simply don't generally occur at the same time for the same person.

Unfortunately, this perspective can be difficult to see in an age of social media that invites us to compare our difficult day at work with another person's lauded day at the beach. It's simply not a valid comparison, but we forget that and assume that our lives aren't good enough (even if we don't use those words aloud).

Further, when perfectionists describe their lives and their feelings in greater detail, it is often clear that what they mean is that they aren't happy all the time. They experience moments of happiness, sure, but what about when happiness fades? Ben-Shahar laughs that people sometimes criticize him for being a 'happiness expert' who isn't continually bursting with joy. When he talks about his failures or fears, people sometimes express surprise that he considers himself happy despite such undesirable experiences. "Underlying both reactions is the assumption that truly happy people are somehow immune from feeling sadness, fear, anxiety or from experiencing failures and setbacks in life. The pervasiveness of this assumption—across generations, continents, and cultures—made me realize something astounding: I was surrounded by Perfectionists."[372]

Consequences of perfectionism include "low self-esteem, eating disorders, sexual dysfunction, depression, anxiety, obsessive-compulsive disorder, psychosomatic disorders, chronic fatigue syndrome, alcoholism, social phobia, panic disorder, a paralyzing tendency to procrastination, and serious difficulties in relationships."[373] None of these consequences are desirable in the workplace, although employees and leaders often feel pushed to be 'perfect' in their work responsibilities because mistakes are not tolerated well.

If you see in yourself—or in the employees you manage—tendencies of perfectionism, consider trading those tendencies for realistic optimism. This is critical to generating a successful work environment. Instead of rejecting failure, painful emotions, and imperfect reality, try accepting them. While setting high standards, keep your goals grounded and take time to feel gratitude for accomplishments along the way. Be willing to see the journey as an irregular spiral rather than a straight line—learning is just part of the process and, especially when you're taking on new responsibilities or clients, you might feel like you're moving one step forward and two steps back. Take failure as a form of feedback and be open to suggestions. Adapt. Find benefits rather than faults and be open to the idea that good enough is really . . . good enough.

Brian Tracy compares each of us to pilots who are flying to a designation of health, happiness, and prosperity. Airline pilots spend much of their flight time keeping the plane on course in the face of headwinds, downdrafts, storm fronts, turbulence, and more.[374] Steven R. Covey echoes this theme, suggesting that when the plane takes off at an appointed time toward a predetermined destination, it is in fact "off course 90 percent of the time." Yet it arrives on time at the right destination. Pilots integrate feedback constantly and patiently bring the plane back on track.[375]

Similarly, in our lives and careers, we need to make constant course corrections on route to our destination. If we are unhappy that we may be off course 90 percent of the time, then we will never be happy. Focus on constant course improvement, not perfection. Brian Tracy advises: "The key to success is for you to keep your mind fixed clearly on the goal but be flexible about the way of achievement. Be open to new inputs and ideas. Learn from every experience. Look for the good in every setback or difficulty."[376]

Happiness does not equal perfection. Happiness can and must be had in imperfect circumstances—acceptance makes that possible. Such acceptance forms the basis for success at work; it is the root of confidence and healthy growth.

2. Be Fully Present

A study by Harvard psychologists showed that "we spend about 47% of our waking hours thinking about what isn't going on. And that this typically makes us unhappy. The solution? To focus on whatever we are doing and the experience we are having in this very moment. In other words, to develop the skill of mindfulness."[377]

The New York Times defines mindfulness as "paying attention to the present moment in an accepting, non-judgmental way . . ."[378] Research has shown it is a reliable method for reducing stress at work. "We are encouraged in the workplace to be attached to an array of technological wizardry 24-7," says Janice Marturano, founder of the Institute for Mindful Leadership and this information overload can produce anxiety, disconnection and overwhelm.[379]

Regarding happiness, being mindfully present doesn't necessarily mean sitting still and relinquishing the need to do anything; rather, it means being fully aware and focused. The New York Times puts it this way: "The goal of mindfulness isn't to stop thinking or to empty the mind. Rather, the point is to pay close attention to your physical sensations, thoughts, and emotions in order to see them more clearly, without making so many assumptions or making up stories."[380] Mindfulness is about savoring each moment of our workday, regardless of the pace and place—appreciating what we already have and where we already are, and moving forward from there.

Happiness has varying qualities. Some happiness is experienced moment-to-moment, which is often different from the happiness you feel when you look back and remember a time when you worked hard to accomplish some project at work—not every one of those moments of grit and sweat felt happy at the time, but they added up to something worthwhile. Nobel Prize winner Daniel Kahneman described this distinction as "being happy *in* your life" versus "being happy *about* your life."[381]

As you cultivate happiness that builds your life and career success, look at both variations. Harvard Business Review indicates on this topic: "An evening spent with good friends over good food and wine will be experienced and remembered happily. Similarly, an interesting project staffed with one's favorite colleagues will be fun to work on and look back on."[382] The point we're drawing out here is that you can build both moment-to-moment and long-term-review happiness as you focus on finding happiness in each step of the journey.

The good news is that happiness in your career can occur now. Today. In every email and every step of the way. It's in your warm smile as you present to your customers. It's in the scent of fresh coffee and the pleasure of helping a client solve a problem. It's in the relationships you build over time with your colleagues, vendors, and customers—

happiness shows up as you integrate and create meaningful experiences day to day and year to year. But ultimately, happiness shows up because it's inside of you. It is your way of being and state of mind—and it is the grounds for your success.

Happiness is defined as 'the state of being happy.' It's a state of mind and a way of being—not dependent on external surroundings. In fact, if we correlate happiness with our material possessions or our achievements or if we relegate it to someday when something finally happens, then happiness may never arrive. Brian Tracy reiterates: "Life is very much a study of attention. Whatever you dwell upon and think about grows and expands in your life. The more you pay attention to your relationships, the quality and quantity of your work, your finances, and your health, the better they will become and the happier you will be."[383]

3. Release Roadblocks and Re-Program FOMO

One successful business leader teaches his employees that eliminating the "should've," "could've," "would've," "if only," "someday I'll," and "have-to" from our daily lives is the first step to living in a state of happiness.

When we arrive on this planet, we have all the tools and skills we need to be happy; nobody comes pre-programmed for despair. Yet, we often struggle to access our inner calm because of the baggage we accumulate over time: we feel unhappy or unsuccessful because we put roadblocks in our own way. Your mind might fight back at this idea: 'You're saying that I'm a business leader and yet I'm putting roadblocks in my way to happiness? Whatever. Why would I do that? The roadblocks are just there—they're because of my parents, my children, or my (ex) spouse . . . They're because of my genetics or my income or my location. But certainly, they're not intentional.'

We're not saying that the roadblocks you face are your fault. And we're not discounting the role of the things you can't control—you have no power over your family, your genetics, etc. You have some power over your income and location on the planet but if you are looking to any of these things to create or impede your happiness, then you are assigning power over your internal state of mind to external factors.

For example, if you're only happy when your boss approves of your work and you get good sales numbers, then . . . occasionally you will achieve a happiness high. But most of the time, you've surrendered your ability to feel internally at peace with yourself to circumstances beyond your control.

This mentality is part of our social programming—and it's a huge part of the consumer culture in which we live. Every day on Facebook, Instagram, or any media of choice, we're shown advertisements of 'happy' people visiting beautiful beaches we're not visiting, eating delicious lunches we're not eating, and wearing stylish outfits we're not wearing. We sit in our homes and offices, skimming social media, and seeing people we know enjoying healthy food, getting fit, standing with smiling children, traveling the world falling in love, or doing any number of things we want but may not be doing at that moment. We compare our coffee-stained, email-laden reality with their sunny beach photos and it's no surprise that we come up short on the happiness spectrum.

One nickname for this mentality is "FOMO," which stands for "fear of missing out." It's the anxiety we experience that some exciting or interesting event may be currently happening elsewhere (especially given what we see on social media). Or, FOMO creates compulsive concern that we might miss an opportunity for social interaction, experience, or satisfaction, and thus we may live with regret.

In fact, in the hospitality industry, we actively use FOMO to make our sales—through words, slogans, and images, we tell potential purchasers things like, 'Don't you deserve to have a vacation? What if your children grow up and you haven't taken family vacations together? What if your year passes and you simply slave at work while others (on your social media feed) get to relax at the beach? How is that fair? Don't worry, you can be happy by purchasing our special package, which is on sale today and includes . . .'

Have you noticed that advertisers are always willing to sell us the perfect solution to our FOMO worries? They draw imaginary links between dollar signs and what people want ideally, such as to be loved, beautiful, and successful. They imply: buy this suit and you'll be successful. Buy this dress and you'll be beautiful, and the man of your dreams won't be able to resist you and you'll finally feel loved as you deserve to be. Buy this vacation and you'll be a good parent. Travel to this resort and you'll be a hip trendsetter. The list goes on.

The solution to this is simpler than it sounds: let go. Re-program your fear of missing out into an appreciation of each moment. FOMO can only exist on false promises of being happy someday. Someday, after you put in enough time, you'll earn a corner office and you'll be successful. Someday, after you sweat enough, you'll have a fit body, and you'll be worthy of companionship. Someday, when you've got more time, you can play with your kids and be a good parent.

What about today? Why save happiness for later whenever someday arrives—IF that's even happiness in the first place? Counter FOMO by checking in with your supportive, caring relationships at home and at work. "Happiness or unhappiness in life comes from your relationships with others, and it is your relationships with others that make you truly human. They are the real measure of how you are doing as a human being."[384] As you focus on your relationships and dig deeper into each moment, you'll find and create the internal space to slow down, refuel, and enjoy your work.

Take time to evaluate what makes you happy and consider happiness as the organizing principle of your life. "Compare every possible action and decision you make against your standard of happiness to see whether that action would make you a happier person or an unhappier person. Soon, you will discover that almost all the problems in your life come from choices that you have made—or are currently making—that do not contribute to your happiness."[385] As you discover what contributes to your happiness, know that you must pay the price and put in your time along the way. Not every step of the journey will feel 'happy,' but each step is leading you to a place you desire to be.

4. Introduce New Rituals

Dr. Ben-Shahar jokes: how many times have you made a list of new year's resolutions and fulfilled them all? Put your hand up high. Anyone? Now raise your hand if you brushed your teeth today. Why the difference? Nobody fulfills their new year's resolutions and yet everybody brushed their teeth this morning. The difference is this: you didn't need self-discipline or willpower to brush your teeth—it's routine. New year's resolutions rely on willpower and discipline, and they get foiled by enemies like junk food and laziness. Real change happens when we introduce new rituals into our lives.[386] Here are three happiness-generating rituals you might consider introducing into your workday.

Journal Gratitude

First, consider keeping a gratitude journal. Gratitude has been shown to enhance peace of mind. Deepak Chopra advised: "Gratitude opens the door to the power, the wisdom, the creativity of the universe. You open the door through gratitude."[387] Cicero taught: "Gratitude is not only the greatest of virtues but the parent of all the others."[388] And one anonymous saying holds: "It's not happiness that brings us gratitude; it's gratitude that brings us happiness."[389]

Such a journal could happen on a blank computer document or on a piece of scratch paper—no fancy notebook needed. Experts recommend jotting down five things that make you feel grateful or happy every morning. If you feel ambitious, you could increase the number or frequency of the entries. It's more powerful to write specific items, such as "I'm grateful that my co-workers brought me soup on Tuesday," rather than simply, "I'm grateful for my co-workers."[390] If you can't physically journal your points of gratitude, try to at least make a mental note.

Include what matters to you personally and savor surprises that delighted you. Maybe your boss gave you some helpful feedback or a colleague brought extra sports tickets to share. Take time to let your mind linger on each of these happiness-inducing entries and absorb the sensation of gratitude. By highlighting gratitude, you push out negative emotions—both cannot exist simultaneously.

Savor Peace of Mind

Another simple ritual is just this: savor peace of mind. Anytime you feel it, focus on it. You can jot down these feelings in your gratitude journal, but simply noticing the feelings is a sufficient ritual. Recall the wisdom that we see more of what we focus on, so the more we focus on feeling peaceful, the more peace we are likely to experience. Brian Tracy says unequivocally that peace of mind "is the highest human good. Without it, nothing else has much value."[391] And the greater your overall peace of mind, the more likely you are to earn a good living, save regularly for the future, and ultimately achieve financial independence.[392]

Tracy correlates increased peace of mind with increased relaxation, positivity, and health."[393] When you have more peace of mind, your relationships improve. You become more friendly, optimistic, and confident. As you feel better about yourself internally, your work improves—you become a more grounded boss and more capable co-worker. As such, cultivating peace of mind can support well-being in your personal life and in your career.

Redesign Your Office Desk for Joy

Synonyms for happiness include joy, contentment, and pleasure. As you look around your desk or office space, do the items you see actively augment your joy, contentment, and pleasure? Designer Marie Kondo recommends that we keep only the things that speak to our hearts and discard all the rest. "By doing this," she says, "you can reset your life and embark on a new lifestyle."[394]

Consider making a habit or ritual of periodically picking up and holding each item in your office that you've voluntarily put there (or collected). Ponder: How does this make me feel? Does it increase or reduce stress? Does it increase my happiness and functionality? Often when we 'declutter' our spaces, we make piles of stuff to toss. Kondo teaches instead a positive, joy-centric approach: "We should be choosing what we want to keep, not what we want to get rid of."[395]

The question of what you want to own and surround yourself with—at work and at home—is the question of how you want to live your life. If we want to be in a state of ease, love, joy, and appreciation no matter what is happening in our lives, then we need to take ownership of our spaces and create them so that they augment our happiness.

Why take time with office 'housekeeping'? The theory is that if we can increase the calm and happiness we experience while sitting at our desks and in our offices, this calm will translate to the other work we do as business leaders. "Whenever we're in a state of love, peace, and joy in our lives, we can extend that to others," teaches Dr. Eva Selhub.

Try it and see if your interactions with your co-workers and colleagues shift toward the positive.

5. Look Inward and Release What Doesn't Serve You

"Throughout all of history," Brian Tracy proclaims, "self-knowledge has gone hand in hand with inner happiness, positive thinking, and outer achievement. To perform your best, you need to know who you are and why you think and feel the way you do."[396]

Many world traditions teach that self-study is our most efficient means of recognizing our habits and thought processes. Often, such study requires us to walk through our personal history to understand our present ways of being. For example, from our earliest understanding of ourselves, we pick up ideas that we are 'good' or 'bad' and we correlate those with our sense of who we are as adults (and ultimately as business leaders). Maybe our parents said we were "bad" when they meant that what we did at that moment was "bad," but we internalized it subconsciously as though we were "bad." Children don't know the differences, but the emotional programming we pick up when we're young informs our understanding of ourselves into adulthood—and it can hold us back from success in life and in work.

For instance, when we carry unresolved guilt and shame, this amps up our fear of failure because we see mistakes as "bad" rather than as necessary areas for growth and pivoting. Sometimes it encourages us to continually seek external validation and approval. This unsupportive internal programming holds us back from bringing our best selves forward—we feel less confident in ourselves, and less able to take risks and to learn. In short, if we are not comfortable with our value internally, then we have a hard time bringing anchored confidence to our work and our relationships.

Kintsugi is a Japanese art of repairing broken pottery with golden lacquer. Instead of throwing away a broken pot, artisans gather the pieces and put them back together using a special, vibrant mending technique. Rather than repairing by hiding the cracks, artists highlight the cracks in gold.

Philosophically, kintsugi treats breakage and repair as part of the history of the object—so much that the repaired pot with golden cracks can be more valuable than it was initially when it was 'perfect.' No one of us is perfect—we all bear the scars of our history and decisions, try as we might to hide them. What if, instead, we allowed these scars to become witness to our growth and our strength? Would they add to our acceptance of self and overall happiness?

Instead of needing to hide our imperfections, we would focus on the wisdom built through years of falling down and standing back up again, thereby putting together the pieces of our lives. This doesn't mean that we begin airing our dirty laundry in public; rather, it has to do with acceptance of the growth that comes from difficult times. Often, those difficult experiences shape the unique skills and mental processes that we rely on in business leadership—including strength, courage, vision, and hope.

Mirroring the essence of kintsugi, Dr. Selhub teaches this mantra of self-forgiveness: "I forgive myself for being human. I forgive myself for making mistakes and I truly love myself . . . so I can be in this place of peace and then extend that to others."[397] Self-forgiveness is an existential issue, Selhub holds. It's not about particular things that have happened in our lives or what people have done to us. Rather, on a deeper level, it's about embracing our cracks and recognizing that they are often boot camps of learning and growth. They are worth being colored gold.

Researcher Brené Brown corroborates: "Owning our story can be hard but not nearly as difficult as spending our lives running from it. Embracing our vulnerabilities is risky but not nearly as dangerous as giving up on love and belonging and joy—the experiences that make us the most vulnerable. Only when we are brave enough to explore the darkness will we discover the infinite power of our light."[398]

As a positive foundation for business leadership, happiness comes from looking deep within ourselves, releasing what is negative, and accepting who we are. It comes from interrogating our often-childish constructs, re-scripting negative stories, and accepting ourselves as human. As we forgive and infuse love into the darker parts of ourselves, we recognize how incredible it is to be present on this

190

planet, to learn and grow, to live this life and discover, and to experience both pain and joy.

You may wonder what all this 'self-forgiveness mumbo jumbo' has to do with the workplace. Let's consider: how important is it for a leader to take ownership of mistakes and turn them into growth in his or her career? Pretty important, generally. If employees struggle with a long-ingrained fear of mistakes, how likely will they be to step up in taking on new projects? How likely will they be to succeed in managerial roles?

Not very likely because without taking time to ferret out and embrace their inner cracks, these employees can only be limited to safe spaces. They will avoid new territory and come down hard on themselves when there are letdowns or setbacks. They will also be hard on their team members, perhaps accusing others or focusing on where the team fell short rather than where they pulled through. In the long run, working or managing through fear and terror generally reduce happiness and productivity.

It's true in life and in work that: "Because true belonging only happens when we present our authentic, imperfect selves to the world, our sense of belonging can never be greater than our level of self-acceptance."[399]

Business leadership requires a certain vulnerability. While celebrated leaders often demonstrate a sense of bravado and confidence, these qualities (when authentic) are rooted in a self-awareness of their vulnerability.[400] In fact, Brown describes vulnerability as "the birthplace of innovation, creativity, and change."[401] While some people conceive of vulnerability as weakness, Brown's research has found that vulnerability is rather one of the most accurate measures of courage. It is the combination of uncertainty, risk, and emotional exposure—which are inherent in sales and customer service roles, which require employees and leaders to put themselves out there each day and connect with clients on a personal level.

While leaders should observe proper boundaries in their sharing, they should be as candid as is appropriate with their trusted group and with the company. Appropriate vulnerability is grounds for authentic relationships, and it thus encourages cooperation and trust in teams. This is absolutely relevant in the world of business. It is a foundation for building success through happiness.

Key Takeaways

The cost of unhappiness is real. Economists have put a monetary price on misery and alienation: a Gallup poll estimates that employee unhappiness "costs the US economy $500 billion a year in lost productivity, lost tax receipts and healthcare costs."[402] In light of that, happiness-oriented initiatives in the workplace seem like a no-brainer. However, they can backfire on occasion because they highlight how unhappy employees may feel.

For example, in many ways, happiness can be hard to define and harder to measure. "Is it action or contemplation? Is it in our minds or in our senses? . . . When we wonder whether we are happy, we are already not happy—we suffer by seeking to eliminate suffering." [403] By seeking to eliminate pain, we inevitably focus on it. We consume and collect hoping that one day we will finally arrive. As employees and leaders, we may spin around the hamster wheel trying to improve ourselves and succeed but, if we can't do that, at least we can upgrade our car and have the hottest new vehicle among our neighborhood or friends.

If we mistakenly seek enduring happiness outside of ourselves, we may inflict upon ourselves unrealistic desires or ineffective behaviors. We may try to buy happiness, or barter for it from our relationships. We may expect happiness to come from our jobs and social worlds, so we are often trying to fake it in hopes of making it. At some level, while the promise of happiness appears like a blessing, it can be experienced like a debt we will never be able to repay. We may feel angry with ourselves for not meeting the 'established' standard of happiness. French philosopher Pascal Bruckner wrote: "Unhappiness is not only unhappiness; it is, worse yet, a failure to be happy."[404]

Practical Approach to Success Through Happiness

Brian Tracy suggests a practical solution: "Take the brush of your imagination and begin painting a masterpiece on the canvas of your life. It is for you to decide clearly what would make you the happiest in everything you are doing."[405] He elaborates: "Decide what is right for you before you decide what is possible. Create your ideal life in every detail. Don't be concerned about the process of getting from where you are to where you want to go. For now, just focus on positive thinking and creating a vision of your perfect future."[406] One Jamaican riverboat guide summed it up like this: 'There are no problems, just situations.' And in a popular song years ago, Bobby McFerrin put it this way: "Don't worry; be happy."[407]

The five strategies we have discussed in this chapter can go a long way toward helping you define and cultivate happiness as a foundation for success in your business leadership career. Accepting reality and mistakes as natural will help reduce performance anxiety and enable you to enjoy your activities more. Accepting painful emotions as an inevitable part of being alive means that you experience them, learn from them, and move on. You don't waste precious time and energy trying to suppress them.

As we invest time into self-study and introduce new, healing rituals into our daily lives, we will grow our sense of gratitude and contentment. We'll be better positioned to let go of the roadblocks we put into our path including wanting things to be perfect, wanting things to be different than they are, or being blind to the present moment. We'll be more at ease in our skin and thus more able to connect with our co-workers and clients. These strategies can support business leaders in leading rich and fulfilling careers. As we accept real-world limits and constraints, we can set attainable goals, and we'll be thus able to experience, appreciate, and enjoy success through happiness.[408]

14

Mindfulness in Management

Today's business leaders are mentally on call nearly 24 hours a day. A clear mind is what enables quick thought, decision making, and discernment between one course of action and another. Your mind is conditioned to analyze data, envision future results, and recall past endeavors—both successful and less successful. Having a clearer, calmer mind enables you to generate greater focus and productivity.

Unfortunately, our minds are often clouded with chatter—have you noticed the voice (or maybe voices) in your head continually commenting on life as it passes by? It judges, complains, and worries all the time. We may not like to admit it, but our minds may feel more productive when they're re-examining, re-living, and re-processing past and future occurrences.

Our busy brains often come up with a lot of commentary—they generate Twitter-type announcements and lengthier speeches for every aspect of the day: "Have I booked my flight to the conference yet? I must remember to tell my assistant to handle that for me." "I have spent so much time training this team and here we are again, not quite pulling in the results that I was projecting . . . I wonder what I can do next to help improve their performance?" "I think I need another cup of coffee . . . or a nap."

Sometimes our mind chatter turns quite personal and we encounter an internal critical voice that points out negative aspects of what we've done. This critic likes to say that we are not good enough, that others don't like us, or that we will never get it right. In your career, you've probably already found ways to manage your inner critic, but it will still pop up at inconvenient times, like right before you're about to give a speech, or during an award ceremony. It will ask destabilizing questions like: "Who do you think you are? They're listening to you, but they have no idea that you're not as confident as you seem. You don't deserve the recognition."

Chapter Roadmap

Wouldn't it be easier to lead in business without so much input from the inner critic? Wouldn't it be helpful to cut through the unproductive mental chatter and find clarity of mind for decision making in the long and short term?

While it's generally impossible to entirely banish mental chatter and the inner critic, our goal in this chapter is to enhance performance by drawing attention to the words in our heads and controlling the inner dialogue we have with ourselves. While some may wonder if this subject is too "soft" or "touchy feely" for leadership training, rest assured that top performers in business, sports, and all aspects of life learn to control and harness their inner voices and perceptions for maximum performance and success.

We'll provide concrete strategies for transforming the inner critic into an inner coach and thereby improving our capacity for business leadership.

- First, we'll look at mental chatter and the words we say to ourselves via the lens of the 'monkey mind,' unpacking that Eastern philosophical metaphor as applicable to the Western business world.

- Second, we'll provide a useful framework for noticing the mental chatter for what it is (mere thought patterns), right as it arises. That awareness is key. In this section, we'll turn our attention to a concrete example: understanding the inner critic—the negative words we say to ourselves.

- Third, we'll discuss the process of actively releasing our automatic identification with our unproductive thoughts, thereby mitigating the power that those thoughts have over us. In this section, we'll provide ten techniques for transforming the negative inner critic into a positive inner coach.

Taken together, these strategies—gaining awareness and actively releasing—enable modern business leaders to understand the often-chaotic mind patterns and harness a deeper awareness from which to manage their teams and companies.

Mental Chatter and Monkey Mind

Many Eastern philosophical traditions have dedicated centuries to the study and practice of calming the mind. Instead of reinventing the wheel, we'll borrow functional concepts and perspectives from those traditions and adapt them to modern Western business leadership.

One of the foundational metaphors in these Eastern writings involves monkeys: teachers often conceptualize the 'chatter' that fills our minds like the behavior of monkeys. In North America, where monkeys generally aren't part of everyday life, we may not as automatically connect with this metaphor, but let's consider it anyway because it is helpful.

For example, in rural India, monkeys stalk through village areas and congregate in trees or on fences. They run this way and that, chasing anything that catches their attention. They're attracted to any scent of food and are completely unconcerned about grabbing a bag of trail mix or a plastic water bottle from the hand of an unsuspecting person. If you happen to have fresh fruit with you, beware because crafty monkeys will watch for a moment when they can sneak in and snatch it.

Monkeys and baboons often line the roads and cross in herds—some are unhurried and stubborn, while others dart around, trying to escape oncoming cars. In the forests, monkeys swing through treetops and gather in groups. They have so much to say! They chirp and shriek to each other, sounding vocal alarms when they see worrisome people or unfamiliar things. Their eyes and bodies seem to be in motion all the time—looking for food, chasing each other, playing together, carrying babies, or hurrying to the next location.

How does this monkey metaphor relate to the modern business world? Just as monkeys swing through the trees, grabbing one branch and letting it go only to grab the next, our minds grab onto and release thoughts continually. We worry about the past and plan for tomorrow. We consider our plans, dreams, goals, and lists.

We miss today entirely.

For example, have you ever consciously listened to the chatter in your mind when you enter a room before a meeting begins? Granted, the room may be loud with people conversing, but often what's in your head is louder. "I hope my notes are in order. Did my assistant remember to order the right supplies? Why does his shirt look wrinkled? That reminds me: I need to pick up my dry cleaning on the way home tonight. Where did I put the numbers for the reporting session today? Oh, right, they're in my file here. Ok, seventeen people are present and accounted for. Why are three people late for this meeting? I guess I'll have a word with them after. Where's my coffee?" And out loud: "Good morning, everyone. Welcome to today's staff meeting."

These endless thoughts are like babbling mental monkeys: they swing through trees with a life of their own, catching branch after branch, often with no real destination in mind. Some of our thought-monkeys have specific names or emotions, such as fear, hope, anger, and desire. Others are more nebulous and difficult to pin down if you look at them. Whether we're fully aware of it or not, this rushing stream of thought drags us along, asking us to attend to each thought as though it were the most significant thing.

If we identify with our busy thoughts, we not only miss other aspects of life around us, but we also miss cultivating our true identity because we assume the chatter is who we are. Eckhart Tolle writes: "Most people spend their entire lives imprisoned within the confines of their own thoughts. They never go beyond a narrow, mind-made, personalized sense of self that is conditioned by the past."[409]

Research shows that humans have around fifty thousand separate thoughts each day—many of them on the same topic.[410] Because of our innate capacity for thinking, our minds seek out stimuli. As we identify with the fluctuations in our minds, life can feel like a roller coaster ride. Left unchecked, these mental monkeys will limit our ability to lead in the business world. We'll get tangled up in their detail, noise, and movement, and we'll be less able to see the bigger picture—about our companies and about ourselves.

However, two strategies can help calm the mental chatter and reconnect with the present moment: awareness and release. As we gain awareness, we begin to release our identification with our thoughts—we see them as monkeys playing, not as ultimate reality. In making this distinction, we begin to lead from a place of grounded inner clarity. This is the most centered and empowered space for business leadership, creativity, compassion, and decision making.

Gaining Awareness

Forbes defines mindfulness as moment-to-moment awareness. "When you are mindful, you become keenly aware of yourself and your surroundings, but you simply observe these things as they are. You are aware of your thoughts and feelings, but you do not react to them in the way that you would if you were on 'autopilot.'"[411] Such autopilot reactions would be like climbing up the forest trees with the monkeys. Rather, by "not labeling or judging the events and circumstances taking place around you, you are freed from your normal tendency to react to them."[412]

Several prominent companies have implemented mindfulness programs for employees, including Apple, Google, McKinsey and Co., Procter and Gamble, General Mills, and more. These companies invite leaders to recommit themselves daily to their vocation as a leader and to be fully present in each moment.[413] However, to fully be present and lead effectively, leaders must recognize and tame the monkey-mind chatter that tries to take center stage in our subconscious awareness.

Recognition is the first step. Eckhart Tolle teaches, "When you recognize that there is a voice in your head that pretends to be you and never stops speaking, you are awakening out of your unconscious identification with the stream of thinking. When you notice the voice, you realize that who you are is not the voice—the thinker—but the one who is aware of it."[414] It sounds simple—especially for talented, logical business leaders—just to become aware that our minds are chattering all day long, but often we imagine that the thoughts we think are 'ourselves.' For example, we assume that when we *feel* angry, we *are* angry. But there's a space between what we feel or think and who we are fundamentally.

When we get still and listen, we become witness to our thoughts rather than identifying ourselves with them. If we identify with our thoughts, we cling to pleasure and flee from pain—running to and fro like the monkeys. However, by taking on the role of a witness, we're more likely to see our thoughts as ever-changing, fleeting, and transient in nature. In other words, we begin to see that our thoughts are not true; they are simply our thoughts. This process is a kind of unlearning.

If the concept of being a "witness" sounds too passive, think of yourself as the commander of a powerful ship on the open seas. You see the waves rising and falling and currents twisting and turning, but you know that the ocean is separate from the boat and you steer the vessel through the changing waters rather than allowing the ship to be thrown off course by the marine conditions.

To see how the rubber meets the road with this theory, let's look at a highly relevant, concrete application. For example, most of us—business leaders included—encounter a negative voice inside our minds that complains, judges, and criticizes. As we noted earlier, we'll call this voice the 'inner critic.'

Noticing the Inner Critic

Negative self-talk comes in many forms, but all are damaging. It may sound realistic or practical, such as, "Well, I didn't do well on that project, so I guess that's just not my strength." It may spiral into fear, such as, "I'm so worried that if I fail to make this deadline, I'll lose my job!" While our inner critic can occasionally be truthful and motivate self-improvement, it tends to do more harm than good by creating stress and limiting our growth.

The inner critic is often involved in blaming, fear-voicing, victimizing, catastrophizing, and criticizing. It tells us that we are lacking in fundamental ways or that we are to blame for everything—including things over which we don't have control. For many of us, the inner critic claims that we are unworthy or unlovable, and that we will never be enough. It limits our belief in ourselves and fuels perfectionism. For some business leaders, this ongoing inner criticism influences depression, creates insecurity, and destabilizes relationships.

Ironically, perhaps, we may invest great effort into achieving success in school, career, and parenting in order to counteract the internal negativity. However, nothing external—not even wealth or prestige—can silence the inner critic. We must take it on from the inside.

To mitigate the inner critic's power, the first step is to draw awareness to its monologue. Listen to what you're saying to yourself in your mind. As you notice the negativity, consider whether you would ever speak these things to a child or a friend—if not, why are you saying them to yourself or your inner child? Cultivating awareness allows you to unhook the inner critic's words from reality.

Actively Releasing

In this section, we will discuss several techniques for transforming the inner critic into a supportive inner coach. But, let's hit pause on the critic for just a minute as we discuss the context of active releasing in general.

Actively releasing our thoughts or emotions doesn't mean avoiding or numbing out. Rather, it means being present and accepting our thoughts and feelings, while at the same time understanding that they are fleeting. It's about letting one moment transform naturally into the next without trying to hold too tightly to what was before. If we attach our happiness to a thought, person, concept, or other external thing, we will end up suffering because all things change over time.

However, if we attach our well-being to our calm internal center, we can experience deep contentment. In short, noticing the rise and fall of our thoughts helps us cultivate a steady center from which we can master our thoughts, rather than being at their mercy.

As we become aware of our thoughts and mental chatter as separate from our deeper understanding, we can begin to unhook from their importance. Put another way, as we see our thoughts like monkeys jumping, shouting for attention, and so on, we can either identify with them and join their shouting, or we can realize that we are aware of their shouting so there is a deeper part of us that is witnessing the chaos. That deeper awareness doesn't need to be disturbed by the chaos and it doesn't need to identify with it. It can notice the chaos for what it is and choose not to join in.

Seeing that choice is critical because so many people don't realize that they have the choice. Something happens and they react immediately, believing that reaction is the only option. For example, if you're driving to work and the car in front of you is going too slowly for your liking (or for the speed limit on the road), you can choose how to react— you can begin shouting in frustration or you can realize that there is a 'frustration monkey' jumping around in your mind. Pause long enough to see that thought-monkey for what it is, and you'll realize that you have options in how you respond. You could jump around and shout with it, or you could just drive calmly without being disturbed. Your power to choose is anchored in your deeper awareness.

If you choose the former course of action, you will feel emotions rising in association with frustration. If you choose the latter course, your frustration thought-monkey will get bored and go on to the next thing, leaving you in peace for a moment.

This same releasing process works in business day to day: for instance, if you receive an email that troubles you, hit pause in your mind. Notice your reaction as simply a reaction. Realize that you can choose how you respond—you can fire back an angry, frustrated message, or you can take a deep breath and draft something more productive. Maybe you'll want to pick up the phone to understand more of the situation. Seeing these options shows that the immediate frustration is not reality. Reality is deeper inside you and it is the place from which you lead best.

Until we draw awareness to our stories, though, they can control us. We spend time thinking about something, generating feelings about that thing, and then reacting to our thoughts with more feelings. Pretty soon we get wrapped up in our story about what happened far more than connecting with reality. In the workplace, when we make decisions based on the stories we are telling ourselves, we are not effective business leaders. However, if we notice thoughts or stories going on in our minds but take a minute to reconnect with what is real, we can tap into a quieter, more grounded place inside ourselves that is not distorted by our reactions. This is the most effective place for decision making and leadership.

Ten Techniques for Transforming Inner Critic into Inner Coach

To see how the rubber meets the road, let's pick up again the concrete example of the inner critic. Here are ten 'active releasing' techniques that business leaders might use for transforming the inner critic into an inner coach. They involve recognition and re-scripting. Not every technique will work for every person, so feel free to pick and choose those that suit you. As you find these successful in your life, you will also see their application in your work and leadership because each of the people you manage faces similar sorts of issues. Not only will you be able to see these issues with a clearer mind, but you will also be empowered to strengthen your teams by sharing your insights and techniques.

1. Discern Common Origins

As the critic begins its tirade, it can be helpful to start at the beginning and discern common origins. For example, sometimes you'll realize that your inner critic says exactly what your mother, father, or your teachers said to you when you were young. "I can't believe you screwed up again on this simple task." "You're always a mess." "Why can't you get things right?" Your inner critic internalizes these words and mirrors them back to you as you age. While it's never helpful for adults to speak so negatively to children, most of us encountered someone as we were growing up who preferred to accuse or label us than to encourage us. Journaling, conversation, or therapy can help make connections with the past.

Now, maybe you didn't receive any negative programming but rather created your own. This often happens when you notice discrepancies in the world around you—particularly in media. For example, Facebook can leave us comparing everyone else's best trip, meal, or selfie to our worst. We might see photoshopped magazine images and then look in the mirror and make subconscious decisions like: "I'm not good looking." Or, "I don't have a car like that one so I must not be successful." Thus, your inner critic might have collected thoughts not related to past moments, but rather to past impressions.

You might notice in your career moments when you have felt limited by some unnamed, negative sense inside. In an odd way of attempting to keep yourself safe in the future, your inner critic internalizes past negativity and reflects it to you to help you avoid future failures. For example, when you have an opportunity to give a speech, your inner critic may intervene: "Remember how you froze up during your sixth-grade speech? Better sit this one out."

If you believe the critic although decades have passed, you might turn down the opportunity by saying what you decided in that past moment, even if it's no longer true in the present: "Oh, I must not be good in front of people." Surely over time you've become more comfortable in front of people than you were in elementary school, but the inner critic blocks you from growth or new opportunity via its words of critique.

Just recognizing the common origins of the critical words—whether in your former authority figures, decisions, or failures—can be the first step in disempowering them.

2. Re-script Negative Words to Suit the Present Moment

As you begin to understand the origins of your inner critic, you can watch for situations in the present that mirror situations from the past—and you can deliberately respond differently. For example, maybe you enthusiastically accept the invitation to speak at your company. This will be a 'trigger' space where your inner critic will remind you of past failures but you can actively say in response, "That was years ago and I feel prepared to handle it now. Calm down. Thanks for your concern, but I can do this."

By re-scripting the critic's words, it's almost as if you invite the critic to evolve with you—to see you as a capable adult and not a frightened child. This re-scripting works as you notice situations where you may have responded from a place of fear or limitation in the past—guided by your inner critic—but you deliberately respond differently in the present moment. Now, you don't have to accept every invitation to speak in public, for example, but at least you can recognize that you've grown and you can treat yourself with compassion. Heeding negativity means losing opportunities; transcending your former boundaries brings new growth.

3. Challenge the Critic: Stand Up for Yourself

Another technique for unhooking the inner critic's words from reality is to ask questions. When you begin to hear the critical monologue, ask "Really?" "What is true about this, if anything?" "Why are you telling me this?" "What are you trying to accomplish?" "How is this situation I'm in similar to situations in the past?" "Is there some deeper concern here that I'm not seeing?" "What are you trying to protect me from?" As you ask questions and interrogate the critic's statements, you'll begin to discern the intention behind the critical words.

Now, while you can safely acknowledge any truth from the critic, you can do so in a way that doesn't compromise your confidence or positivity. For example, if the critic says that you're a failure because you didn't do well at a project, you might speak back to it: "I know that project didn't go well, but I've got a plan to do better on the next one. I talked with my boss and she supports my work. Every failure is a learning opportunity and I am growing. I'm not a failure even though the project didn't go as planned."

Try looking into a mirror and speaking aloud the inner critic's words— how does that feel? Do you sense indignation rising? Who would ever be allowed to talk to you that way? While recognizing any truth in the situation, stand up for yourself and reframe the criticism into gentler language. For example, imagine what you might say to a friend or child if you were listening to her speak aloud the inner critic's accusations— many of us respond more gently to friends or to our children than we do to ourselves, so this can be an instructive thought process.

Even if you are a successful team leader, you might be surprised to listen to the negative words you speak to yourself inside your mind. The good news is that you can take control at any time and notice the difference. Re-scripting the critic's negative words into positive words will mitigate the critic's power over time. It's a means of 'dancing' with the critic and building positive outcomes.

4. Name and Limit Your Inner Critic

If you have a particularly active inner critic, try giving it a funny nickname. Then you can label it: "Mr. Negative is just yacking here again." Naming the critic distances it from being something worth taking seriously, and using a comical name distances you from identifying with it.

Also, try imposing limits. Give Mr. Negative only 15 minutes per day to provide advice and critique, then he must shut down. If he tries to exceed the 15-minute limit, remind him that the time is up and he's welcome to stop by tomorrow. It sounds goofy but this is a method of taking control of the situation and validating your needs—not allowing the critic to have an unlimited open mic in your mind. If he can't say something nice, he doesn't get to say anything at all. Some critique can be useful, but not if it's the focus of your mental chatter.

Think about it like you're holding a meeting at your office. You may invite team members to speak critically of an initiative, but then you will set boundaries and invite them to shift gears toward discussing solutions or alternatives. Successful business leaders let critique inform growth, but they don't camp out in negativity.

5. Zoom Out

Try switching from short-term focus to a more long-term perspective—is a failure on a project as tough as your inner critic wants to make it out to be? Many world-class athletes and business leaders point to key failures as turning points for their ultimate success.

For example, best-selling author Tim Ferriss interviews world-class athletes, businesspeople, strategists, and others, and one of the pet questions he asks these uber-successful people is: "What is one of your favorite failures?" In every case, the responses include stories of when the person felt at the lowest point but then pivoted, buckled down, let go, or shifted in some way that enabled their performance to make massive strides. It's the time when they got cut from the championship team, re-evaluated their training, and made the next year with stronger times than ever before. It's the time when they didn't receive funding or got fired from their jobs, changed strategy, started a new company, and had more fun earning more money than ever before.

Time and again, these themes show how a change in perspective can be key to unhooking the power of the inner critic who only wants to focus on short-term failure and blow it out of proportion. Zooming out mentally shows the bigger picture and often a new track to success.

6. Switch Criticism for Encouragement

As you begin to track the origins and methods of the inner critic, it's time for you to cut his hours and replace him with positive input. Replacing even just one instance of negative self-talk with positive reinforcement is a step in disempowering the inner critic and empowering your inner coach. When the inner critic tells you, "No, this isn't going to work. Remember last time when you dropped the ball?" Bring out your inner coach and invite him or her to speak: "Yeah, last time you dropped the ball, but this time is different. You've learned from that and you're more experienced now. You understand the situation and I think you have the capability to make it happen. Give it a shot."

Over time, those positive internal messages will accumulate and begin to outweigh the words of the critic. You are the owner of your story—you can oversee how you choose to organize and frame your narrative. You can see yourself as someone who is lacking and unlovable, or as someone who is worthy of love and belonging and who is learning along the way. Tap into positive memories and fuel yourself by reinforcing your success and value. By choosing to paint yourself in your eyes as someone who is enough, you hush the voice of the inner critic. It doesn't ever fully go away, but you can set healthy boundaries. In so doing, you will begin to live—and lead—on your terms, which is exactly what will help you thrive in the workplace.

7. Bring Your Positive Coach to Yourself

Positive self-talk also boosts your skills as a business manager. For example, let's imagine that a person you manage didn't meet a defined target. When you found out, you immediately called him into your office, expressed your frustration, and demanded that he close the gap as much as possible. Now you're sitting in your office feeling upset because the targets weren't met and upset at yourself for ripping into your employee. In that moment, how could your inner coach walk *you* through a positive learning process (without letting the inner critic speak his mind)?

Imagine what a coach might say to a star basketball player in a similar situation: "Hey, I know you're frustrated because your teammate dropped the pass and you were hoping to make the shot—we all were. But you've got to see that if you get angry with him like that, he's less likely to perform well in the future. Take a minute and cool off. Then go talk to him and try to repair the working relationship. Now, I know you have good intentions and you want this team to succeed. As your coach, I appreciate that! You've also got the capacity for building strong team relationships; I've seen you do it before. Now, go—fix this up and let's make the next shot!"

Where your inner critic might jump to extremes and say that you 'always' lose your temper with the people you manage, your inner coach acknowledges your challenge and encourages you to make a positive resolution. The critic accuses and tears down, but the coach creates a safe space for growth. Instead of speaking harshly to yourself, try adopting a tone that people would use if they were reassuring a friend or child. Speak calmly and compassionately to yourself, even when you hit a setback as a leader. A warm tone helps you accept yourself just as you are, which boosts self-esteem and ultimately enhances your performance.

By cultivating your inner coach, you begin to develop a new relationship with yourself. You feed the voice of truth and kindness rather than the voice of negativity. You become emotionally invested in new, positive routines and habits so they become easier to sustain over time.

When the inner critic says you are missing the mark, you can pause and notice the criticism, and then turn on your inner coach. Find one positive thing to say to yourself about your efforts to lead productively. Think through any positive changes you can make, and just keep on going. The critic mires business leaders in the small, petty things, but the coach builds leaders into the best possible versions of themselves. This makes all the difference for your employees and your company.

8. Recognize Cognitive Distortions

Cognitive distortions arise when our thoughts misrepresent the facts of what occurred. The distortion brings increased pain and upset because it confuses our understanding of reality. Some common cognitive distortions include:

- Black-and-white thinking, or believing that everything is bad because one situation is bad, regardless of any contributing factors
- Emotional reasoning, or taking your feelings as fact and forgetting the other relevant facts
- Catastrophizing, or seeing the future with only pain or hopelessness and forgetting the positives in your life

It doesn't take much imagination to see how cognitive distortions can create problems for business leaders. At a fundamental level, leadership is all about relationships—with yourself, with your team, or with people you manage. If you are susceptible to distortions such as black and white thinking, you'll find yourself categorizing actions as 'good' or 'bad' without fully seeing the nuances and subtleties. You'll risk alienating teammates with your criticisms, just as your inner critic alienates you with its tirades. Although children are taught initially to see the world in terms of black-and-white absolutes, adults—and particularly successful leaders—need to dance with the shades of gray to be successful. Your inner coach can help you become adept at this dance.

As you notice the simple cognitive distortions listed here in your inner critic's words, you'll be able to transform them into useful coaching insights. For instance, if you're tempted to automatically label a team member's failure to retain a key account as "bad," you might pause and notice any black-and-white thinking, emotional reasoning, and catastrophizing. That awareness enables you to detach from the thought long enough to interrogate it. Although the team member lost the account, maybe you can make a call and save it. Or, maybe another account will take its place and you will still meet your targets. Perhaps this transition is merely a stepping stone . . . anything is possible, but recognition of cognitive distortions is the first step.

9. Check In with Your Body and Intuition

This technique might feel a little outside the box for Western business leaders but try it on for a moment. Have you noticed that when your critic is speaking, negative sensations can show up in your physical body? Some philosophies and alternative medical practices hold that our emotions show up in the physical tissue of our bodies—and if we can access those negative emotions via our physical bodies, we'll be able to let them go much more effectively than if we focus solely on accessing them via reasoning.

Dr. Pert, a neuroscience researcher trained at Johns Hopkins, found that emotions trigger the release of compounds called peptides, which are stored in the body's tissues, organs, and muscles. She concluded that "unexpressed emotions are literally lodged in the body," and that "your body is your subconscious mind."[415] Along these lines, Tolle teaches: "If you really want to know your mind, the body will always give you a truthful reflection, so look at the emotion, or rather feel it in your body."[416]

For example, if you feel an emotion build in response to a negative statement from your inner critic, can you find that emotion in your body? Often, challenging emotions show up in the solar plexus or gut area. Sometimes, you can gently push on those spaces (or stretch them) and feel that the emotional discomfort has created tangible physical discomfort. As you locate the emotion in your body, try gently asking: "What is your message?" "What are you telling me?" Or, more simply, "What do you need?"

This patient, open questioning can reveal surprising insights. Not only is it a compassionate way of listening to yourself, but it is also a literal means of transforming the critic into a coach. By listening to the message, you allow it to release. You're taking the message and acting on it, healing it, and moving it out. Your physical body returns to a state of equilibrium as your mind calms. Forbes advises: "By settling into your body and noticing how it feels, you center yourself in the moment you're living."[417]

For business leaders who learn to check in with their bodies and read the physical signals, this method can almost function as a sort of shorthand. For example, imagine a busy situation where there's a decision you must make. Noticing the sensations in your body can immediately clue you into whether you're feeling stressed about the decision (and maybe need to take more time to evaluate), or whether you're feeling at peace and energized about the decision. Checking in regularly can improve your physical well-being, emotional equilibrium, and workplace performance.

10. Believe in Yourself

Psychologist Albert Bandura characterized people's belief in their ability to succeed at a task or situation as self-efficacy. Self-efficacy is closely linked to how perseverant you are: if you don't believe you can manage a task or improve yourself, then what's the point in trying?[418] Turn on an internal motivating dialogue that tells you that you can manage the task, situation, or challenge at hand. Telling yourself, "I've got this," and "I believe in myself" can significantly improve your chances of success.

This shift might be subtle at first, but it gets more pronounced over time. As you switch negativity for positivity and heed the voice of your inner coach, you will set an example for the people you manage. You'll more often become the wind beneath the wings of a great idea. You'll regularly provide positive and constructive feedback, coaching, and guidance for your teams. As they benefit from your positivity, they'll begin to incorporate your example in their work.

Key Takeaways

In sum, these techniques are a way of practicing mindfulness when it comes to our internal critical voice and actively transforming negative emotions into positive emotions. Being mindful of our emotions and thoughts helps us stop identifying so completely with them. We learn to see a thought but not to chase it, and not to believe that it constitutes who we are. Tolle suggests: "Here is a new spiritual practice for you: don't take your thoughts too seriously."[419]

Ultimately, while we can't fully banish our mental chatter, we can begin to dance with it and tame it. As we learn to recognize patterns in the chatter and listen to whatever truth may be inherent in them, we can release our attachment to them to return to the present moment. This is how we can learn to live with the noisy thought-monkeys without being disrupted by their movement.

Dr. David Brendel of the Harvard Business Review notes: "At its very core, mindfulness culture will be a huge step forward for Western cultures if it stays focused on creating opportunities for individuals to discover their personalized strategies for taming anxieties, managing stress, optimizing work performance, and reaching genuine happiness and fulfillment."[420] Further, he indicates that mindfulness in the workplace can help executives reduce stress, avoid burnout, enhance leadership capacity, and steady their minds when making important business decisions, career transitions, and personal life changes.[421]

The techniques in this chapter are worthwhile because they help us reduce the suffering that we may experience when we automatically identify with thoughts, pleasure, pain, and the chaos of day-to-day work and life. Awareness, release, and stillness teach us to see that there is a deeper reality. As we transfer that awareness into our workplaces, we become better leaders because we lead from a place of greater emotional and physical self-control. Our relationships become stronger because we can acknowledge and speak to people from a deeper place within ourselves. We waste less time in rumination and we make decisions that are grounded. As we understand the words we say to ourselves and begin to control those conversations, we take on a power that reinforces our ability to lead productively. Try it out for yourself and see.

15

Meditation for Business Leaders

In partnership with Harvard University, researchers interviewed more than 35,000 leaders in 72 countries and 250 C-suite executives seeking a neurological perspective regarding skills that contribute to success in leadership. Results were conclusive: two of the key skills that influenced leaders' success were mindfulness and compassion.[422]

Across the nation and around the world, more and more top business leaders are beginning to take on meditation and mindfulness practices. For example, Jeff Weiner, the CEO of LinkedIn, sees compassion as a centerpiece of his management style. He describes how, in the business setting particularly, "compassion requires slowing down and taking the time to truly listen to others. It means understanding where they're coming from, caring about the struggles they're facing, and the baggage they're carrying."[423]

Along these lines, Arianna Huffington, founder of the Huffington Post, says that we live in an "unmanageable world,"[424] where, as leaders, it's difficult to make good decisions. In her view, this is not because leaders lack IQ, but because they struggle to tap into their "inner wisdom"—to disconnect from their omnipresent devices and reconnect with themselves.[425] Mindfulness meditation is one specific, effective means for bringing leaders home to their inner wisdom. It's not the only answer, but it shows up again and again in research regarding the habits and routines of top leaders in any field, so it is worth our focus.

In the early 1990s, a business professional was having dinner with one of the owners of several luxury resorts and asked, "What are some of the reasons that you and the developer have experienced so much success?" That owner could have elaborated on the superior quality of the hotels, marketing, financing, employees, and several other conditions, all of which would have been true. However, the owner explained that the most important factor was one thing: each day, that owner spent time in solitary meditation clearing the mind and envisioning possibilities individually and for the company.[426] These concepts work.

Chapter Roadmap

In this chapter, we'll weave together several themes regarding how leaders can enhance their success in the workplace by practicing mindfulness meditation. We'll provide research-based information regarding how meditation supports business leaders in cultivating focus, productivity, and financial decision-making skills. We'll describe how a leader's meditation practice can improve not only his or her health but also the way that teams and employees function under his or her management. It turns out that a leader's empathy and compassion can grease the wheels of cooperation, communication, and collaboration.

For those who are interested in what a simple meditation practice might include, we will cover four skills that leaders are using to calm their minds for as little as five minutes per day. And we will conclude with stories of top business leaders and entrepreneurs who meditate daily and believe that this practice tangibly improves their careers.

As a clarification, this chapter is not designed to encourage you to take on any practice that feels uncomfortable for you. Rather, this chapter is designed to show you how some leaders incorporate this skill into their careers and, in fact, credit meditation with a great deal of their business success. Meditation is only one factor in success, of course, but it is one of the most common factors across the board for top performers and leaders in any industry. Thus, we dive into it here.

Meditation and the Modern Business World

Author Tim Ferriss interviewed 140 people who were at the top of their fields or industries and was surprised to learn that about 90 percent of those people had some type of morning mindfulness or meditation practice.[427]

Bridging the gap between stereotypes and the business world, Ferriss explained with some humor: "Meditation has a branding problem. A lot of people think of yoga instructors playing didgeridoos and swinging dream catchers over their heads. . . . But, at the heart of it, meditation is a simple practice that is about training the mind's control over its emotions."[428] It's about decreasing emotional reactivity so leaders can be proactive in creating their day and their work. Business Insider notes that meditation has a tangible positive effect on the amygdala—the part of the brain that is responsible for emotions, fight-or-flight impulses, and memory.[429]

In the context of this chapter, the words stillness, meditation, and mindfulness all point to the same target outcome but some people react differently to the different words. Here, we will use the word 'meditation,' but, if you prefer, feel free to mentally substitute a word that resonates better with you such as contemplation, reflection, introspection, focus, awareness, centering . . . essentially any process that allows you to quiet mental and emotional disturbance. While these words can connect with both Eastern and Western religious practices, we are not discussing religion here. Rather, our goal is to discuss the productive application of mindfulness meditation in the modern business world.

Illustrating Mindfulness in the Workplace

To illustrate mindfulness, renowned teacher Thich Naht Hanh uses the metaphor of washing the dishes. Instead of rushing from dish to dish with only the end goal in mind of getting to an empty sink, Hanh suggests that we should be aware and enjoy the process. For example, imagine holding a dish—maybe a ceramic bowl—in your hands. Notice the shape and feel of the bowl, and the color and the pattern of the warm water as it flows over the shape. Notice soap bubbles foaming over the bowl, running down into the sink, and draining away. Notice the movement of your hands in rinsing the dish and picking up a towel to wipe off the water droplets until the bowl is ready to hold the next meal.

"I know that if I hurry in order to be able to finish so I can sit down sooner and eat dessert or enjoy a cup of tea, the time of washing dishes will be unpleasant and not worth living. That would be a pity, for each minute, each second of life is a miracle," says Hanh.[430] Further, he advises, "If I am incapable of washing dishes joyfully, if I want to finish them quickly so I can go and have dessert or a cup of tea, I will be equally incapable of enjoying my dessert or my tea when I finally have them."[431]

In our busy workplaces, washing dishes is analogous to our work. We go about the day getting to the bottom of the pile and achieving results. Nobody wants to spend all day washing a bowl; we must clip along, bowl to bowl to bowl. We set up production lines and systems so a person specializes in just one thing. We incorporate machines to speed and automate processes. All of this is 'progress' and improves the quantity of items produced, processed, organized, shipped, and ultimately sold. Numbers and targets are met; management is satisfied; and work goes on day to day. We focus on getting more done rather than on each thing we get done as we do it.

Comparing washing the dishes mindfully to doing our work mindfully, the idea is not to completely slow down or reduce productivity. Rather, the idea is to be present with each step along the way as it is happening. Our minds are wired to do one thing at a time. We like to talk about multitasking, but research shows that this is more a matter of switching rapidly among tasks (and often becoming less efficient at each one) rather than doing multiple things simultaneously. Is there space amid the busy series of events in our high-pressure industries to be present with each task? To hold each dish, so to speak? To focus fully on each email, conference, and conversation?

When we start to think of *how* to cultivate that focus in the workplace, then mindfulness moves from a simple concept to a bigger challenge. Our minds are somewhat like monkeys, shifting quickly from thought to thought, jumping, chattering, etc. To hold steady attention on one thing or one task—just for a single minute—can feel like a herculean task.

Try this: just choose one thing to notice for an entire minute. For example, notice your inhale and exhale. Keep your attention just there and nowhere else for an entire minute. As thoughts arise, notice them, and let them pass. Chances are you will gently notice the first breath, and the second. But by the third breath, your mind has run off: you're drafting email in your head. You're wondering why your colleague said that thing earlier. You've moved from presence into thinking.

Leaders are curious. Leaders analyze, process, adjust, and win. Those skills and capabilities are what raised you to a position of leadership and they're critical to your success . . . but they don't necessarily allow you to be present in a single moment. How can you cultivate the skill of presence? Be mindful of each moment.

For example, if focusing on your breath seems a little too 'touchy feely,' then try being aware of responding to one email. Consider the words you are choosing. Feel the computer keys under your fingertips. Hear the clicking sound those keys make as you push them. Watch the words flow across the screen. Notice the brightness and color of the display. Sense the position of your feet on the floor.

As you write your message, what is happening with your breathing? Are you holding your breath, breathing shallow, or inhaling deeply? Perhaps appreciate the miracle of shooting a message around the world in mere seconds . . . distance that would have taken a paper letter months by slow boat just a few decades ago. These simple things bring mindfulness to each moment. Just sending email can be something that anchors you in the present.

Seven Benefits of Meditation in the Workplace

Before we jump into the *How* of meditation, however, let's talk about the *Why*. Why bother cultivating presence? You've got enough on your plate and you don't have time to focus on 'mindfully washing the dishes.' Honestly, you don't have time to read this chapter; you've got people to manage and email piling up.

In this section, we'll describe seven critical workplace skills that leaders who meditate tend to cultivate:

- Make better leadership and financial decisions
- Respond with calm
- Create an internal anchor
- Improve your health
- Enhance empathy
- Cultivate emotional intelligence
- Boost productivity

Make Better Leadership and Financial Decisions

According to Forbes, "Research shows that 15 minutes of mindfulness-based meditation results in more rational thinking when making business decisions. Studies have also found that leaders who focus on mindfulness at work have happier employees and improved morale. In addition, mindfulness meditation can help reduce chronic lower back pain and insomnia."[432]

Another study noted that participants who spent just 15 minutes in "mindfulness" meditation, such as focusing on their breathing, were 77% more likely than others to resist what's known as the "sunk-cost bias"—the tendency to stick with a less-than-optimal strategy merely because they've already invested significant resources into it.[433] Researchers concluded that meditation correlates with leaders making better financial decisions.

Rich Pierson, cofounder of the meditation app called Headspace, notes that as business leaders and managers learn to meditate, they find greater ease in every area of life: "If you can focus on a subtle, boring object like your breath, then focusing on a work problem is a walk in the park."[434] Meditation is like an exercise for your brain in cultivating quiet, calm, focus, and stillness.

Respond with Calm

According to Harvard Business Review, meditation boosts emotional intelligence by helping leaders learn to regulate their emotions.[435] For example, leaders may find themselves feeling frustrated when things don't happen their way or according to their timeline. When expectations aren't met, leaders who don't practice controlling emotion may turn quickly to anger or upset. Blood pressure rises, as does tension in the office. However, leaders who cultivate mindfulness can keep their calm—especially at critical moments of communication.

Dr. James Doty, a neurosurgeon at Stanford University's School of Medicine, describes the value of mindfulness in business leadership.[436] As a CEO of a company he founded with a colleague to sell a medical device, Doty recalls an interaction he had where mindfulness made the difference between keeping a key investor and losing that investor. At a meeting with stakeholders, a vital investor became angry and unreasonable. Because of his mindfulness practice, Doty took a few breaths and responded with empathy by listening to the investor's situation, expectations, and desires. Because Doty listened without reacting with upset, this investor became an ally in making the company a success. It ultimately went public at a value of $1.3 billion USD.

That story may not sound incredibly remarkable: so a CEO listened to an investor? That is what CEOs are supposed to do, right? What is remarkable is that the leader's ability to stay calm and present and listen to the person's needs made a difference in the success or failure of the company. When the stakes were high, mindfulness carried the day.

Create an Internal Anchor

In one article for the Harvard Business Review, the executive chairman of Ford Motor Company indicates that he takes time to meditate each day, no matter what. During his close call with bankruptcy nearly a decade prior, Ford recounted, "The practice of mindfulness kept me going during the darkest days."[437] He credits meditation with helping him improve not only productivity but also his ability to make decisions with compassion and kindness.

Meditation can provide perspective and a bigger-picture view that is helpful for business leaders when their companies are facing a challenge in the marketplace. Such perspective is also helpful when leaders notice that the industry is shifting around them and their companies must pivot and enter a new phase of the business to stay afloat.

Cultivate Empathy

"The best way to take care of the future is to take care of the present moment,"[438] teaches Thich Nhat Hanh. If we define mindfulness simply as being present in the moment, then mindful leaders may be aware of the space and feeling in the office, focused on each task at hand, one at a time. They are focused on the person with whom they're speaking. They breathe easily, sitting attentively yet with ease. In this observant state, leaders find not only that their productivity increases, but also that their empathy increases.

Oprah Winfrey notes the power of empathy in leadership: "Leadership is about empathy. It is about having the ability to relate to and connect with people for the purpose of inspiring and empowering their lives."[439] Empathetic leaders take time to intentionally support colleagues even when the environment is pressure laden. They proactively cross the silences or disconnects that can occur in cubicles and in remote workplaces. They actively acknowledge, listen to, and show kindness to the people who surround them.

For example, in an annual review, an empathetic leader covers vital information yet also holds a real conversation, listening to the employee and connecting outside the realm of numbers. It doesn't have to be a long session with a box of tissues, but it is a minute or two where leader and employee share space, sit together, and assess how they can support each other's goals.

While investing time in people may seem to take time away from deadlines, infusing kindness into the workplace serves to heighten both camaraderie and productivity. For example, teams who get along well do much better with their assignments. Less time is lost in emotional friction and the wheels of collaboration can spin freely, linking diverse colleagues in diverse work environments to improve performance. Executives have found that mindfulness in the workplace builds trust and cohesion.

Enhance Emotional Intelligence

A regular mindfulness and meditation practice can help leaders cultivate their own—and their employees'—emotional intelligence. CEO of Six Seconds Joshua Freedman explains: "Emotional intelligence is a way of recognizing, understanding, and choosing how we think, feel, and act. It shapes our interactions with others and our understanding of ourselves. It defines how and what we learn; it allows us to set priorities; it determines the majority of our daily actions."[440] Each day you show up at your workplace, your emotional intelligence is called into play as a leader. Research suggests emotional intelligence is responsible for as much as 80 percent of our success.[441]

The most successful and effective leader is not necessarily the one who has the smartest strategy or the best spreadsheet. Rather, the most effective leader is one who consistently uses empathy and emotional intelligence to inspire others—to support employees and colleagues and cultivate human potential.

Improve Your Health

Research has revealed that the exercise of being present improves business leadership. Want to be a more effective leader? Get present. Want to connect better with your colleagues and teams? Get present. Want to feel calmer inside and reduce stress? You already know the answer. Get present. Being present as a leader tends to correlate with reduced stress, waste, and frustration. It lowers anxiety and blood pressure. It is also linked with increased intelligence, positivity, immune function, and heart function. It boosts efficiency, productivity, and connectivity among teams and colleagues.

One study on mindfulness concluded: evidence supports the use of Mindfulness-Based Stress Reduction and Mindfulness-Based Cognitive Therapy to alleviate both mental and physical symptoms in the treatment of cancer, cardiovascular disease, chronic pain, depression, anxiety disorders, and in prevention in healthy adults and children.[442] Because employees and leaders suffer from depression, anxiety, and health problems, mindfulness-based training can be a helpful solution.

Boost Productivity

As a business leader, you may wonder about the wisdom of what seems like doing less—sitting, clearing your mind, breathing, etc.—in a world that compels you to do more, faster. If your long to-do list is still miles from complete, how can you responsibly unplug, close your eyes, and tune into your breathing? Even five minutes seems too long when email is piling up and people are waiting for a response. Robert Kistner has said ironically: "Sometimes we are too busy to do the things that will make us less busy."[443]

However, the New York Times cites growing scientific evidence[444] that when we build in more time for naps, breaks, and vacations, we become not just healthier and happier, but also more productive. These breaks—long or short—help to reset our mental capability and combat the sense of overwhelm that we feel at work. How many times have you checked your email first thing in the morning while lying in bed? It is rather obvious that we are going to feel chaotic inside when we are on screens, devices, and email from the moment we wake up to the moment before we fall asleep. Our goal is to be responsible and responsive to our clients, colleagues, and bosses. Yet, what is the price?

If meditation is so helpful, what's the hold up? Why don't more people do it? One of the main reasons is that people think they are too busy to pause for mindfulness. On that point, the words of U.S. President Abraham Lincoln are helpful: "Give me six hours to chop down a tree and I will spend the first four sharpening the axe." [445] Similarly, as to inner preparation, Martin Luther wrote: "I have so much to do that I shall spend the first three hours in prayer [meditation]."[446] Dr. Stephen R. Covey applies this principle in today's business practice, reminding us: "We must never become too busy sawing to take time to sharpen the saw."[447]

The parable of the woodcutter is on point: A woodcutter strained to saw down a tree. A young man who was watching asked, "What are you doing?" "Are you blind?" the woodcutter replied. "I'm cutting down this tree." The young man was unabashed. "You look exhausted! Take a break. Sharpen your saw." The woodcutter explained to the young man that he had been sawing for hours and did not have time to take a break. The young man pushed back: "If you sharpen the saw, you will cut down the tree much faster." The woodcutter said, "I don't have time to sharpen the saw. Don't you see I'm too busy?"[448]

While there is no one-size-fits-all solution, one survey counted eighteen million adult Americans[449] who have chosen to incorporate meditation into their lives and work. Even in the realm of meditation, there is no one-size-fits-all practice. If you asked ten people who meditate what their meditation practices entail, you'd get ten different answers. Yet, those answers would have some commonalities—and that's what we want to summarize for you here.

Simple Meditation Technique

If any of those benefits seem worth your time, let's talk about the single most tried and true method for cultivating presence as a leader: meditation. Here are four simple suggestions for business leaders who are beginning a meditation practice:

- Find stillness
- Look inward
- Tune into your breathing
- Notice thoughts that arise and return to center

Find Stillness

While some leaders prefer walking forms of meditation, people generally choose meditation that involves physical stillness. Turn off or silence your devices. Pick a chair or sit on a cushion if you enjoy sitting on the floor. Feel how your body is connected to that seat through the bones and tissues. Feel how your weight presses down and your spine rises. Reach tall through the crown of your head. This erect posture transforms us from hunched over desks and screens to lifted, quiet, and relaxed. It allows both blood and breath to flow more smoothly.

Look Inward

Let your eyelids close. All day long, your eyes take in the sights, colors, and motion of the world around you. You track data and messages on brightly-lit screens. Now, as your eyelids close, you begin to turn your gaze inward—to become aware of your inner landscape and emotions. Although you are still aware of the sounds around you, simply closing your eyes signals to your body that it is in a safe and more contemplative space.

Tune Into Your Breathing

Notice the rise and fall of your chest—or the expansion and softening of your ribs as you draw in a breath and let it go. All day long we catch shallow breaths where we can; we rarely think about the steadiness and rhythm of our breathing. When we're sitting for meditation, our only job, so to speak, is to simply watch the breath. Notice how the air moves in, and how your lungs fill. What portion of your lungs fills first? Upper? Lower? Notice if the air lingers and then how it moves out of your body. Feel your lungs release and rest before drawing in more air. Realize that air moves in and out of your lungs without your conscious effort; it is simply part of your existence on this planet.

In this attention to the breath, you don't need to change your breathing. While there are fancy patterns of holds, quick inhales and exhales, alternate nostril breaths, and more that you can learn if you want to get into a breathwork practice (sometimes called pranayama), they are not necessary. For simple meditation, simple breathing is the best choice.

Notice as Thoughts Arise and Then Consciously Re-Center

As thoughts begin to chase across your mental awareness, they jump up and down for your attention. They might chatter and shout at each other like monkeys. Initially, you may feel like you need to follow them, chase them away, or take notes because they're reminding you to call your mother and pick up the dry cleaning. But as you relax and simply watch without becoming attached to them, the thoughts will pass and new thoughts will arise.

It's like watching clouds float across the sky. You see the movement and shape of vapor, all without being, or attaching to, the clouds. You are the watcher, not the puffs of vapor. If you become distracted or find that you've chased a specific monkey-thought up a tree, notice that without judgment and simply return to your quiet watching. It helps to re-focus attention on your breathing because this will shift attention away from the monkeys.

The goal is not to make the mind go blank; rather, it is to unhook our instant identification with our thoughts. Arianna Huffington writes: "Meditation is not about stopping thoughts but recognizing that we are more than our thoughts and our feelings."[450] In each of us, there is a dimension of understanding that is deeper than our surface-level thoughts. You could call it presence, awareness, consciousness, or any number of things. It is the part inside of you that is aware of the thinking going on inside your head. It is the listener—the one who knows that the stuff of the thoughts is mere stuff. It is the witness that the thoughts passing across your mind are mere thoughts but that they don't define your essence. Ram Dass teaches: "Be still. The quieter you become, the more you can hear."[451]

It's impossible to remove the fluctuations of the mind because the mind is always thinking—that's what it does. But it is possible to begin to slow the mind down and un-identify with those thoughts. Find the gap between: "I *feel* angry" and "I *am* angry." You can feel angry without taking it on as a state of being. You can watch it and question it and learn from it. You can use your feelings for insight without being overwhelmed by them.

And that's it—those are the basics. Like lifting weights strengthens your muscles, meditation strengthens your mind and inner core. Your mind learns to do one thing at one time: in this case, your mind must simply exist and watch without getting attached to the chaos. Your mind learns also that it is more stable than the thoughts that arise day by day. You begin to identify with the calm behind all the thoughts. You understand your nature as the one who is aware of the thoughts— you begin to identify more with the witnessing presence, and less with the monkeys jumping up and down.

Don't get boxed into thinking that you can only meditate when you are closing your eyes, sitting cross-legged on a yoga mat, chanting "OM" and burning incense. We can practice mindfulness in every moment and even while on the go, doing dishes, walking,[452] running,[453] and exercising.[454] Harvard Business Review even advocates practicing mindfulness while driving during the daily commute.[455] It seems that there is no situation where you are conscious and cannot practice mindfulness. In fact, the more demands there are on your attention, the more valuable is your mindfulness. The possibilities are unlimited.

More Positive Results

Leaders who meditate or engage in mindfulness practices consistently report positive outcomes. The American Psychological Association has aggregated some of these empirical results, including the following:[456]

- *Less rumination.* How much time do you spend dwelling on past failures and current challenges? Mindfulness meditation can reduce ruminating thoughts, which in turn can help you think more clearly and positively.

- *Reduced stress.* People who practice daily meditation also show fewer signs of stress. This makes meditation imperative for those in prominent decision-making roles, such as business leaders or team managers.

- *Improved memory.* Better working memory and retention correlate with regular meditation practices.

- *Better focus.* Meditating in short sessions can help you focus on your work better throughout the day, reducing distraction and sharpening cognition.

- *Greater emotional control.* People who meditate show less emotional reactivity. They gain greater control over their emotions and are less likely to behave impulsively. This control aids in making logical, calm decision making.

- *Enhanced self-observation.* Because meditation cultivates self-observation and introspection, business leaders who meditate generally recover faster when negatively provoked. They learn to interrogate automatic pathways and break bad habits.

- *Greater relationship satisfaction.* People who meditate report higher levels of satisfaction in their personal relationships and lower levels of relational conflict.

As business leaders, when we tap into our quieter dimension, we find stillness underneath the turbulent surface that is ruffled up by chaotic thought, activity, words, email, social media, or anything we see or hear and react to. We begin to let ourselves out of the conceptual thought-prisons that limit our minds.[457] Instead, we fuel what is timeless about ourselves and our surroundings. Being able to see the larger picture without believing that our thoughts are equal to reality is a hallmark of talented leadership—it is the source of outside-the-box thinking.

Learning More

While we have listed the basics here in this chapter, some business leaders choose to take on a more structured meditation practice by attending classes or retreats. Meditation studios are becoming well-established, and resources, instruction, and teachers are easily discoverable online. We are not promoting any specific type of meditation or any specific teacher, but common search terms may include "mindfulness meditation," "vipassana," and "transcendental meditation."

For those who prefer a more independent approach, there are a variety of apps with guided instruction and lectures. Because the apps change frequently and we are not promoting a specific type of mediation here in this chapter, we won't provide a list of recommendations. However, a simple search online or in your smartphone's app store will return many results from which you can choose. Many apps offer initial lessons for free so you can experience a teacher and decide whether his or her style seems like the right fit for you.

Key Takeaways

Once considered an 'alternative' life choice, meditation has hit mainstream in the last few decades. Meditation can make you a better leader, and it costs nothing. It's mind training. Look around at top business leaders—ask them about their success practices—and you'll find meditation popping up again and again. One list includes:[458]

- Oprah Winfrey, Chairwoman and CEO of Harpo Productions, Inc.
- Russell Simmons, Co-Founder, Def Jam Records; Founder of GlobalGrind.com
- Rupert Murdoch, Chairman and CEO, News Corp
- Bill Ford, Executive Chairman, Ford Motor Company
- Arianna Huffington, President & Editor-in-Chief, Huffington Post Media Group
- Padmasree Warrior, CTO, Cisco Systems

Further demonstrating that meditation is mainstream at work, sources indicate that Apple offers meditation classes at its main campus. Nike employees have access to relaxation rooms, which they can use to meditate. A 2007 program at Google called "Search Inside Yourself" helped more than 500 employees learn how to breathe mindfully, listen to their coworkers, and even improve their emotional intelligence. Yahoo! has on-site meditation rooms and free onsite classes. Deutsche Bank, a global financial services company, has offered meditation classes and quiet spaces onsite for several years, hoping that it will help encourage better decisions and to reduce stress.[459] The list goes on.

In sum, research offers case after case demonstrating the value of meditation for business leaders. According to Harvard Business Review, "research on mindfulness suggests that meditation sharpens skills like attention, memory, and emotional intelligence."[460] Thus, if you take a few minutes for simple sitting practice, you may notice that your critical leadership skills like empathy and emotional intelligence improve. You may find better health and better decision-making capacity. You may feel more calm, productive, and anchored internally. Give it a try.

16

How Values and Tradeoffs
Drive Decision Making

How to Choose Wisely . . . Or, How to Choose Less Stupidly

Why do smart business leaders often make stupid decisions in their careers and personal life? On a human level, one answer is that leaders have too much on their plates to consistently make great decisions. Psychology Today reports that most people make "roughly 2,000 decisions per hour or one decision every two seconds"[461]—and many of these decisions happen on autopilot. Think of small, unnoticeable decisions like petting the dog or ignoring a text. Just ordering a coffee involves as many as 15 decisions: espresso or Americano? Grande or tall? What kind of milk? Steamed? Cappuccino, macchiato, latte . . . And all those decisions happen before a leader even sets foot into the office where larger decisions await, like launching a marketing campaign or hiring a new employee.

No wonder decisions slip off the rails from time to time—maybe leaders invest in a new idea based on a gut feeling rather than on factual research. Oops. Maybe we hire someone we like instinctively without analyzing well whether he or she can do the job. Double oops. Even with the best of intentions, we all make mistakes and leaders are no strangers to poor decision making at times. In his book entitled *The Road Less Stupid*, Keith Cunningham indicates that dumb decisions tend to be instinctive and informed more by emotion than by logic. Cunningham notes that "stupid" decisions carry an inherent "dumb tax,"[462] which includes lost time, money, and reputation.

Rather than stressing that every decision we make must be a home run, Cunningham suggests that leaders can succeed primarily by avoiding stupid decisions. In fact, he goes so far as to claim that: "the key to getting rich (and staying that way) is to avoid doing stupid things."[463] Put another way, developing the mind muscle to avoid making bad decisions is a critical skill for leaders who want to succeed.

Chapter Roadmap

This and the upcoming two chapters are focused on smart decision making, which is designed to tackle vexing questions like: why do we get derailed by making bad decisions even when we have good intentions? Is there some way to hardwire smart decision-making processes? To answer these questions, this series is divided into three parts, which cover theory and practice. Here's a quick overview:

- Part I (this chapter) analyzes decision making on a *conscious* level. It covers how we conceive of decisions as stupid or smart, and it describes the relevance of values, tradeoffs, and thinking time.
- Part II takes this a step farther by analyzing decision making on a *subconscious* level, including the way that areas of our brains inform how we make decisions that have evolved in response to external stimuli. This section pulls back the curtain and helps us see *why* we make the decisions we have made.
- Part III puts theory into practice by describing Cunningham's practical five-step method for avoiding stupid decisions: 1) finding the unasked question; 2) separating the problem from the symptom; 3) checking assumptions; 4) considering second-order consequences; and 5) creating the machine.

Values Define Smart and Stupid Decisions

What Makes a Decision Smart or Stupid?

Let's begin by defining terms: what makes something a good decision or a stupid decision? Other than obviously terrible decisions like hiring Enron to handle your financial statements, most decisions are good or bad based on a subjective set of criteria. In the broad scope on an organizational level, good decisions are objectively those that increase profit, growth, and business reputation while minimizing superfluous costs and inefficiency. Smart decisions achieve desired outcomes, improve client relationships, and facilitate return on investment. Stupid decisions are things you regret or wish you hadn't done—they are the risky moves that didn't pay off or the investment that led to losses rather than gains. On a personal level, stupid decisions are choices that made your life worse, weakened your leadership, or diminished your overall career trajectory.

Your Values Define What Decisions You View as Stupid and Smart.

As leaders, we hope that our decisions will create a trajectory of growth and value according to our desired subjective outcomes. We're using the term 'subjective' here because each organization measures value differently. For example, value could mean anything from expansion of product placement, to expansion of markets, to expansion of consumer demographics, to an increased number of products/services overall, and so on. Or, an organization might define value more in terms of enhancing reputation, increasing diversity and inclusion, and so forth. In short, how you define your values and goals will have everything to do with what you label as a smart decision. This applies at both the organizational and individual levels.

Further, what is a great decision for one person could be a stupid decision for another person. On a personal level, our life values come into play as we assess decision opportunities—do we value accumulating money and education? If so, then choosing to spend years in school to enter a high-paying profession would be a smart decision. But if we instead value backpacking the world or accumulating time with our friends and family over accumulating money, then trading most social time to study for exams for the better part of a decade would be a stupid decision. Three-time #1 New York Times bestselling author Mark Manson writes that values "are the measuring sticks by which we determine what is a successful and meaningful life."[464]

Organizations tend to be clearer than people on what they value. Organizations generate charts and lists of values, which they post on signs and discuss in meetings. On the other hand, people can sometimes feel confused about values because of the word "should." We are told throughout our lives that we 'should' do _____ (you fill in the blank) but, in reality, we spend our time doing _____ (again, you fill in the blank). What we do is a clue to our values because chances are that our behavior will ultimately align with our values. Why? Because time is finite. We can do only one thing at a time, and how we spend our time in the long run shows us what we truly value. Each activity, however brief, is a clue to what we value most: maybe we spend five minutes talking with our parents, cleaning the sink, making a call, or zoning out watching TV. As the years add up, our behaviors both reflect and create our identity.

We'll propose here that there are not inherently *good* values and inherently *bad* values—for proof, look around the world and see how different civilizations and groups enshrine different values. Rather, we'll propose that there are *types* of values that consistently lead to good and bad decisions. For example, stupid decisions stem from destructive values that are outside your realm of control, whereas good decisions stem from constructive values that are within your realm of control and based on evidence.[465] These values about values, so to speak, can help us honestly assess our values and make fewer stupid decisions along the way.

Values Can be Found on the Flip Side of Success

Most leaders focus on what they want to accomplish. We set goals and psych ourselves up for how great success will be. Manson suggests that we flip that around: instead of asking what reward we want, we should ask ourselves instead, "What pain do you want? What are you willing to struggle for?"[466] By re-orienting our gaze to what we are willing to suffer through to achieve what we think we want, we will more clearly see what we value and what rewards we are likely to achieve.

For example, you can't become an Olympic athlete without years of practice. If you don't want to suffer through practice sessions, weight training, endless coaching, and injuries, then maybe you don't really want to become an Olympic athlete. And that is fine—most of us won't be willing to suffer through the journey to attain that goal. The beauty of this question is that it helps us assess whether we are strong enough to survive the journey toward what we think are our goals.

Tradeoffs are inherent in decision making since we can't have it all. As you know from experience in leadership, decisions inherently involve a matter of tradeoffs. Every good decision involves making what we hope is a good trade—giving up one thing to invest in something else that will bring more benefits. Manson suggests that another way to make smart decisions is to consider lack: "What is *worth* giving up in each moment for something else? What is the something else worth pursuing?"[467] Just above, we were considering what is worth suffering through to get a reward.

This is the flip slide: what is worth not having to get your desired reward? Put another way, suffering is what we *have* in the day-to-day grind of pursuing what we want—the long practice hours, injuries, stress, etc. Giving up is what we *don't have* in the day-to-day grind of pursuing what we want—vacations, free time with family and friends, normal schedules, etc. Answering those questions will direct you toward the highest-value tradeoffs.

As leaders, we have a finite number of resources that we can and should invest in decisions that deliver the highest returns. Again, the concept of highest returns goes back to values: on the level of the organization, would you benefit more from investing money into research to develop a better product? Or investing money into marketing existing products to expand your reach? You cannot do all things at once because resources are finite. So, you must prioritize what you value and invest there . . . you will be giving things up, but according to what you value, you will be making a smart decision.

Smart decisions come in a variety of options, though. For example, if your company delivers services that are well established within the US and Canadian markets, good decisions with marketing funds may involve expanding marketing efforts to reach broader consumer demographics within those markets. Or, good decisions may involve customizing branding to appeal to a higher-end luxury market. Or softening branding to appeal to younger consumers and families. Further good decisions may involve establishing marketing efforts in other countries, and perhaps reaching throughout the Americas.

In sum, the way to determine what is a good decision or a stupid decision in this arena is whether it produces the results that you value.

It's easy to see from the lens of tradeoffs that if your organization values appealing to a luxury market consumer demographic, any investment of marketing funds, time, resources, or leadership outside that focus will potentially constitute waste when measured against the larger objective. Waste is a hallmark of a stupid decision. And waste is subjective according to the stated values.

Specific Company Tradeoffs: One Smart and One Stupid

The examples mentioned so far are somewhat narrow, but you get the idea. Think of tradeoffs that are already familiar to you: at a time when movie rentals occurred primarily in stores, Netflix traded the store model for the mail model (before streaming). That tradeoff positioned Netflix to capture the market that Blockbuster stores had dominated for years, and it turned out to be a smart decision. Blockbuster sank and Netflix took the field. After several years, to keep pace with the times, Netflix de-emphasized its mailing rental service and poured resources into video and television streaming service. Here, Netflix outdid itself and streaming is the primary consumer method. Tradeoffs paid off and we judge Netflix as having made smart business decisions.

On the flip side, consider Kodak. At a time when digital photography was taking off, Kodak considered alternatives reinvested in film rather than digital photography. You already know the way that tradeoff turned out, and the film industry has rendered Kodak obsolete. In other words, although investing in film was Kodak's mode of success for several years to that point, it turned out to be a stupid decision considering the shifting consumer and technology market. Bad tradeoff.

Importance of Thinking Time

Other than re-thinking our values (and the organization's values, to the extent we have the need to do so and the power to do so), what else can we do to avoid stupid decisions? According to Cunningham, "thinking time" is the best way to improve one's options in business and avoid doing stupid things. In fact, strong leaders take time to practice, learn and research, test out ideas, correct what went wrong, and keep at it over time. Warren Buffett has been quoted as saying, "I insist on a lot of time being spent thinking, almost every day. . . . This is very uncommon in American business."[468] Why? We are continually subject to information overload and distraction deluge—email, social media, text, people knocking on the door, etc. To think clearly, Fast Company "recommends carving out at least 30 minutes a day to just think, especially if you're in a creative or leadership role."[469]

Thinking helps us identify when we are generating ideas with strong emotional pull and then investing in those ideas without dedicating enough time to considering the long game. Using a metaphor from baseball, we are tempted to swing at bad pitches with the hope of a home run rather than insisting on hitting strikes. Although we may have talent and ambition, bad pitches are bad pitches, and striking out is worse than walking to first base. Buffett clarifies, "I do more reading and thinking, and make [fewer] impulse decisions than most people in business."[470]

Why should someone of his status spend so much time pondering? "I do it because I like this kind of life." That type of life is steady and successful—and, in leadership, winning is more about making smart decisions day by day rather than swinging for wild hail Mary home runs. So, how can you create a Buffet kind of life and head in the right direction from the get-go? No baseball players would swing at a bad pitch if they could see that the pitch was bad from the outset. They get confused or they misjudge the ball, or they overestimate their talent or reach.

In short, if they had more time to think they would probably make much better swing decisions. Alas, baseball players don't have the luxury of thinking time as a ball moving at extreme speeds comes whizzing in their direction. But business leaders are a different story. Although the pace of office life is quick, you can and must carve out time to dedicate to thinking if you want to swing for strikes.

Key Takeaways

Here, we have discussed values, tradeoffs, and thinking time—things of which our conscious minds can be aware and can analyze. We have seen that our values are subjective and that effective leaders will determine what constitutes a smart decision for the organization depending on whether it aligns with corporate values. From this lens, leaders can ask what tradeoffs will be required to create the value-based outcomes they desire. Plenty of thinking time is needed to effectively assess values and tradeoffs, and we recommend that leaders book time into their schedules for such analysis.

In reality, most decisions have a percentage of stupidity and a percentage of smartness, and a few drops of wild luck left to chance. But by thinking intentionally and being clear on their values, leaders can hedge bets in their favor when it comes to conscious tradeoffs to make smart decisions (and avoid stupid decisions). In Part II, we will dive into aspects of human brain evolution and psychology to analyze subconscious drivers that are 'beneath the surface' of conscious thought as leaders make decisions. Buckle up.

17

Brain Evolution and
Subconscious Decision Making

Does Brain Chemistry Affect Parole Hearing Outcomes?

Did you know prisoners whose cases are heard in the morning are more likely to have their parole applications approved?[471] Is this because prisoners whose cases are heard in the morning are consistently more reformed than prisoners whose cases are heard in the afternoon? Looking into the data, researchers found that these results are likely correlated with the reviewing judge's body chemistry. In the study, they documented judges' two daily food breaks and found that the percentage of favorable rulings dropped gradually from about 65% to nearly zero as blood sugar levels sank. Then, favorable rulings jumped abruptly up to 65% after another food break.[472]

Beyond blood sugar levels, researchers found that case rulings throughout the day could also be correlated with the judge's level of decision fatigue.[473] Doctors define decision fatigue as the phenomenon such that "'after making many decisions, your ability to make more and more decisions over the course of a day becomes worse . . . The more decisions you have to make, the more fatigue you develop and the more difficult [making good decisions] can become.'"[474] The point is that throughout the day, decision making absorbs a great deal of energy—both consciously and subconsciously—and such fatigue can set the stage for smart people to make less-than-smart decisions. Who else makes many significant decisions throughout a day? Business leaders.

This type of data doesn't boost consumer confidence in the justice system, but the results apply across the board: where humans are involved, then human body chemistry and fatigue are involved. We aren't trying to demean judges or the justice system here; rather, we are pointing out that grand decisions like "judicial rulings can be swayed by extraneous variables that should have no bearing on legal decisions"[475] . . . such as blood sugar levels.

What's true of the courtroom is equally true of the office board room. Business professionals are not immune to decision fatigue and indeed may face it more frequently when they must make higher quantities of weightier decisions. Since Keith Cunningham implies that leaders who succeed will focus on making fewer stupid decisions, smart leaders will proactively become attentive to what is going on underneath the surface of the conscious mind that is influencing their decision making. Put simply, smart decisions must harness both conscious and unconscious mind levels.

Chapter Roadmap

Welcome to the second chapter of the trio on smart decision making. These are designed to tackle vexing questions like: why do we get derailed by making bad decisions even when we have good intentions? Is there some way to hardwire smart decision-making processes? By way of reminder, Part I analyzed decision making on a *conscious* level. It covered how we conceive of decisions as stupid or smart, including the relevance of values, tradeoffs, and thinking time.

This chapter—Part II—goes a step farther by analyzing decision making on a *subconscious* level. It explains how the decision-making areas of our brains have evolved to respond to external stimuli. It also highlights the influence of emotion, thereby pulling back the curtain to help us see *why* we make the decisions we make.

In the final chapter, Part III will put theory into practice by describing Cunningham's practical five-step method for avoiding stupid decisions: 1) finding the unasked question; 2) separating the problem from the symptom; 3) checking assumptions; 4) considering second-order consequences; and 5) creating the machine.

Brain Evolution Drives Decision Making

Hindsight is 20-20

On the level of the organization, smart decisions increase profit, growth, and business reputation while minimizing inefficiency and extra cost. Smart decisions achieve desired outcomes, improve client relationships, and facilitate return on investment whereas stupid decisions are the reverse: things that increase cost, reduce efficiency, and overall bring a sense of regret. Many decisions are only effectively labeled smart or stupid in hindsight when time has borne out the results of those decisions and highlighted any faulty underlying assumptions. On a granular level, it becomes evident that no action produces only good or bad results: you invest some here to get some there, but sometimes it's two steps forward and one step back.

Time shows what we failed to assess at the outset, or what was hidden from our view. As days and years pass, things that were hard to predict in advance at the outset—such as market conditions—may swing in our favor or may turn against us . . . and affect the ultimate label of "stupid" or "smart." Sometimes decisions are in fact smart at the outset, but then judged in hindsight as stupid because they didn't pan out. Perhaps industry changed in ways that the decision failed to predict. Perhaps key people didn't follow through. Perhaps assumptions that seemed sound at decision time turned out to be faulty. It's not possible to account for all external changes that might occur, but it is possible for internal factors.

To be fair, few of us sit at our desks thinking, "How about I make a really stupid decision today? It's got to be one that will cost my company money and dampen my reputation. Awesome!" Further, few of us approach the weekend thinking, "I know what will be fun—I'll go out, drink until I black out, pick a fight, then try to drive myself home, and wake up in jail. Perfect!" Not one of us has made such a plan, and yet these things happen to the best of us.

Sometimes Even the Best Intentions Get Hijacked

So, how do 'stupid' decisions happen? Even with the best of intentions, most of us have made many, many stupid decisions over our lives and careers—decisions that have cost us money, time, health, and relationships (to say nothing of peace of mind). Generally, this is not because we are stupid people by nature. Rather, these decisions are influenced by brain chemistry and unregulated emotions.

For example, regarding basic evolution and brain chemistry, humans have evolved with a logical part of the mind and a less-logical part of the mind. (In case you couldn't tell, this is not a scientific treatise; it's a practical, rubber-meets-the-road discussion.) The logical part of the mind—the cerebral cortex—is the one we trust for smart decisions because it analyzes, studies, considers consequences and potential outcomes, and puts a plan into effect.[476] It makes charts and wisely allocates resources. Smart leaders learn how to harness the power of this logical mind to make and effectuate good decisions.

But the less-logical part of the brain is the wild card. This part is influenced by the amygdala—by attraction, by Ponzi schemes, and by powerful emotions like fear and desire. Along these lines, Brian Tracy says, "Everything you do is triggered by an emotion of either desire or fear."[477] The amygdala is a part of the brain that encodes memory and emotions.[478] Psychology Today refers to it as the "lizard brain"[479] because it is dominated by instinct and impulse rather than by rational thought. Here's an easy way to understand it: the "limbic system is about all a lizard has for brain function. It is in charge of fight, flight, feeding, fear, freezing up, and fornication."[480]

These lizard brain responses are essential to survival and have evolved to help humans survive over centuries. The lizard brain responds to perceived threats with aggression and fear to protect the organism. It also runs our deep-seated, often mysterious emotions of desire and pleasure.

In many good ways, this illogical part of the mind is what makes us fundamentally human—somehow our non-flawless, un-robotic, unpredictable nature often fuels surprise and creativity. Artists might describe themselves as 'being in the zone' where they are running on mere sunlight and core creativity as they paint. Business leaders might dive deep into a project so all that matters is forward movement and connecting the dots at the expense of all else. Transcendentalist poet Walt Whitman wrote it thus: "Urge and urge and urge, always the procreant urge of the world."[481] His ultra-famous "Song of Myself" poem celebrates many things, including aspects of human behavior that we might construe as the delicious, wild, uncontrollable lizard brain.

Yet, for all its mystical and poetic beauty, the lizard brain is not the best analytical place from which to make decisions. If you think back over your life to any one or two particularly stupid decisions that cost you money, time, or reputation, chances are that this less-logical side of the brain took the steering wheel at a critical 'trigger-influenced' moment and played a role in instinctual decisions.

Subconscious Emotions Drive Decision Making

How Well We Deal with Emotions Can Affect How Often We Make Stupid Decisions

Often, this less-logical part of the brain pushes us subconsciously to act in ways that our conscious minds know are stupid. Peeling back the layers of 'stupid' decision making, we usually find at the root a large emotion such as desire, pain, or fear (perceived threat). Of those, desire and fear are straightforward—we know what we want, and we know what we fear. But pain is sneaky because it often masquerades as something else, such as frustration, anger, shame, etc. The experience of pain might be fresh, such as with a relationship loss or an office misstep. Or, the pain might have occurred years or decades ago in childhood, and the mind is still processing it as an encoded memory. Pain can be rooted in fear of abandonment, as well as in fear of failure. These fears throw sand in the air, so to speak, so we cannot see situations or ourselves clearly.

In the personal realm, pain and fear usually inspire us to check out.
Where are we going with this discussion? Here's the point: pain is one excuse that our less-logical minds use to accomplish hijacking. In the personal realm, we tend toward the *flight* response on the fight-flight continuum. This is the cue that says essentially: "I'm feeling too much pain/fear/anger from some experience or memory, so I need to [do this distraction behavior] to numb out." We can each fill in the brackets with our 'favorite' distraction. When feeling pain, fear, and anger, we run from those emotions and invoke behaviors of numbing out,

starting fights, eating too much or too little, gambling, compulsive shopping, using substances, or risky sexuality—you name it. If a behavior enables us to mask pain rather than to face it, that behavior is likely someone's favorite 'stupid decision.'

Although such decisions in the personal realm may seem separate from the office realm, they can directly impact a leader's reputation and character. As a case in point, the 'me, too' movement highlighted such concerns related to misplaced sexual expression, often in a workplace setting. The gist of it is that healthy, well-adjusted leaders don't make the sorts of decisions that end up criticized by such movements.

In the workplace, pain and fear usually inspire us to fight.
In the business leadership realm where we have less flexibility to simply numb out with behavior, pain and fear tend to inspire reactive decision making. In other words, we respond to perceived threats with the *fight* response on the fight-flight continuum. For example, if leaders obtain data showing that a competitor is far and away beating their company on first-quarter sales, then leaders may feel anger and may act out that anger with blame.

Harvard Business Review reminds leaders that in moments of peak anger, decision making can be impaired and provides this advice: "Resist the temptation to respond to people or make decisions while you're emotionally keyed up. Practice walking away from the computer or putting the phone down, and return to the task at hand when you're able to think more clearly and calmly."[482] Along similar lines, Robert Kistner notes: "When you are in crisis management mode, nothing gets accomplished."[483]

Peeling Back Anger and Pain to Identify Fundamental Emotions Can Mitigate Reactivity.

Leaders who avoid reacting and instead sit with tough emotions like anger can find that underneath it lies something like pain or sadness. We worry because we came in second place. We worry about what others and the boss will think since we didn't succeed. In many ways, our fears and worries come down to fundamental security concerns like, "Will I be good enough? Will I be able to succeed and inspire others? Will my boss see me as contributing something of value?"

Leaders can then focus on reassuring themselves amid sadness or calming the fear rather than acting out anger and reactivity in decision making. Likewise, in the personal realm, if we can sit with discomfort instead of numbing out, we will have a far better chance of avoiding stupid decisions and keeping our heads straight.

At this point, however, we'll leave the rest of the clinical psychology and theory to the expert doctors and therapists. The point of our discussion is that humans make decisions in ways that are not entirely logical and not entirely emotional. Rather, we are a beautiful, jumbled-up mix of the two. We're a complex mix of feelings, brain chemistry, achievements, lizard brain urges, hopes, heartaches, desires, fears, and dreams. And that messy, existential mix sometimes leads to less-than-genius decision making—particularly if we let the less-logical brain take the steering wheel.

Key Takeaways

So, what's the fix? How do we take conscious control of decision making? The key takeaway is this: smart leaders evolve beyond lizard brain leadership. Highly reactive leaders get themselves into more sticky situations and make more stupid decisions than do people who practice being with pain/difficult emotions and not letting the emotions control their thoughts or reactions. Think for a minute about your friends, family members and colleagues. Do you agree? Fortunately, knowing how brain evolution and subconscious factors can hijack decision making, we can proactively hedge our bets. Here are two methods leaders can implement to put themselves back in the driver's seat for conscious and un-stupid decision making: notice and diffuse the trigger, and invest time to think.

Notice and Diffuse the Trigger

When you feel uncomfortable sensations arising in the body—like tightening fists, shortening of breath, rising heart rate, and contracting muscles—simply realize that an emotional trigger is occurring. This is the lizard brain doing its evolutionary job. Don't worry about it, but don't let it take over, either. Before reacting to situations by embodying or acting out variations of anger, conscious leaders should look underneath the anger for a source of pain, fear, or desire. Is there a threat? A fear of failing? A fear of looking bad in front of others?

Instead of reacting to that negative emotion by acting out or making less-than-logical decisions, take a few moments to acknowledge the root fear or pain. By bringing a sense of understanding and even compassion to yourself in such moments, we can help diffuse the intensity of the emotion so that we will be less likely to experience hijacking and more likely to respond calmly. By spending time understanding the root fear and settling the emotions prior to making decisions, leaders will make far smarter decisions on an interpersonal level and on an organizational level.

As an easy way memory cue, clinical psychologist Tara Brach developed an acronym for this method of moving through challenging feelings, called "RAIN"[484]:

- Recognize what is happening
- Allow the experience to be there as it is
- Investigate with interest and care
- Nurture with self-compassion

Put another way, you can take responsibility and stay in the driver's seat of decision making by noticing the trigger as it arises and patiently responding to it internally. That proactively shifts how we feel about ourselves so we are less likely to respond from the lizard brain when triggers occur.

Along these lines, Brian Tracy advises: "The happiest people in the world are those who feel absolutely terrific about themselves, and this is the natural outgrowth of accepting total responsibility for every part of their lives."[485] Taking full responsibility is particularly important as business leaders because we cannot afford to make 'stupid' decisions that compromise our reputation and our organization.

Invest Time to Think

One of the best ways to avoid making stupid decisions is by investing time to think. Brian Tracy quotes Aristotle as saying "Wisdom (the ability to make good decisions) is a combination of experience plus reflection. The more you think about your experiences, the more vital lessons you will gain from them."[486]

In fact, tapping into the power of 'thinking time' as the solution to stupid decision making is the premise of Keith Cunningham's book: *The Road Less Stupid*. Proactive and focused thinking harnesses the conscious brain, which has evolved beyond lizard brain responses, and which forms the reliable base of successful leadership analysis.

Therefore, to improve leadership thinking time, Cunningham suggests five steps.[487] We've summarized them here in a nutshell:

- Create questions that enhance clarity and generate options. More options make for smarter decisions.
- Get clear on what obstacles are preventing success—not all obstacles are problems; rather, they can be blind spots.
- Check assumptions. There are facts and then the stories that we make up regarding the facts. Figure out which are which.
- Identify what is at stake if things go wrong; clarify and measure risks.
- Draft a plan to move from where you are to where you want to be. Include the necessary people and funds.

We will spend the entirety of the next chapter unpacking these five steps.

18

Five Actionable Steps for
Making Smart Decisions

Because unfamiliar circumstances can be a birthplace of creative decision making (much like how necessity is the mother of invention), Harvard Business Review researchers created an experiment wherein they put retail marketing professionals into military research work for two weeks. It's easy to see how retail and military are vastly different worlds; where is the conceptual overlap designed to produce creative decision making? In both environments, professionals must "work with large volumes of data from which it was critical to identify small trends or weak signals."[488]

It's no surprise that patterns become more evident when we get out of the box and see familiar patterns from different angles. Although the study did not provide detailed information regarding the type of military information that the retail professionals encountered and analyzed, the study did point out an effect on creative decision making. At the conclusion of the experiment in the military environment, the marketing professionals "discovered that there was little difference between, say, handling outgoing disaffected customers and anticipating incoming ballistic missiles."[489]

What a wild juxtaposition! Nonetheless, as the marketers analyzed data and came up with creative solutions to anticipate ballistic missiles, they found overlap in the process used to "detect a potential loss of loyalty and take action before a valued customer switched to a competitor. By improving their strategy, the marketers were able to make smarter decisions and thereby retain far more high-volume business."[490] So, what's the key takeaway? Harvard Business Review notes that "leaders are susceptible to *entrained thinking*, a conditioned response that occurs when people are blinded to new ways of thinking by the perspectives they acquired through past experience, training, and success."[491] Relying solely on entrained thinking can be one basis for making bad decisions.

Chapter Roadmap

This is the third of three chapters focused on smart decision making by tackling questions like: why do we get derailed by making bad decisions even when we have good intentions? Is there some way to hardwire smart decision-making processes?

By way of reminder, Part I analyzed decision making on a *conscious* level. It covered how we conceive of decisions as stupid or smart, including the relevance of values, tradeoffs, and thinking time. Taking this a step farther, Part II analyzed decision making on a *subconscious* level. It explained how the decision-making areas of our brains have evolved to respond to external stimuli. It also highlighted the influence of emotion, thereby pulling back the curtain to help us see *why* we make the decisions we make.

Here in Part III, we will put theory into practice by detailing Keith Cunningham's practical five-step method for avoiding stupid decisions, as outlined in *The Road Less Stupid*:[492]

1. Find the unasked question: Create questions that enhance clarity and generate options. More options make for smarter decisions.
2. Separate the problem from the symptom: Get clear on what obstacles are preventing success—not all obstacles are problems; rather, they can be blind spots.
3. Check assumptions: There are facts and then the stories that we make up regarding the facts. Figure out which are which.
4. Consider second-order consequences: Identify what is at stake if things go wrong; clarify and measure risks.
5. Create the machine: Draft a plan to move from where you are to where you want to be. Include the necessary people and funds.

Find the Unasked Question

For this first step, Cunningham cleverly refocuses leaders on finding questions rather than on finding answers: "Having the right answer is smart. Having the right question is genius."[493] When things go wrong, we don't make the sale, or we must manage unforeseen human resources issues, most leaders look for answers, rather than for questions. We want to know why this happened or who is at fault. But those aren't the right questions to be asking if we want to solve root issues.

For example, Cunningham shares, "When we get stuck, we tend to think the reason is because we don't have the right answer. My experience is that finding the 'right' answer is rarely the problem. What keeps us stuck are inferior questions that produce tactical or unattractive choices."[494] That is what he means when he suggests finding the unasked question—the question that highlights possible solutions or improvements.

Break What Needs to Be Broken

If Cunningham is correct that "a problem is simply an unanswered question," then finding the right questions is key to solving the problems that leaders need to solve. To ramp up our question-finding skills, Cunningham suggests a basic architecture we can use as a template. He recommends that we frame problems with two questions:[495]

1. How might I _____?
2. So that I can _____?

This two-step template encourages leaders to adjust their thought process from "what needs to be fixed" to "what needs to be broken."[496] The most comprehensive solutions will generally involve breaking things (stopping certain practices) and starting other things (initiating new practices). Harvard Business Review seconds Cunningham's process: "Good leadership requires openness to change on an individual level. Truly adept leaders will know not only how to identify the context they're working in at any given time but also how to change their behavior and their decisions to match that context."[497]

As leaders fearlessly pull previously unasked questions into the light, those questions not only simplify the problem at hand, but they also increase the various possibilities available to solve the problem. Peter Drucker advises, "Most serious mistakes are not being made as a result of wrong answers. The truly dangerous thing is asking the wrong question."[498] In short, as you invest time into designing better questions, you will see better solutions to the problems you must solve as a leader.

Listen to Your Intuition

In addition to relying on facts, don't silence your hunches and instincts because these are clues toward deeper realms of knowing—they highlight things that aren't always obvious on a fact level. Admittedly, "in the age of big data, trusting your gut often gets a bad rap. Intuition—the term used to refer to gut feelings in research—is frequently dismissed as mystical or unreliable."[499]

For example, saying "I have a bad feeling about this" is probably the least convincing standalone argument in a business meeting, but "studies show that pairing gut feelings with analytical thinking helps you make better, faster, and more accurate decisions and gives you more confidence in your choices than relying on intellect alone."[500] Thus, smart leaders will learn to leverage both feelings and facts in decision making.

In fact, Harvard Business Review points out that when leaders approach decision making on the level of intuition, the brain works in tandem with the gut to tap into information stored in memory, past experiences, and preferences to inform a wise decision grounded in context. A feeling in the pit of your stomach can steer creative processes and can prompt leaders to make deeper factual analysis of a situation. "In this way, intuition is a form of emotional and experiential data that leaders need to value."[501]

Leverage High Sensitivity as an Asset

Some leaders are gifted in realms of sensitivity, which informs intuition. You may already be familiar with research regarding sensitivity as a temperament trait: the National Library of Medicine "suggest[s] that sensory processing sensitivity (SPS), found in roughly

20% of humans and over 100 other species, is a trait associated with greater sensitivity and responsiveness to the environment and to social stimuli."[502] Some studies correlate higher SPS levels with higher intellect, which is an asset, but there are plusses and minuses of sensitivity. For instance, leaders with high SPS may struggle for internal equilibrium in "normal" busy, loud, crowded, or chaotic office environments.

However, from the lens of decision making and leadership, Harvard Business Review indicates that "the trait of high sensitivity contributes to perceiving, processing, and synthesizing information more deeply, including data about others' emotional worlds."[503] In sum, although leaders who are highly sensitive may have been taught by societal criticism to devalue and mask this trait, it is a strength because having access to multiple levels of sensory data boosts intuition. If you have it, use it because it will help you find the unasked questions. If you don't have it, consider inviting a colleague with high SPS onto your decision-making advisory team.

Separate the Problem from the Symptom

As a leader, what would you say are the top five problems that you're up against? As an experiment, grab a pen and jot down your ideas. Not enough sales? Too many complaints? Lack of employee motivation? High turnover? Lagging revenues?

When asked to articulate their largest, most vexing problem, most business leaders "erroneously identify their problems as the gap between where they are and where they would like to be."[504] The top five problems you wrote down are likely representations of the gap.

Cunningham clarifies, "The gap is not your core underlying problem; it's the *symptom*. The symptom is what indicates something is wrong, but it does not shed any light on what is causing it to show up."[505] In other words, knowing what you want (the gap) does not explain why the gap is there (root cause). Although the gaps are frustrating, trying to bridge the gaps does not actually close the gaps.

Clarify Root Causes

Instead, we must shift our focus from the symptom to the obstacle that occupies the gap, which limits our ability to move from where we are to where we want to be. "It is the obstacle that is the problem, not the dissatisfaction with your current circumstances!"[506] Cunningham exclaims. Depending on how you label the problem, you build solutions and systems to fix that problem. Misdiagnosing the problem wastes time and money.[507] As you look for reasons and causes behind the symptoms you're experiencing, consider subcategories and distinctions, and seek clarity about the underlying obstacles. "Find the drip; fix the leak."[508]

If you're not clear on root causes, you might make progress by initially moving forward according to best guesses, but if you're not going in the right direction, then it doesn't matter how much mileage you cover. A flurry of activity is not the same as progress: "Just because you're sweating doesn't mean it's working."[509] Three questions that bring clarity:[510]

- Context: "What are the possible reasons I am noticing this symptom?"
- Add: "What isn't happening that, if it did happen, would cause the perceived gap (symptoms) to either narrow or disappear?"
- Stop: "What is happening that, if it stopped happening, would cause the perceived gap (symptoms) to narrow or disappear?"

As you consider these three questions, you'll find clarity on the unasked question that will help you correctly diagnose the root cause and problem/obstacle so that you can design an effective solution. Where possible, seek input from people who are honest and willing to tell you what they see as the truth, even if it's hard for you to hear. "Few things are worse than running the wrong direction enthusiastically."[511]

Along these lines, Brian Tracy says, "Superior leaders are willing to admit a mistake and cut their losses. Be willing to admit that you've changed your mind. Don't persist when the original decision turns out to be a poor one."[512]

Ferret Out Blame When It Locks Problems in Place

Here's a counterintuitive reason that we stay stuck in the gap: sometimes we unconsciously enjoy our problems. We make up juicy stories where we are victims of forces beyond our control, and these stories inform our identity. When we blame others, we shift responsibility to some other person, power, or company. We believe we can't be in our current problems because of our own doing. Identifying with a victim narrative allows us to avoid responsibility and garner sympathy; however, it does not enable us to make changes.

"Retelling your story [in which you are a victim] does not help you change it. Nor does it help you discover a solution."[513] Instead, believing yourself to be a victim keeps you stuck in a disempowered state. If this sounds familiar, ask yourself: would you rather blame others (and thereby be disempowered) or would you rather solve the problem (and thereby be empowered)? By letting go of blame, leaders will be more able to remove obstacles and separate problems from symptoms.

Check Assumptions

Assumptions are like blind spots. As you spend time contemplating a problem, ask yourself: What am I missing here? What am I unable to see? Cunningham says: "This question is powerful because what I don't see is what costs me money."[514] To begin to see what is in your blind spot, Cunningham suggests that leaders ask more questions to root out assumptions that are "highly unrealistic, overly optimistic, or just plain stupid."[515] As assumptions come to light, leaders should take time to see how those assumptions inform proposed courses of action. This will help check assumptions for their odds of success.

Put another way, leaders can ask: if we take this action, which is rooted in this assumption, what are the chances of us meeting the goal we have set? If the odds of success are low, you might get lucky, but that is overall not a reliable course of action. A simple illustration is: if I buy this lottery ticket (the action) because I think that today is my lucky day (the assumption), what are the odds that I will win the jackpot (the goal)? Left unchecked, this type of blind-spot assumption leads to actions that cost money without producing returns . . . except for the one person who does hit the jackpot, and who then pays half of it in taxes. A lottery ticket doesn't cost much, but a high-level business decision rooted in blind spot assumptions may cost much more.

Focus on Facts

Harold Greneen, who formed a conglomerate at ITT, said, "'The most important elements in business are facts. Get the real facts, not the obvious facts or assumed facts or hoped-for facts. Get the real facts. Facts don't lie.'"[516] When considering the facts, come up with a hypothesis, and then creatively look for its opposite. This will help negate confirmation bias. In the last section, we noted the power of tapping into intuition.

However, have you noticed that other things—such as confirmation bias—masquerade as intuition? Just because something is familiar doesn't mean it is intuitively right. As you harness facts to reveal flaws in your thinking, you'll ferret out weaknesses in your products and sales approaches long before they cause trouble within the domain of your leadership.

Instead of *reacting*, smart leaders *act*. Make time for due diligence. Because we spend much of our day responding to stimuli—from alarm clocks to email chimes to people's comments in meetings—take time to pause. Reacting is going about on autopilot, informed by prior circumstances and awareness. As leaders realize they are reacting on autopilot, it's easy to interrupt the process.

If a reaction is on auto, take a moment to think. How long you think depends on the magnitude of the decision. Which brand of office supplies to buy? Short thinking time. Which investment to make? Longer thinking time. Investing time into decision making is the heart and soul of due diligence—"this means taking the time to make the right decision. You may be wrong, but it won't be because you rushed."[517]

Allocate Time to Think

Brian Tracy teaches: "Aristotle once said that wisdom—the ability to make good decisions—is a combination of experience plus reflection. The more time that you take to think about your experiences, the more vital lessons you will gain from them."[518] Careful analysis takes time, and time tends to be scarce as leaders' calendars are packed full each day. Cunningham preaches: Get a chair. Get a journal. Set aside some time and let the ideas flow. Silence your phone and close the door. Set a timer. Sip water and pace as needed. Jog your creativity in ways that work best for you so that you can spark idea after idea.

Don't worry about refining ideas while you are generating them—in fact, that is counterproductive because it turns off the faucet. Analysis comes later, after you're finished brainstorming and feeling around in the dark for unseen assumptions that are driving the strategy. Shift ideas this way and that to see how they add up in different formations. Generate lists of what you could do to effectuate your ideas. Try drawing diagrams or even flow charts. Visual people might benefit from drawing on large whiteboards, making shapes and circles, and linking those with lines.

Whatever it takes, invest some effort into examining underlying assumptions and tinkering with them. Then go do something else— leave the chair and set down the journal. Go get lunch or do something entirely different. Yet, allow a little space for further tinkering after your thoughts percolate and new ideas bubble to the surface. You can always return to your notes, and you may find that things that had seemed hazy before now have a new lens of clarity. These instructions are intentionally vague so that you can try them on for your specific circumstances. Spending time checking assumptions will help you refine the questions and move toward viable solutions.

Consider Second-Order Consequences

Considering second-order consequences asks us to take a mental leap beyond 'what happens next?' into 'what could happen after that?' To illustrate this concept, Cunningham recounts a story of the British who decided on a course of action to eradicate venomous king cobras in New Delhi. In their logical plan, they offered a generous bounty for every cobra that people killed and brought for collection. But they failed to ask, "What might happen next?" Initially, the program was quite successful, and many cobras were exchanged for rewards. However, as the number of cobras in the area declined, "some entrepreneurial Indians realized they could breed these snakes in captivity and thus continue to receive the bounty."[519]

That's a daring and creative workaround! HBR researchers note: "Conditions of scarcity often produce more creative results than [do] conditions of abundance."[520] Snake breeding became an innovative and logical income stream—for people who had the guts to do it. In any case, when the British learned about the cobra cottage farming industry, they stopped offering the bounty. Again, they should have asked, "What might happen next?" With the bounty gone, the farmers had no economic reason to continue raising venomous cobras, so they released them into the wild. In sum, the unforeseen second-order consequences of this brilliant plan actually doubled the number of king cobras around New Delhi.[521]

When we make decisions from inside of our familiar thinking or comfort zone, we lean on short-term assumptions. "The very act of thinking long term sharpens your perspective and dramatically improves the quality of your short-term decision making."[522] As a metaphor, instead of solving a problem with duct tape (a short-term fix), leaders who focus on longer-term fixes will consider potential consequences and create solutions that may take more effort today but will build a better tomorrow.[523]

Try Crystal Ball Brainstorming

Possibilities of second-order consequences become exponential rapidly, so here are a few questions to keep you focused. Get out your journal and ask yourself:[524]

- *What's the upside?* This tends to be easy to answer since we are already convinced of what we might gain if all the pieces line up in our favor. What's the upside of what might happen next?
- *What's the downside?* Put on your 'pessimist' thinking cap here and ask what might go wrong with the plan. Get creative. Take it a step further and ask: What's the downside of the next second-order consequence?
- *Can I live with the downside?* This is your classic risk analysis considering risks and benefits. The most stringent question is: If all risks materialize and none of the benefits materialize, is the process still worth the effort? We all hope for a sunny day,

and we'll take a few clouds, but if it's a total rainout, is it still worth the investment? If so, then what are you waiting for?

While we can't generally control the consequences of our decisions, we can invest more time in choosing wisely with an eye toward facts, risks, and future unintended consequences. Although mistakes are inevitable, you can usually avoid throwing good effort after bad.

Create the Machine

After clarifying the core problem and obstructing obstacles, shift your focus toward creating a mechanism that will reliably move you from where you are to where you want to be. Build new processes or adapt currently existing methods to address the obstacles you have identified. Stop doing what wasn't working and put the pedal to the metal where effort will bring greatest reward.

Allocate Resources

"Shoes that don't fit are not a bargain at any price. A good idea that can't be executed is a bad idea."[525] As you shift priorities, be sure to also shift resource allocation accordingly. Set up for yourself the keys to flawless execution: consider if you need new or updated practices, standards, metrics, processes, teams, or accountability structures. As we have learned in prior chapters, be sure to measure what matters because what gets measured gets mastered. In fact, Cunningham goes so far as to say that "measurement is THE key to sustainability and a culture of accountability"[526] (emphasis in original).

Prioritize Efficient Processes

Abraham Lincoln is credited with saying: "Give me six hours to chop down a tree and I will spend the first four sharpening the axe."[527] In other words, at the outset, "better decisions free up your time and improve results."[528] Along those lines, Robert Kistner notes that sometimes we, as leaders, are "too busy to do the things that will make us less busy," but "when we live in crisis management mode, nothing gets accomplished."[529] Smart leaders get out of crisis management mode by creating efficient processes which produce efficient outcomes.

Adjust for Situational Complexity

"When the right answer is elusive, however, and you must base your decision on incomplete data, your situation is probably complex rather than complicated. In a complicated context, at least one right answer exists. In a complex context, however, right answers can't be ferreted out."[530] For example, Harvard Business Review compares decision making approaches when the matter involved is complicated. Consider these metaphors that highlight complexity and flux: is the matter more like a Ferrari or more like a rainforest? A Ferrari is a complicated machine and "an expert mechanic can take one apart and reassemble it without changing a thing. The car is static, and the whole is the sum of its parts."[531]

On the other hand, no mechanic on earth can take apart and reassemble a rainforest. A rainforest "is in constant flux—a species becomes extinct, weather patterns change, an agricultural project reroutes a water source—and the whole is far more than the sum of its parts."[532]

The key idea here is that the contemporary business environment is more like a rainforest than like a Ferrari—it is the "realm of 'unknown unknowns'" and it is constantly in flux with shifting global market and technological trends. What was unheard of a few years ago is standard practice today. This environment requires a more experimental mode of leadership (with correlated failures which are natural to the startup of new processes), which does not rely exclusively on past practices and defined outcomes.

"Remember that best practice is, by definition, past practice. . . . Since hindsight no longer leads to foresight after a shift in context, a corresponding change in management style may be called for,"[533] advises Harvard Business Review. Regarding timing and complexity, "there is always a trade-off between finding the right answer and simply making a decision."[534] Invest plenty of time to think, but don't let too much thinking inhibit reasonable forward motion.

Key Takeaways

These five steps will help leaders make smart decisions and take the road less stupid by finding the unasked questions, separating problems from symptoms, checking assumptions, considering second-order consequences, and building a well-oiled machine for execution. Add these five steps to the two prior chapters about Smart Decisions regarding conscious and subconscious decision making, and leaders are well prepared to customize decisions around values and tradeoffs.

We'll tie up this chapter with advice from Brian Tracy: "The better you think, the better decisions you make. The better decisions you make, the better actions you take. The better actions you take, the better results you get."[535]

19

Boosting Resilience in Leadership

Stress and the Workplace

In a 2016 study cited by Harvard Business Review, "a quarter of all employees view their jobs as the number one stressor in their lives, according to the Centers for Disease Control and Prevention. The World Health Organization describes stress as the 'global health epidemic of the 21st century.'"[536]

Our current global business culture is one of increasing complexity. A few years ago, IBM Institute for Business Value surveyed 5,247 business executives from 21 industries in over 70 countries who reported that the "scope, scale and speed"[537] of their businesses were accelerating. This is especially true as the competitive landscape is "increasingly disrupted by technology and radically different business models. The result is at times a frenetic way of working."[538]

While this acceleration can create room for growth and expansion, it can also come with a tangible human toll for business leaders: "Being hyper connected and responsive to work anytime, anywhere, can be extremely taxing."[539]

In fact, the Centers for Disease Control found in a 2016 study that fully one-quarter of employees viewed their jobs as "the number one stressor in their lives."[540] In our constantly connected, highly demanding careers, stress and burnout are widespread.

Good Stress Versus Bad Stress

Stress presents business leaders with a duality of "challenges *as well as* opportunities."[541] In other words, depending on the intensity and type of stress, stress in the workplace can be either helpful or harmful—"good stress" can accompany exciting growth opportunities, while "bad stress" can harbor challenges that inhibit productivity and healthy functioning. Even though our immediate physical experience of good stress and bad stress may be the same—raised heart rate, adrenaline, constricted breathing, etc.—the duration and overall outcomes differ.

On one hand, "good stress" accompanies a type of challenge that "can make us healthier, motivate us to be our best, and help us perform at our peak."[542] We may feel this type of vibrant tension when we're excited about a prospect: our pulse quickens and we feel more alive even if we know that it will be a long climb to the top, so to speak. In life, good stress might be triggered by a mountain climb, first date, or competition. In the workplace, this helpful stress might show up when we are presented with a new challenge, intriguing project, or chance to make a difference through an enormous personal investment.

Good stress invites us to reach beyond what we consider our limits—to stretch and grow. It is the sort of stress that athletes tap into when they are training, building muscle, and achieving new heights. When stress is at a manageable level in the workplace, employees and leaders alike can see positive impact in terms of growth and achievement. In other words, good stress in our daily work environments and schedules can have a positive effect on our well-being and productivity.

On the other hand, when stress rises too high to motivate performance, or lasts for too long a time and overloads us, stress can become a source of burnout, fatigue, or chronic disease. This "bad stress" or "distress" often accumulates when we work in reaction mode indefinitely, responding to surprises or things that we perceive as threats. In reaction mode, we're continually swinging hard, solving crises, and trying to catch a breath. There's no room for the good stress involved in creation because we can't even find solid footing throughout the day.

For example, in life, bad stress might rise if we get in a car wreck or receive bad news about the health of a loved one. In the workplace, bad stress accumulates when we are always putting out fires, in essence, and unable to return to a centered space. When bad stress occurs over time—even throughout a career—it becomes "chronic" and causes unhealthy strain, thereby diminishing happiness, productivity, and physical stability.

Along those lines, Harvard Business Review cites a survey of more than 100,000 employees across Asia, Europe, Africa, North America, and South America, which "found that employee depression, stress and anxiety accounted for 82.6% of all emotional health cases in Employee Assistance Programs in 2014, up from 55.2% in 2012."[543]

Becoming Unstoppable: Transforming Bad Stress into Good

Now, this information about good stress versus bad stress is probably already clear to business leaders—we all know the feeling of strain that accompanies our jobs when we exist in response mode constantly. However, have you noticed that some leaders seem to manage stress more easily than others? This may have something to do with their nature and intensity tolerance levels, but it may have even more to do with their mindset. Brian Tracy explains: "A common thread runs through every successful person. No matter who they are or what they are doing. Every single one of them, without exception, has developed that wonderful quality of resilience that has enabled them to bounce back, to persevere, and to finally become unstoppable."[544]

Because the pace and intensity of contemporary work culture are in crescendo, resilience skills are critical for today's business leaders. Resilience is a "'positive adaptation' after a stressful or adverse situation."[545] In the workplace, resilience shows up in many ways, but it is fundamentally the "ability to mentally or emotionally cope with a crisis or to return to pre-crisis status quickly. Resilience exists . . . in people who develop psychological and behavioral capabilities that allow them to remain calm during crises/chaos and to move on from the incident without long-term negative consequences."[546] In other words, resilience is the actual technique and daily practice of becoming unstoppable.

Thomas Edison is a well-known example of being unstoppable, one of the greatest inventors in history with over 1,000 different patents. It is said that it took Edison over 10,000 failed attempts to perfect the light bulb. His attitude was to redefine his experience saying: "I have not failed. I have just found 10,000 ways that won't work."[547]

Chapter Roadmap

The key takeaway from this chapter is that resilience is a skill that enables business leaders to transform "bad" stress consistently and productively into "good" stress. To flesh out this idea, let's divide our discussion into two parts:

1. First, what is resilience in the workplace? Because resilience can be rather slippery to define concretely, we will approach it from several angles, including redefining disruption, cultivating the skill of bouncing back, and learning from failures.

2. Second, how do we as business leaders become resilient? Here, we will provide several concrete strategies that leaders can use to boost resilience in their lives and careers. Initially, we will zoom out and look at the bigger picture of how business leaders can respond to negative stressors effectively. Through the lens of mindfulness in the workplace, we'll consider how successful leaders discern lessons from challenges and take control of their mental dialogue to build this mindset over time.

   Then, we will zoom in and consider several other practical, real-time techniques for optimizing cognitive effort and mental agility in the face of stressors. For example, we will explain why it is critical for leaders to build in breaks and recovery time, and to be kind to themselves and others during stressful times. While there's no single solution or silver bullet for cultivating resilience skills, every leader can make shifts in perception and practice to increase his or her abilities. Some shifts can be implemented immediately but others evolve as a long-term mindset.

Resilience in the Workplace

What is resilience in the workplace? In this section, we will look more closely at various aspects of resilience in the workplace, including the ability to redefine disruption, bounce back from challenges, and learn from failure. These traits are not merely available to a select few; rather, they are learnable with practice. Such adaptation has been the root of human success over time.

The word 'resilience' comes from the Latin word 'resalire,' which means "springing back, or rebounding. This captures the essence of resilience from an individual's perspective; an ability to recover quickly. But being resilient is more than just bouncing back to where we were before. If we are resilient, we stretch ourselves, spring forward and, because of the challenges we face, emerge stronger."[548]

U.S. President Abraham Lincoln was a remarkable example of resilience. He was born into poverty and faced defeat throughout his life—losing eight elections, failing twice in business, and suffering a nervous breakdown. "He could have quit many times, but he didn't and because he didn't quit, he became one of the greatest presidents in the history of [the United States]. Lincoln was a champion and he never gave up."[549]

Resilience Involves Redefining Disruption

Because plans rarely go perfectly, business leaders recognize that disruption is inevitable in life and in the workplace. From slight hiccups to major changes of course, disruptive events occur along a spectrum of seriousness. They might be relatively small or short-term disruptions like commuter traffic, adverse weather on a significant day, or a lost sale. Or, they might be larger, longer-term disruptions like health challenges, relationship stress, loss of an expected promotion, and so on. We are constantly faced with change. The Greek philosopher Heraclitus said, "Change is the only constant in life."[550]

At the most fundamental level, disruption is about change—generally, changes we did not anticipate or would not choose. Alvin Toffler says, "Change is avalanching upon our heads and most people are grotesquely unprepared to cope with it."[551] Change is tough because many times we can't see it coming and we cannot control when or how it occurs. What we can control, however, is how we perceive and react to it. Maya Angelou wrote: "I can be changed by what happens to me. But I refuse to be reduced by it."[552] Similarly, business leaders can cultivate resilient attitudes, behaviors, and skills so that changes are welcomed and become stepping stones to new opportunities.

Resilience involves redefining disruption as opportunity. It's the moment where we assess the situation, accept it, and begin brainstorming: "Given this challenge, what options and opportunities have now become available?" While that idea may seem a bit cheerful at the outset, resilient leaders are generally optimistic. Responding to change involves taking control of our perceptions and attitudes so that disruption becomes a launching point rather than a roadblock. One applicable military mantra is to "improvise, adapt, and overcome."[553]

Resilience is About Bouncing Back

In the workplace, we often see resilience as a leader's ability to bounce back from disruption or hardship without letting it break his or her spirit. Such leaders seem unstoppable. Brian Tracy teaches: "The most important single quality that you can develop in your lifetime—the one quality that, more than anything else will guarantee you great success— is the quality of becoming 'unstoppable.'"[554] Along these lines, Robert Kistner says: "At the end of the day, I'm a results guy."[555] Being unstoppable and resilient creates results.

How do we become unstoppable? By persisting until "until you succeed. You become unstoppable by refusing to stop. You become resilient by bouncing back from defeats and disappointments. You become like an irresistible force of nature by deciding that that is the kind of person you are."[556] Being unstoppable is not a quality that comes in a week or a month, or from inspirational reading or talks. Rather, it is fully a habit of mind and character that we develop by practicing persistence over and over until it locks in and becomes a permanent aspect of who we are. Bouncing back time after time requires self-discipline to persist and adapt to new circumstances.

In addition, unstoppable resilience is about rolling with the punches and dealing with adverse situations positively and creatively. As a deliberate worldview, resilience is a business leader's skill of seeing a challenge as an opportunity to learn and even advance so it has a minimal cost to his or her physical and mental state. Adapting with resilience decreases the length of time that it takes to recover from stressors, so leaders are ready for the next challenge sooner.

Steve Jobs, the founder of Apple who made "a dent in the universe" said, "I'm convinced that about half of what separates the successful entrepreneurs from the non-successful ones is pure perseverance" and "getting fired from Apple was the best thing that could have ever happened to me. The heaviness of being successful was replaced by the lightness of being a beginner again. It freed me to enter one of the most creative periods of my life."[557]

As a useful metaphor, consider how athletes often assess cardiovascular health by measuring their heart rates while they are resting or performing some baseline activity of their sport. Then, they train in a way that stresses their cardiovascular capacity, like running sprints or performing a challenging skill, and they measure that peak heart rate.

The most resilient athletes are those whose heart rates require less time to return from stressor highs to baseline stability. This recovery time shows the athlete how well his/her body is handling stress, and a shorter recovery time means that the athlete is better able to handle stress. For example, if a soccer/futbol player sprints to take the ball toward the goal, a player with a quick recovery time will be ready for the next sprint to the goal. The longer the recovery time, the more opportunities the athlete misses.

Same in business. Instead of measuring heart rate recovery to assess resilience for business leaders, we could measure stress level recovery time. Like athletes who are warming up, business leaders show up at work with a certain baseline stress level. As the work day progresses, leaders encounter specific stressors—some expected (like key meetings) and some unexpected (like sudden problems). Leaders who have practiced resilience skills can reduce the amount of time it takes them to move from peak stress levels to baseline levels. Like athletes, resilient business leaders cultivate the skill of handling stressor situations and then recovering rapidly to be ready for the next sprint.

Resilience Involves Learning from Failure

In addition to bouncing back and shortening functional recovery time, resilient business leaders need to learn to interpret failure as feedback. Instead of running into a wall and letting it stop them, resilient leaders utilize failure as simply a step in the process of achieving success. Harvard Business Review clarifies: "The most resilient individuals and teams aren't the ones that don't fail, but rather the ones that fail, learn, and thrive because of it. Being challenged—sometimes severely—is part of what activates resilience as a skill set."[558]

Michael Jordan, one of the greatest superstars in basketball history, credits his accomplishments to learning from his setbacks, saying, "I've missed more than 9,000 shots in my career. I've lost almost 300 games. Twenty-six times, I've been trusted to take the game-winning shot and missed. I've failed over and over and over again in my life. And that is why I succeed."[559]

One thing to note: it can be harder for us to learn from personal and professional setbacks if we attribute them to individual inadequacy. Instead of taking setbacks personally, we can dial into reality about the situation by actively identifying other specific and temporary contributing factors. While we strive for excellence, we can temper our tendencies to demand perfection and instead accept that life and work involve a mix of losses and wins. For example, Henry Ford went bankrupt three times before he managed to design his first successful automobile. He subsequently became one of the richest men in the world, and he once said, "Failure is merely an opportunity to more intelligently begin again."[560]

In the same vein, don't be afraid to try again. Success may come after several temporary setbacks and defeats if we keep our eye on the goal. If we know we're heading in the right direction but we encounter failure, getting back up is the key. Margaret Thatcher reminds: "You may have to fight a battle more than once to win it."[561] A touch of persistence allows you to implement the lessons you learn on the first, second, and third tries into the fourth attempt . . . and so on. After spending decades in prison before he became President of South Africa, Nelson Mandela echoes this sentiment: "Do not judge me by my success; judge me by how many times I fell down and got back up again."[562]

Eight Strategies for Cultivating Resilience

How can leaders cultivate resilience in the workplace? Because resilience is multi-faceted, its manifestation varies from leader to leader. In this section, we have collected eight proven strategies that business leaders can use to boost resilience in their lives and careers. Initially, we will take a big-picture view in considering how leaders can productively experience and respond to negative stressors. Through the lens of mindfulness in the workplace, we'll consider how powerful leaders discern lessons from challenges and take control of their mental dialogue.

Then, we will zoom in and consider several practical techniques for optimizing cognitive effort and mental agility in the face of stressors. For example, in addition to ensuring quality focus, resilient leaders prioritize attention breaks and recovery time. Further, they strive to be kind to themselves and others. These daily shifts in practice are instrumental in enhancing resilience skills over the lifetime of a successful career. Granted, not every strategy will suit every leader, but most leaders can benefit from at least a few of these in boosting resilience.

Resilience Booster #1: Get Through the Valley Faster

As we outlined above, resilience involves the skill of bouncing back from challenge or disruption, and getting up when life or work knocks us down. These sorts of knock-down disruptions are generally not positive events—they're things we wouldn't choose and they often derail us from achieving the outcomes we want as quickly as we had hoped. Disruptions mean that we now must invest more time or effort toward our goals, or that we might need to change track altogether. Maybe the grand deal that you worked so hard for just fell through. Or your promotion was denied. Or you're being transferred.

The negative quality of disruption brings with it a natural need for a process that may surprise you in this business context: grieving. According to Elisabeth Kubler Ross, grief involves several distinct and often cyclical stages: denial, anger, blame, bargaining, despair, acceptance, and then thriving.[563] For example, when we first receive really bad news at work, we might feel numb. Our immediate response might be denial. *No. This is not happening!* Denial slides quickly into anger and blame. We look for who's at fault. *Who dropped the ball? I cannot believe that person failed to do what he or she was supposed to do! If only . . .*

Maybe we start bargaining with the powers that be for alternatives, looking for ways to somehow wrench ourselves back on track toward our goals despite the disruption. *Is the deal over or is there some way to save it? Can we re-open the bid for promotion or is it completely closed for the year?* Amid the thrashing, blame, and denial, we slip sooner or later into a degree of depression or despair. *What's the point? There's no way this is going to work now. It's over.* This despair is often correlated with how badly we wanted the specific outcome or how we are impacted by the specific loss.

The experience of despair is like getting stuck in an emotional valley where we are unable to see the larger terrain. In this context, Clay Scroggins suggests that "resilience is a catalyst"[564]—resilience allows us to get through the valley in a shorter amount of time. It also allows us to experience the change with less impact so it's not as heavy on us. Resilience helps us move into the healing phases of grief, wherein we accept the loss or setback, see potential positive outcomes, and transition from merely surviving to actively thriving. Resilience is the skill of getting as smoothly as possible to the other side of the bad thing and choosing to see how we are better for the challenge.

For business leaders who fly regularly, consider this metaphor. Just as every person's life and career will experience unavoidable setbacks that keep us from reaching our desired outcomes as quickly as we would like, every traveler in modern airports will experience slowdowns at the security checkpoints. Even with expedited screening programs, most travelers will still experience some delay ranging from a few minutes to even a few hours depending on various factors that are outside of our control—weather, crowding, technology, etc.

Although we all must go through security screening to get to our gates, we may experience a degree of frustrated denial when we see longer-than-anticipated lines: *"No way! This can't be happening today! I have to board in 25 minutes and this line will take an hour!"* We might look for someone to blame, like the travelers who carry a million items in their pockets, parents with little children and strollers, or the x-ray scanner workers who spend pains-taking extra minutes looking at each bag. At some point, we might start bargaining with people around us to get a step or two ahead in line. Pretty soon, though, we run out of options.

The key takeaway from this metaphor is this: when there is no way we can avoid the disruption or setback, the sooner we move from denial, through blame and/or anger into acceptance, the sooner we begin to thrive. This is the skill of resilience.

While we control what we can by arriving early and preparing our carry-on items for quick screening, we must accept what we cannot control because there is no other lawful way to get to the airplane boarding than going through security screening. Resilience helps us walk more gracefully through this setback with lower stress levels during the wait – and perhaps even have the calm to identify other ways through the maze that we may have not otherwise considered if consumed by unhealthy stress.

Similarly, when there are delays or unexpected failures at work, resilient business leaders take control of what they can control but then they rapidly accept the new state of things, pivot as needed, and continue moving forward toward their desired destinations/outcomes. This ability to bounce back, improvise, adapt, and overcome enables leaders to get through the valley and thrive despite disruptions to their original plans.

Resilience Booster #2: Calibrate for Equanimity at Work

"Adversity in organizational life, sometimes the result of major change, sometimes the provocateur of it, is a way of life today. Leaders need higher levels of resilience in constant reserve to weather this new normal."[565] Regardless of what we're facing, it's ultimately our "reaction to adversity, not adversity itself that determines how [our] life's story will develop."[566]

In the workplace, we can calibrate our reactions toward equanimity as we draw awareness to our present experience and choose our reactions

271

deliberately by lengthening the space between stimulus and response. For instance, if we feel frustrated with a situation (stimulus) and we can draw awareness to that sensation rather than instantly reacting to it (response). The more that we as business leaders can un-automate our automatic responses, the more insight we gain about ourselves and the more control we gain over future outcomes. Why? Because we can consciously choose our optimal response to the stimulus. As we turn off autopilot routines and behaviors in response to setbacks or disruption, we can instead create what we intend to create. Equanimity is synonymous with calmness, levelheadedness, and poise—critical characteristics for successful leadership. Equanimity and mindfulness go hand in hand.

In business, equanimity and mindfulness have been found to benefit leaders in many ways. For example, Harvard Business Review notes that mindfulness predicts the accuracy of judgment and insight in problem solving, and enhances cognitive flexibility. Further, in "dynamic work environments, organizational psychologists Erik Dane and Bradley Brummel found that mindfulness facilitates job performance, even after accounting for all three dimensions of work engagement—vigor, dedication and absorption."[567]

Many organizations view level-headed composure as a core competency, and they infuse mindfulness practice into the rhythms and routines of daily work. For instance, as leaders, we may become more aware of the voice in our minds and transform our inner critic into a positive coach. We may draw awareness to our physical bodies and actively breathe more deeply throughout the day, boosting physical and mental calm.

We may gradually release mind-made labels like 'good' or 'bad' to get in touch with the reality of work situations. Research shows that such calming practices can help employees be more focused, improve collaboration, boost resilience, and manage stress better. Even in online work environments, equanimity can be "effective in decreasing employee stress, while improving resiliency and work engagement, thereby enhancing overall employee well-being and organizational performance."[568] In sum, cultivating equanimity can help reduce stress levels and add up over time to a leadership career of resilience.

Resilience Booster #3: Discern Lessons

Renowned author J.K. Rowling said, "Rock bottom became the solid foundation on which I rebuilt my life."[569] Resilient business leaders actively seek growth even in the lowest or most difficult moments. A helpful first step is to find a purpose for the pain. Instead of asking, "Why is this happening?" resilient leaders ask, "How can I grow through this challenge that is happening?" "What can I learn?" Poetess Mary Oliver wrote about her experience developing this skill of discerning lessons from challenges: "Someone I loved once gave me a box full of darkness. It took me years to understand that this, too, was a gift."[570]

For business leaders, resilience is the difference between the challenge taking you down and taking you where you want to go. When we and our colleagues are facing hurdles—things like job transfer, relationship failure, chronic illness, or discrimination—discussions of resilience may feel pointless. We can't stop the challenges from happening but we can seek discoveries that help us grow.

In fact, as time passes, we might look back on periods of challenge or disruption and feel that we never would have become the leaders we are today without those experiences. Each hurdle we overcome can build our strength if we let it. "Courage is not the absence of fear, but rather the judgment that something else is more important than fear."[571]

Brian Tracy reminds us that "life is like an airplane journey. From the time you take off, you will be off course 99% of the time. All airplanes are off course 99% of the time. The purpose and role of the pilot and the avionics is to continually bring the plane back on course so that it arrives on schedule at its destination."[572] Pilots don't think of turbulence, weather, or being off course as failure, but rather as circumstances to navigate toward the ultimate destination. Smart leaders do the same.

Courageous leaders also follow good examples—other leaders have solved similar problems and we can use their methods and experiences as patterns for what we are working to create. Although disruption can feel insurmountable, there is always room for growth. With this mindset, leaders will become more whole, self-assured, and mature.

Resilience Booster #4: Rescript the Story

Resilience resides in the stories we tell ourselves. Mizuta Masahide, a 17th Century Japanese poet and samurai wrote this famous poem:[573]

> Barn's burnt down—
> now
> I can see the moon.

An alternate translation reads:

> Since my house burned down
> I now own a better view
> of the rising moon.

Most of us would likely respond a little differently to the experience of our homes (or barns) burning down. We'd lament the loss of our possessions and shelter. Amid our grief, we might forget to turn our attention to considering what we may have gained by the house burning down.

However, if we shift our mental dialogue regarding the loss, we may see new opportunities. Maybe the insurance offers a great payout and now we can move from a snowy place to a warm place, or closer to family. Maybe it offers freedom to make a new start is what we needed even though we wouldn't have chosen this loss. In our careers, losing a deal, failing to make a critical sale, or even losing a job can open all sorts of opportunities we would never have otherwise considered.

One accomplished attorney credits his success in part to being laid off from one of the largest law firms in the world during a global economic downturn. That recession and loss of employment were beyond the attorney's control. Rather than treating those seismic events as devastating setbacks, the attorney used them as a springboard to create his own law practice that ended up being much more rewarding in lifestyle and compensation than ever before.

Cultures around the world celebrate finding beauty in seemingly broken circumstances. For example, Kintsugi is a beautiful form of

Japanese art where broken or cracked pottery is repaired with gold and silver adhesives that emphasize imperfection, rather than to hide it. The idea is that if an object has been damaged then its history and richness should be highlighted and honored rather than discarded or hidden because that is what makes it beautiful in its current state. That same concept applies to each of us and is like the Japanese philosophy of "wabi-sabi," which celebrates our flaws and imperfections as badges of beauty and growth.

By re-scripting the stories we tell ourselves and the people around us, we can transform the disruption into opportunity and celebrate new futures rising from the breakage or ashes of the old. Carl Gustav Jung taught: "I am not what happened to me, I am what I choose to become."[574]

Resilience Booster #5: Build Mental Agility Via Decentering

A component of resilience is mental agility: the ability to step back and see the bigger picture. Harvard Business Review makes this comparison: "We often tell our children who are upset to 'use your words,' for example, and it turns out that stopping and labeling emotions has the effect of activating the thinking center of our brains, rather than the emotional center—a valuable skill in demanding, high-performance workplaces everywhere."[575]

Another name for this skill is "decentering." It involves pausing, observing the stress from as neutral a standpoint as possible, and labeling or naming emotions. Getting outside of the mental and emotional turbulence enables us to consider options and various perspectives, and then choose wisely a path to solve the problem. In other words, from a vantage point of naming thoughts and emotions using words, business leaders actively take a cognitive step back from experience and pivot attention to the parts of the brain involved in observation. This action is critical to mental agility and core resilience.

When responding to tough moments and unexpected setbacks, business leaders need not only cognitive agility but also a degree of flexibility. Where an oak tree might break in a strong windstorm, a willow tree will bend and survive. Jodi Picoult teaches: "The human capacity for burden is like bamboo—far more flexible than you'd ever believe at first glance."[576] In flexibility can lie great strength.

Resilience Booster #6: Optimize Cognitive Effort

On a day-to-day basis, try boosting your resilience by doing one thing at a time and eliminating distractions. Our ability to focus builds our ability to bounce back in the face of setbacks with calmer stress levels. According to Shawn Achor, co-founder of the Institute for Applied Positive Research and author of The Happiness Advantage, "We receive 11 million bits of information every second, but the executive, thinking centers of our brain can effectively process only 40 bits of information."[577]

When we are on overload, we're less able to respond resiliently to stressors or to bounce back from difficult situations. Although as business leaders we cannot practically reduce the amount of information we receive, we can take control of how we process the information. For example, we might batch different types of work activities such as strategizing, brainstorming, emailing, or leading meetings. This compartmentalization helps us eliminate time that we might otherwise waste switching from one task to another.

Some leaders dedicate specific times in the day to do specific work activities. This approach helps create space to process information effectively, make decisions, and reduce cognitive strain throughout the workday. Different leaders will find different approaches that work best for their style. Nonetheless, by optimizing focus and tuning out distractions, leaders boost both productivity and resilience.

Resilience Booster #7: Switch Gears Periodically

We all experience ebb and flow in our energy and productivity throughout the day. Research shows that mental focus tends to flow in cycles of between 90–120 minutes, at which point it's helpful for us to step away from work to reset our attention. Even a brief mental detachment can reinfuse our work with liveliness, clarity, creativity, and focus—and these characteristics boost our capacity for resilience as the workday progresses. Resilient leaders organize their cognitive tasks in conjunction with energetic peaks and valleys.

For example, if you notice that a relatively run-of-the-mill workplace challenge is pushing you over the edge, so to speak, then you could use a little more mental reset time. Even if we regularly handle such challenges as part of doing business, it's easier to perceive a mountain in a molehill when we're overtired. By taking breaks, optimizing cognitive tasks, and practicing work-focused mindfulness, business leaders develop mental agility to respond to tasks or difficult situations proactively rather than simply reacting to those situations.

If we take a militaristic, "tough" approach to resilience and grit, we might "imagine a Marine slogging through the mud, a boxer going one more round, or a football player picking himself up off the turf for one more play. We believe that the longer we tough it out, the tougher we are, and therefore the more successful we will be."[578] In addition to demonstrating grit and pushing through challenges, research shows that taking strategic recovery periods boosts our health, safety, resilience, and success. In fact, overwork and exhaustion are the opposite of resilience because they drive up risks and diminish our available cognitive resources. Thus, seasoned business leaders recognize the value of building recovery time into their busy schedules to increase productivity and resilience.

Beyond simply stopping work; rather, recovery involves unplugging and resting both the brain and the body. "If you really want to build resilience, you can start by strategically stopping. Give yourself the resources to be tough by creating internal and external recovery periods."[579] Recovery is about letting go, powering down, and recharging your personal and emotional resources so that you can bring your full heart, mind, and spirit back to work as you power on again.

Harvard Business Review contends that resilience involves a cycle of exerting effort, stopping, recovering, and then exerting more effort. This is "based on a fundamental biological concept describing the ability of the brain to continuously restore and sustain well-being. . . . When the body is out of alignment from overworking, we waste a vast amount of mental and physical resources trying to return to balance before we can move forward." Building into the schedule some strategic time for recovery enables leaders to re-balance themselves before diving into the next project—and often before encountering the next stressor. With recovery, leaders find themselves able to respond more quickly and more positively to stressors as they arise.

Resilience Booster #8: Be Kind to Yourself and Others

Although some managers might believe that putting pressure on employees is a good way to boost performance, the correlated increase in stress brings higher costs than revenues. You probably don't have to think back very far in your career to remember a time when you watched a colleague or business leader 'snap' under stress. Often, as leaders, we set high standards for ourselves and others. When we push ourselves to the limit, even a small internal or external stressor can send us over the edge. Not another lost sale! Not another problem with the photocopy machine!

In these cases, Harvard Business Review recommends that leaders curb misplaced irritability because when "confronted with intense levels of stress amidst turbulent change or the headwinds of a harsh market, leaders' fuses get short. Leaders lacking sufficient awareness of how their behavior is being affected tend to take out their stress on whoever happens to be in the way."[580] These people could be assistants, family members, or other well-meaning employees who happen to be in the way of an onslaught of frustration that they do not deserve.

To keep priorities in check and avoid snapping, resilient businesses proactively infuse compassion into the workplace. Compassion can be defined as simply as kindness. Forbes explains: "Compassion begins with empathy—the ability to discern that someone is under stress or suffering distress, and then the willingness to relieve suffering by taking action."[581] Just a simple acknowledgment of stress can go a long way toward releasing the pressure valve. "Hey Sarah, I know it has been a long week and the sales meeting didn't go as planned. Is there something I can help you with today?"

Research shows that "when organizations promote an ethic of compassion rather than a culture of stress, they may not only see a happier workplace but also an improved bottom line."[582] Compassion improves workplace culture by enhancing bonding, social interaction, positive moods, and even productivity. In terms of physical health, a compassion-centered workplace can go so far as to reduce employees' blood pressure and psychological stress.[583] People who work in such an environment generally feel more engaged with their jobs and more committed to sticking around and producing results over time.

As business leaders show compassion for themselves and for others, they bring the human element back into the busyness of the work environment. Harvard Business Review notes: "Compassion and business effectiveness are not mutually exclusive. Rather, individual, team, and organizational success rely on a compassionate work culture"[584] because this increases happiness and well-being at work, enabling leaders and teams to manage workload stresses better. In short, compassion is a hallmark of resilient leadership.

Key Takeaways

In today's business climate, leaders experience a near-constant demand for resilience and adaptation to complex change. "With the ongoing onslaught of problems leaders face, and change being the only constant in organizational life, leaders must cultivate resilience as an ongoing skill, not just for the 'big moments' of painful setbacks or major change."[585]

As companies, leaders, and managers, we have room to grow in terms of helping our employees (and ourselves) manage workload so that 'good' levels of stress don't become 'bad' levels of overwhelm. Fully 57% of respondents in a Deloitte survey of human capital trends said that their organizations were "weak" in terms of "helping leaders manage difficult schedules and helping employees manage information flow."[586]

As companies build organizational cultures that support and encourage resilience, they will help their employees and leaders manage workloads with greater mental agility and clarity. Because resilience feeds on a broad set of skills and behaviors, leaders who invest in resilience generally see positive benefits in themselves and their teams— including fewer healthcare concerns and missed work days, and higher productivity and positivity. Overall, investment in resilience provides a solid return. As American football coach Vince Lombardi taught his winning teams: "It does not matter how many times you get knocked down, but how many times you get up."[587]

Business leaders with high resilience demonstrate several common characteristics, including "optimism; the ability to stay balanced and manage strong or difficult emotions; [and] a sense of safety and a strong social support system."[588] Resilient leaders make realistic plans and take the steps necessary to follow through. They are confident in their abilities. They communicate and solve problems. Further, they actively manage strong impulses by building in space for reflection between stimulus and response. Resilient leaders demonstrate empathy and compassion for themselves and their colleagues. Resilient leaders are persistent. Microsoft legend Bill Gates reminds us, "It's fine to celebrate success, but it is more important to heed the lessons of failure."[589]

As we discipline ourselves to persist in the face of adversity, we become stronger and more able to bounce back from disruption. We grow more capable of responding quickly and effectively to problems, crises, or unexpected reversals that arise during the workday. We demonstrate confidence and courage because we quickly identify the core elements of a problem and take charge of the situation. Resilient leaders discover the opportunities that reside within any disruption to land on their feet. By showing compassion for ourselves and for our colleagues, we build healthy teams and work environments.

The strategies in this chapter are designed to help leaders take control of mental dialogue, and move more quickly and calmly through setbacks. With these techniques, leaders can improve their capacity for resilience, and boost resilience throughout the teams they manage. As a comparison, if we want to be healthy over time, we take daily steps of eating nutritious food and exercising.

While one day of good food doesn't have a significant impact on its own, a collection of good meals and workouts will add up over time to boost us toward our long-term goal of being healthy. So, too, with acquiring resilience: it's a leadership lifestyle that pays off through daily dedication and practice. It's not an overnight transformation, but the time invested is worthwhile.

In conclusion, Brian Tracy teaches, "I've been down enough times to know that if you don't take positive action to pick yourself up every time you fall . . . eventually you'll stay down. And that's neither positive nor helpful."[590] He reminds us about the process of learning to ride a bike—how, when we were young, we put in our best effort but still fall time and again.

Even when we injured our bodies or pride by falling, we took fresh action: "You got right back up and you tried it again. Eventually success was yours. You were walking or riding like you'd been doing it forever. So, what kept you going during these seemingly daunting setbacks? That's resilience, my friend. The ability to pick yourself up and keep moving on."[591]

20

A Trusted Voice: Robert Kistner's Journey Into Bold Leadership

When you pick up a book on business leadership, you may naturally be curious about the author's story to ensure you can trust what the author says. Accordingly, this chapter is built around several leadership lessons that emerged from and illustrate Robert Kistner's multi-decade career.

From his early days putting miles on well-worn shoes as a new salesman to his current position in the highest roles of management, Robert (known as "Bob") has put in the sweat and effort to ascend the ranks of and ultimately become one of the preeminent leaders in the Mexican vacation ownership industry. Bob's journey makes his voice trustworthy because he understands firsthand the struggles and triumphs of each position along the way.

Chapter Roadmap

In this chapter, we will discuss 10 practical bold leadership lessons that have emerged from Bob's lifelong career:

1. A bold leader knows intuitively when to pivot.
2. A bold leader demonstrates grit.
3. A bold leader understands persuasion and tailors his message to motivate action.
4. A bold leader takes risks and succeeds.
5. A bold leader puts people first.
6. A bold leader develops rapport.

7. A bold leader develops a soul-sustaining spiritual practice.
8. A bold leader cares for community and family.
9. A bold leader takes action.
10. A bold leader demonstrates loyalty.

Ten Leadership Lessons

Lesson 1: A bold leader knows intuitively when to pivot.

In 1979, Acapulco was a bustling town, still leaning on its famous reputation from the jet set of the 1950s and 60s. A trickle of tourists from North America became a raging river, filling hotels and beaches, and kicking the hospitality industry into high gear. Resorts, amenities, and restaurants were going from blueprints to reality as fast as materials and management could come together. With miles of Pacific coastline set against the rising Sierra del Madre del Sur mountain range, Acapulco was the perfect place for a motivated 23-year-old American to begin a career.

Dishes clanged in the kitchen and savory tacos came out on a dime in the restaurant where Bob worked as a young assistant manager. Tourists sauntered in for delicious Mexican food and locals stopped by for a hearty dinner after work. One group of regulars circled their favorite table several times a week for dinner, laughing as they popped open Coca-Cola cans and swapped war stories of selling timeshare. Bob made sure the food was served hot and they roped him in to hear their tales of meeting prospects, persuading buyers to listen, writing deals, and taking home a clean ten percent commission off the top. All in a day's work.

These fun-loving professionals sensed Bob's work ethic as a young man rising in leadership at the restaurant, and they invited Bob to join them in sales. "Come on, man! You have what it takes to make it big. Come by my office and I'll tell you all about it." Tempting offer. But, with a pregnant wife and the need for a regular salary, Bob waved them off with a smile and headed back to the kitchen . . . nevertheless, the idea stayed in his mind.

As is often the case with vibrant young managers, Bob took on extra duties at the restaurant but didn't always see eye to eye with his superiors. He saw many ways the business could improve, but his ideas weren't given much credence and Bob soon felt frustrated. In time, Bob decided to go a different direction professionally. He remembers the day like this: "As I drove from the restaurant toward my house, my mind went back to the conversation I'd had with the timeshare salesmen as they were eating. They seemed to be doing well financially—at least, they spent plenty of money at dinner. I remembered how I felt when they had invited me to work with them." Almost squealing the tires of the car, "I turned my car toward their office to learn more. When I walked through the door, one of the men recognized me and announced to the others, 'This guy starts today. Pick up this model and follow me.'"

And that's how it began.

Lesson 2: A bold leader demonstrates grit.

In the 1980s, timeshare salesmen were street warriors, standing on avenue corners and outside of restaurants, striking up conversation after conversation with passersby. This was long before they worked in beautiful offices and commercial sales spaces. "Back then," Bob recalls, "we stood on the streets with hope in our hearts and a model of the property in our hands." To keep going against all odds, Bob developed a personal mantra: "Every time you hear a 'No' you are that much closer to a 'Yes.'" Worn shoe soles and a farmer's tan were the mark of a job well done.

Where did Bob develop the grit needed to show up day after day, rain or shine, ready to pitch the deal? Raised in a low-income household as one of four children, Bob learned early on the value of hard work. After high school, he joined the Marine Corps, which he says was "brutally important in my life. Everything I know about responsibility and commitment I learned in the Marine Corps. I'm geared to achieve. Challenge me to do something and I'll go show you I can do it." This attitude served Bob well as he began selling timeshare and saw his effort translate into achievement.

From the beginning of his career through today, he lives by the Marine Corps motto: "If you aren't early, you're late!" Even now, he is usually the first one to arrive at meetings and he is known for responding to email messages early in the morning before the rest of the world awakens. "As a leader, I don't have the glory of sitting in a meeting and talking about all the reasons that the situation is not working because the buck stops with me," he reiterates. "Energy and persistence are your insurance against failure." With strong character, Bob translated aspects of his difficult childhood into a solid work ethic and bold leadership skills.

Lesson 3: A bold leader understands persuasion and tailors his message to motivate action.

Bob and his team learned to identify prospective buyers on sight depending on the product they were marketing. "From the moment I joined the team," Bob says with enthusiasm, "I picked up on the business model. Our job was to talk with tourists and educate them about timeshare, which was still new at the time. In exchange for their time, we offered a small token of appreciation: a refreshing, ice-cold Coca-Cola."

With his finger on the pulse of the industry, Bob intuitively began to harness rhetorical ethos, pathos, and logos to motivate potential buyers—and that paid off with sale after sale. Initially, when the sales value proposition heavily leaned on the notion of money savings, Bob would carry a calculator to show buyers how much they could save by investing in timeshare compared with booking a hotel. Dollars and cents (or pesos) savings added up over time and sold the product without further ado.

However, as the market evolved, Bob shifted his rhetorical message away from savings and toward quality and luxury experience. Today, timeshare is "about exclusivity, client experience, specialized service, and even the quality of the sheets," he says. "We have a hundred percent focus on food and beverage. We offer a customized wine list. We produce our own mattresses. This evolution in quality has been huge in sales and marketing. Customers walk into the room and say, 'I wish I were staying here.' Luxury sells."

Combining good people skills with an attention to detail, Bob discovered how to connect with potential purchasers on a personal level by identifying what mattered to them, and then tailoring his sales pitch to those things. For example, when speaking with a couple, Bob asked about their hobbies and their family. Was the man wearing an expensive watch? Did he dedicate time to golfing? Perhaps he valued luxury items and could be persuaded by a sales pitch focused on luxury and quality. Was the woman wearing a necklace with the multi-colored birthstones of her children? Did she show him photos of her grandchildren? Perhaps she would be receptive to a sales pitch focused on fun family time and shared memories on a luxurious vacation at a beautiful resort.

Far more than just writing contracts, Bob crafted a vision that revolved around the memories with loved ones, the joy of witnessing young children grow, and the prospect of returning to the cherished resorts alongside future generations to enjoy warm Mexican hospitality. "The product just sold itself," laughs Bob.

Why all this focus on timeshare sales in a book about business leadership? Well, Bob became a great leader as he cultivated wisdom to read and understand people. Working the ground level of sales required Bob to keep pace not only with industry trends but also with the desires of potential buyers. These skills transferred to interpersonal leadership roles as Bob worked his way up in management because he needed to read people every day and persuade them on a personal level to perform on the level of the organization. In short, a leader who can craft a vibrant shared vision and motivate others to see through the same eyes is a leader who succeeds year after year.

Lesson 4: A bold leader takes risks and succeeds.

As Bob grew in experience, he transitioned to a sales gig that was primarily aimed at a local demographic even though his Spanish was not perfectly fluent because he was still relatively new to living in Mexico. Bob's first manager in this position cautioned him, "Look, I'm going to hire you but you're not going to make it because you don't speak Spanish and we only sell to Mexican nationals." Other salesmen might not have taken the risk given these odds but Bob believes that "striving for impossible is the only way to succeed on what is possible."

If you tell a guy like Bob that he's not going to make it, you had better buckle up. With characteristic resilience, Bob transformed this daunting language barrier into a sales strength. How? Bob recalls: "The language gap actually worked in my favor. Local buyers were polite and felt they should listen to the foreigner who was struggling through the sales pitch. Even more, they then felt obligated to help me out by purchasing the product, which was relatively inexpensive." With a sense of pride, Bob recalls, "I wrote a couple deals a day and I got 10% commission in cash, which was great for my family."

Lesson 5: A bold leader develops rapport.

In 1982, when Bob was still working in Acapulco, he met a few developers who changed the course of his career. One was a visionary investor, who had a marketing agreement with one of the first large timeshare companies in the US, which marketed properties in Hawaii, snow country, and so on. "In the late 1970s," Bob recalls, "the idea of timeshare really started catching on. Mazatlán was the most advanced market in the 1980s for sales and marketing. Now it is a mostly national destination, but back then there were more American tourists than Mexican tourists."

How did this market enable Bob to grow in leadership? "A few guys and I went over to a new soon-to-open sales operation in Acapulco to look at the deal and help start that market there. Right away, I got a job as a salesperson." After two years, Bob became the assistant manager and began making good money. Markets are constantly shifting, and when the deal in Acapulco started to wind down, a key developer turned his sights to Mazatlán because it had six or seven timeshare projects with competitive marketing, whereas Acapulco had only two. He called Bob into his office and said: "We're doing a big project in Mazatlán, and we need to put together marketing and sales. Can you get the crew out there?"

He didn't even need to ask.

Developers rely on excellent salespeople and Bob didn't fail to deliver. In fact, Bob talked all 20 guys on his Acapulco team into going to Mazatlán. This success is evidence of Bob's ability to develop rapport up the food chain (with the developer leaders) and down the food chain (with those he managed). When Bob's sales team arrived, they lived at the hotel on the third floor and opened a dedicated timeshare sales room. This high-energy team worked hard during the day and played hard during the night. It was a time of energy and growth in Bob's career.

Throughout his work in Mazatlán, and again after returning to Acapulco, Bob continued to cultivate solid personal rapport with the other leaders, and this opened doors to new opportunities. As Bob took on increasingly senior roles in management, his teams followed him to new markets. Soon, Puerto Vallarta became the hot location and Bob received an offer to be the assistant sales manager for a new salesroom. "Get on a plane and I'll reimburse your ticket," the developer said. "Come see the place and you can help me get the sales stuff ready." Bob recalls, "When I flew out there, only one building was open and the second building was about 70 percent finished. There was one little palapa restaurant near the pool." One of Bob's talents is seeing the finished product even when the beginning is barely underway. He jumped in with both feet: "I wrote the first sale for that place and the rest is history."

Lesson 6: A bold leader puts people first.

Soon, Bob was leading teams on the front lines of timeshare growth in Puerto Vallarta. From street contacts to sales rooms, and from board rooms to offices, Bob motivated his teams to excellent performance. How? Bob developed a people-first philosophy of management. He advises leaders: "People are the most valuable asset. Your business is your people, particularly in the tourism business. You're putting those people in front of your clients and if you haven't done a good job with your people, they're not going to give great service to your clients."

Sales represents an intensely human side of marketing and leadership, and Bob trained new recruits to follow in his steps. "I wish I lived in a world where I could hire all superstars. But I don't; no leader does. Instead, I live in a world where I grow my people to superstar status." By investing in creating high performance teams, Bob creates results: "No top producer can out produce a team of top producers. So, it is more important to create a team of top producers than to just produce."

As Bob stepped into executive management for teams across borders with employees in the US and Mexico, he invested time in listening to clients: "Client surveys are a mirror. If I have employees that are happy and smiling, they're delivering that to the clients." This information helped Bob improve operational logistics, customer service, and workplace satisfaction to enhance the success of the organization. By putting people first—both colleagues and clients—Bob created a reliable network of feedback and growth.

Lesson 7: A bold leader develops a soul-sustaining spiritual practice.

Bob believes in the power of spirituality to enhance bold leadership. "I think the world would be a better place if more executives had a relationship with a higher power. I'll tell you why. Connecting with your higher power gives you the ability to let go of things. You realize you're not all powerful, and that realization surprisingly helps in business. It eliminates resentment and bad attitudes."

When people push back against the idea of connecting with god or a higher power, Bob responds practically: "I think spirituality is very personal. I know it's a difficult subject to talk about, particularly in business. Most people don't want to have anything to do with it, and I disagree with that. I think that there is room to allow your spiritual relationship to drive you in the right areas. I know it has in my life, particularly where charity is involved."

For example, Bob takes time every day to prepare himself spiritually to face the challenges inherent in the business day by strengthening his relationship with his higher power. "Keeping balance in your working lifestyle is all about dedicating time to get yourself in the right space," he advises. "I've become more jealous of my time in in the sense that I try not to have any meetings before nine o'clock because I hate feeling rushed." Despite being a busy leader at the apex of management, Bob dedicates the first three hours of his day to a morning routine designed to create mental space and centeredness.

Upon waking around 4:00 a.m., "First, I look at what's up on email. Then I walk around the terrace, breathing in fresh air, letting go, and focusing on my thoughts. I make an espresso and start reading a structured reflection about the Bible, which helps me think about my relationship with God. I use the word 'God' but it could be anybody. Some people prefer the phrase 'higher power.' The point is to connect with a power larger than self." Being a leader within his family, Bob collects some of the inspirational information he reads and sends it out to his four children "to help them start their day right." To anchor his physical health, he laces up tennis shoes and hits the gym or walks three to five miles.

Some people might wonder how he has time for this practice, but Bob responds: "When I get to work, my mind and body are in the right space and I never have a problem with focus." He cautions: "Sometimes we are too busy to do the things that make us less busy." Bob's morning routine provides mental space and fortitude to help him start the day intentionally and prioritize family relationships. Further, his daily spiritual practice inoculates him against reactive stress and enables him to keep balance with the pace of work. It's a means of channeling his strong private faith into bettering his organizational leadership. Bob sums up: "Spirituality is an important part of my life. It helps me be myself every day."

Lesson 8: A bold leader cares for community and family.

As a successful leader, Bob helps give back to the community. In 1999, he collaborated with timeshare buyers and resort developers to establish the Eagle's Wings Foundation, a California nonprofit foundation that helps alleviate poverty in communities surrounding the timeshare resorts. Led by an executive committee and board of directors representing the community as well as the resorts, Eagle's Wings reviews and approves grants.

As of 2023, Eagle's Wings has received well over eight million dollars (USD) in donations of cash and other tangible items from timeshare developers and buyers. With Bob's assistance and the support of other founders and donors, Eagle's Wings collects items that are no longer needed at the resorts but are still in good shape—such as mattresses, microwave ovens, towels, sheets, lamps, pillows, furniture, small appliances, and so forth—and offers them inexpensively to local families. In short, Eagle's Wings represents its founders' dedication to service and enhancing the communities. That is the kind of leadership that will not be soon forgotten.

Another more private way that Bob 'pays it forward' is by delivering leadership to his family and his four children. He describes how his parenting philosophy informs his leadership philosophy: "I believe a lot of who my kids are today has to do with their ability to make mistakes. When my children were young, I believed my job as a parent was to set up some barriers. I didn't give the kids a one-lane road, more like an eight-lane highway. I let them make mistakes—not the mistakes that could destroy their life, but the kind of mistakes that could teach and transform them."

The ability to learn lessons in low-stakes environments teaches children to make good decisions when the stakes are high. Bob laughs: "Some people thought I allowed my kids too much freedom, but they are doing okay today even if there were some tough moments."

The same philosophy is relevant in workplace leadership, says Bob: "I give my people space to grow, learn, and make mistakes. I try to keep them from making a company-destroying decision, but I give them space to learn and grow." In this way, Bob supports his children and his employees in becoming more grounded, capable people. What a wonderful way to care for community and family.

Lesson 9: A bold leader takes action.

Leaders are often running a million miles an hour and it is easy to become overwhelmed. "When you are in crisis management mode, nothing gets accomplished and being overwhelmed will defocus you because you're trying to think of too many problems at one time. At the end of the day, I'm a results guy," Bob describes.

So how do you put that into practice? Bob's golden rule for avoiding worry and overwhelm is to act: "Whatever the problem is, I ask myself 'What can I do about this right now about this?' If there's nothing to do right now, then I take it off the table. I don't worry about it. If there is something to do right now, I do it. Perhaps the action is to set up a meeting. I pick up the phone and arrange the meeting. Taking action helps me focus on the particular issue and let go of what I cannot control. This is the number one key to not having stress in my life."

In terms of applying his golden rule to organizational leadership, Bob takes executive action regarding operation and logistics, human resources, commercialization, and so on. He knows how to bring the right people into the business, how to train and motivate them, and how to help them grow their careers.

From brand management to client satisfaction, Bob has committed his professional journey to providing excellent company service and quality people connection. What if there is nothing that Bob can do about a problem when it arises? "If there is no action to take at the time, I don't worry because what is the point of worrying when there is nothing to be done? Take the action you need to take and you'll never feel overwhelmed," he counsels.

Lesson 10: A bold leader demonstrates loyalty.

Rubbing shoulders with developers and front-line salespeople, Bob's unique perspective over decades highlights the value of loyalty. Bob summarizes, "I've been in the same job for 40 years. You find the right business, the right company, and the right people and stay there. Many of my friends in the business jumped to the next deal and fished for a position and they're still doing that. I came to work at one place and I stuck it out. I've been promoted and demoted. But overall, I have given my life to this and it has taken care of me in return." Bob's practical approach also highlights his loyalty to his business partners, who are not only his mentors but also his family.

Staying in one business over time is not without its challenges. Bob advises that having the right attitude is everything: "The word 'fair' is an opinion and if you let it influence your personal decisions you're always going to lose. You do not get what's 'fair;' rather, you get what you negotiate." Bob saw people walking around demanding to be treated fairly, rather than focusing on delivering value. He counsels: "Don't focus on everything you do for the company; know that you're replaceable. The reality is that we are all replaceable. Just because I did something yesterday doesn't mean I should be rewarded tomorrow. Loyalty doesn't equal results." But loyalty paired with hard work can deliver a successful career spanning many decades.

Key Takeaways

Consider how these ten lessons can inform and up-level the framework of your own leadership. Wise leaders learn from those who have gone before, implementing tried and tested techniques to bring the best of themselves to their organization. Bob's story is just one among many, and yours will be another story of great leadership.

From years in the crucible of sales and management, Bob emerged as a bold leader with heart and talent. As vice president of one of the premier timeshare hotel brands in Mexico, he is one of the rare people who knows the view from top levels as well as the view from the ground level. He has an executive perspective on the financial side of success, including business development and wealth, and he also understands the human side of success, including community and social investment. That mix of experience positions him to lead effectively now and into the future, and it makes his voice one you can trust.

One author said of Bob, "You came forward as a warrior from the past. Now you have the future in your pockets."[592] As Bob looks to the future, he is focused on sharing his leadership lessons and vision with the world. He proactively inspires and guides new and experienced salespeople, and he believes that if you teach employees how to better their lives, they will be more likely to stay with the organization. Having dedicated years in senior management to producing inspirational leadership blueprints for businesspeople related to topics such as marketing, coaching, serving, and so on, Bob will motivate generations of leaders to come.

Endnotes

[1] Ibarra, Herminia and Scoular, Anne. "The Leader as Coach." Harvard Business Review. Published Nov.-Dec. 2019; accessed March 2020: https://hbr.org/2019/11/the-leader-as-coach.

[2] *Id.*

[3] Westfall, Chris. "Why Coaching Matters: How Leaders Can Become Better Coaches and Build Stronger Teams." Forbes. Accessed March 2020: https://www.forbes.com/sites/chriswestfall/2019/07/04/coaching-matters-how-leaders-become-better-coaches-build-stronger-teams/#26a79fcd405e.

[4] *Id.*

[5] Kistner, Robert. "Strategy 2020." Published Feb. 2020.

[6] Collins, Gary. "45 Coaching Quotes." Inspirational Words of Wisdom. Accessed March 2020: https://www.wow4u.com/coaching/.

[7] Ibarra, Herminia and Scoular, Anne. "The Leader as Coach." Harvard Business Review. Published Nov.-Dec. 2019; accessed March 2020: https://hbr.org/2019/11/the-leader-as-coach.

[8] Mahalo, Tom. "45 Coaching Quotes." Inspirational Words of Wisdom. Accessed March 2020: https://www.wow4u.com/coaching/.

[9] *Id.*

[10] Nelson, Bob. "45 Coaching Quotes." Inspirational Words of Wisdom. Accessed March 2020: https://www.wow4u.com/coaching/.

[11] Pulsifer, Byron and Pulsifer, Catherine. "45 Coaching Quotes." Inspirational Words of Wisdom. Accessed March 2020: https://www.wow4u.com/coaching/.

[12] Ibarra, Herminia and Scoular, Anne. "The Leader as Coach." Harvard Business Review. Published Nov.-Dec. 2019; accessed March 2020: https://hbr.org/2019/11/the-leader-as-coach.

[13] *Id.*

[14] Madison, I. "45 Coaching Quotes." Inspirational Words of Wisdom. Accessed March 2020: https://www.wow4u.com/coaching/.

[15] Dixon, Phil. "45 Coaching Quotes." Inspirational Words of Wisdom. Accessed March 2020: https://www.wow4u.com/coaching/.

[16] Hagen, Tim. "The Conversation Crisis: We Are in Need of Conversational Leaders." Forbes. Published Jan. 2020; Accessed March 2020: https://www.forbes.com/sites/forbescoachescouncil/2020/01/30/the-conversation-crisis-we-are-in-need-of-conversational-leaders/#1ae6b53910e6.

[17] *Id.*

[18] Ibarra, Herminia and Scoular, Anne. "The Leader as Coach." Harvard Business Review. Published Nov.-Dec. 2019; accessed March 2020: https://hbr.org/2019/11/the-leader-as-coach.

[19] *Id.*

[20] Dryden, Gordon. "45 Coaching Quotes." Inspirational Words of Wisdom. Accessed March 2020: https://www.wow4u.com/coaching/.

[21] Winkelman, Nick. "The Language of Coaching." LinkedIn. Published June 2019; Accessed March 2020: https://www.slideshare.net/nwinkelman/the-language-of-coaching-a-story-about-learning.

[22] Wooden, John. "45 Coaching Quotes." Inspirational Words of Wisdom. Accessed March 2020: https://www.wow4u.com/coaching/.

[23] *Id.*

[24] Westfall, Chris. "Why Coaching Matters: How Leaders Can Become Better Coaches and Build Stronger Teams." Forbes. Accessed March 2020: https://www.forbes.com/sites/chriswestfall/2019/07/04/coaching-matters-how-leaders-become-better-coaches-build-stronger-teams/#26a79fcd405e.

[25] *Id.*

[26] Wooden, John. "45 Coaching Quotes." Inspirational Words of Wisdom. Accessed March 2020: https://www.wow4u.com/coaching/.

[27] Kistner, Robert. "Strategy 2020." Published Feb. 2020.

[28] Boyatzis, Richard, Smith, Melvin, and Van Oosten, Ellen. "Coaching for Change." Harvard Business Review. Published Sept.-Oct. 2019; Accessed March 2020: https://hbr.org/2019/09/coaching-for-change.

[29] *Id.*

[30] Kistner, Robert. "Strategy 2020." Published Feb. 2020.

[31] *Id.*

[32] Ibarra, Herminia and Scoular, Anne. "The Leader as Coach." Harvard Business Review. Published Nov.-Dec. 2019; accessed March 2020: https://hbr.org/2019/11/the-leader-as-coach.

[33] *Id.*

[34] Kistner, Robert. "Strategy 2020." Published Feb. 2020.

[35] Westfall, Chris. "Why Coaching Matters: How Leaders Can Become Better Coaches and Build Stronger Teams." Forbes. Accessed March 2020: https://www.forbes.com/sites/chriswestfall/2019/07/04/coaching-matters-how-leaders-become-better-coaches-build-stronger-teams/#26a79fcd405e.

[36] *Id.*

[37] *Id.*

[38] *Id.*

[39] *Id.*

[40] Kistner, Robert. "Strategy 2020." Published Feb. 2020.

[41] Wooden, John. "45 Coaching Quotes." Inspirational Words of Wisdom. Accessed March 2020: https://www.wow4u.com/coaching/.

[42] Boyatzis, Richard, Smith, Melvin, and Van Oosten, Ellen. "Coaching for Change." Harvard Business Review. Published Sept.-Oct. 2019; Accessed March 2020: https://hbr.org/2019/09/coaching-for-change.

[43] Kistner, Robert. "Strategy 2020." Published Feb. 2020.

[44] Cagneey, Brian. "45 Coaching Quotes." Inspirational Words of Wisdom. Accessed March 2020: https://www.wow4u.com/coaching/.

[45] Tracy, Brian as quoted in Brown, Joel. "45 Highly Inspirational Quotes." Published May 2014; Accessed March. 2020: https://addicted2success.com/quotes/45-highly-inspirational-brian-tracy-quotes/.

[46] Kistner, Robert. "Strategy 2020." Published Feb. 2020.

[47] McGannon, Don. "Leadership." Accessed March 2020: https://goleansixsigma.com/leadership-is-not-a-position-or-a-title-it-is-action-and-example/.

[48] Carucci, Ron. "How to Actually Encourage Employee Accountability." Published Nov. 2020; Accessed April 2021: https://hbr.org/2020/11/how-to-actually-encourage-employee-accountability.

[49] *Id.*

[50] Jensen, Michael C. "A New Model of Integrity: An Actionable Pathway to Trust, Productivity and Value." Harvard Business School Negotiation, Organization and Markets Research Paper. Published Nov. 2009; Accessed April 2021: https://www.scribd.com/document/77538419/A-New-Model-of-Integrity-2009-Jensen-Erhard.

[51] Tracy, Brian. "Brian Tracy Quotes." Brainy Quote. Accessed April 2021: https://www.brainyquote.com/authors/brian-tracy-quotes.

[52] Tracy, Brian. "No Excuses!" As quoted in The Ripening. Accessed April 2021: http://www.theripening.com/2016/01/notes-quotes-no-excuses-brian-tracy.html.

53 Christensen, K. "Integrity: Without it Nothing Works." Published March 2014; Accessed April 2021: https://poseidon01.ssrn.com/delivery.php.

54 Tracy, Brian. "No Excuses!" As quoted in The Ripening. Accessed April 2021: http://www.theripening.com/2016/01/notes-quotes-no-excuses-brian-tracy.html.

55 Jensen, Michael C. "A New Model of Integrity: An Actionable Pathway to Trust, Productivity and Value." Harvard Business School Negotiation, Organization and Markets Research Paper. Published Nov. 2009; Accessed April 2021: https://www.scribd.com/document/77538419/A-New-Model-of-Integrity-2009-Jensen-Erhard.

56 Forstmoser, Peter. "Integrity in Finance." Swiss Banking Institute. Published Nov. 2006; Accessed April 2021: http://www.nccr-finrisk.uzh.ch/media/pdf/ethicalfinance/EFRS06Forstmoser_pres.pdf.

57 Emerson, Ralph. "No Excuses!" As quoted in The Ripening. Accessed April 2021: http://www.theripening.com/2016/01/notes-quotes-no-excuses-brian-tracy.html.

58 Tracy, Brian. "No Excuses!" As quoted in The Ripening. Accessed April 2021: http://www.theripening.com/2016/01/notes-quotes-no-excuses-brian-tracy.html.

59 Forstmoser, Peter. "Integrity in Finance." Swiss Banking Institute. Published Nov. 2006; Accessed April 2021: http://www.nccr-finrisk.uzh.ch/media/pdf/ethicalfinance/EFRS06Forstmoser_pres.pdf.

60 Id.

61 Tracy, Brian. "No Excuses!" As quoted in The Ripening. Accessed April 2021: http://www.theripening.com/2016/01/notes-quotes-no-excuses-brian-tracy.html.

62 Id.

63 Hubbard, Elbert. "No Excuses!" As quoted in The Ripening. Accessed April 2021: http://www.theripening.com/2016/01/notes-quotes-no-excuses-brian-tracy.html.

64 Moneyball Film. Wikipedia. Accessed April 2021: https://en.wikipedia.org/wiki/Moneyball_(film).

65 Mauboussin, Michael. "The True Measures of Success." Harvard Business Review. Published Oct. 2012; Accessed April 2021: https://hbr.org/2012/10/the-true-measures-of-success.

66 Welch, Jack. As quoted by AZ Quotes, "Leadership Vision." Accessed Feb. 2020: https://www.azquotes.com/quotes/topics/leadership-vision.html.

67 Kistner, Robert. On Leadership. Business Leadership Interview.

68 Tracy, Brian. "Goals! How to Get Everything You Want Faster Than You Ever Thought Possible." Downloadable report accessed Oct. 2018: https://www.briantracy.com/.

69 Mauboussin, Michael. "The True Measures of Success." Harvard Business Review. Published Oct. 2012; Accessed April 2021: https://hbr.org/2012/10/the-true-measures-of-success.

70 Id.

71 Id.

72 Results-based Accountability Guide. Results Leadership Group. Accessed April 2021: http://www.dhs.state.il.us/onenetlibrary/27896/documents/by_division/dchp/rfp/rbaguide.pdf.

73 Id.

74 Tracy, Brian. "Leadership Success Blog." Accessed April 2021: https://www.briantracy.com/blog/leadership-success/leadership-quotes-for-inspiration/.

75 Kistner, Robert. On Leadership. Business Leadership Interview.

76 Jensen, Michael C. "A New Model of Integrity: An Actionable Pathway to Trust, Productivity and Value." Harvard Business School Negotiation, Organization and Markets Research Paper. Published Nov. 2009; Accessed April 2021: https://www.scribd.com/document/77538419/A-New-Model-of-Integrity-2009-Jensen-Erhard.

77 Christensen, K. "Integrity: Without it Nothing Works." Published March 2014; Accessed April 2021: https://poseidon01.ssrn.com/delivery.php.

78 Carucci, Ron. "How to Actually Encourage Employee Accountability." Published Nov. 2020; Accessed April 2021: https://hbr.org/2020/11/how-to-actually-encourage-employee-accountability.

79 Welch, Jack. As quoted by AZ Quotes, "Leadership Vision." Accessed Feb. 2020: https://www.azquotes.com/quotes/topics/leadership-vision.html.

[80] Sinek, Simon. "Why good leaders make you feel safe." TED2014. Accessed March 2019: https://www.ted.com/talks/simon_sinek_why_good_leaders_ make_you_feel_safe.

[81] *Id.*

[82] *Id.*

[83] *Id.*

[84] Tracy, Brian. "Motivating People Toward Peak Performance." Effective Manager Seminar Series: Nightingale-Conant Corporation, 1988.

[85] Collins, Jim. As quoted in "Get the Right People on the Bus." The Wunderlin Company. Published Aug. 2013; Accessed March 2019: http://wunderlin.com/get-the-right-people-on-the-bus-2/.

[86] Jonze, Spike. "Hiring." Brainy Quote. Accessed March 2019: https://www.brainyquote.com/search_results?q=hiring.

[87] Tracy, Brian. "How to Hire and Fire." Effective Manager Seminar Series: Nightingale-Conant Corporation, 1988.

[88] Eisenhower, Dwight. "Motivation Quotes." Brainy Quote. Accessed March 2019: https://www.brainyquote.com/topics/motivation.

[89] *Id.*

[90] Tracy, Brian. "Motivating People Toward Peak Performance." Effective Manager Seminar Series: Nightingale-Conant Corporation, 1988.

[91] *Id.*

[92] *Id.*

[93] Tracy, Brian. "Creating a Productive and Happy Work Environment." Accessed March 2019: https://www.briantracy.com/blog/general/creating-a-productive-happy-work-environment.

[94] Tracy, Brian. "Motivating People Toward Peak Performance." Effective Manager Seminar Series: Nightingale-Conant Corporation, 1988.

[95] Manwani, Harish. "Profit's not always the point." TED2013. Accessed March 2019: https://www.ted.com/talks/harish_manwani_profit_s_not_always_the_point.

[96] *Id.*

[97] *Id.*

[98] Sinek, Simon. "Why good leaders make you feel safe." TED2014. Accessed March 2019: https://www.ted.com/talks/simon_sinek_why_good_leaders_ make_you_feel_safe.

[99] *Id.*

[100] Tracy, Brian. "Motivating People Toward Peak Performance." Effective Manager Seminar Series: Nightingale-Conant Corporation, 1988.

[101] Tracy, Brian. "How to Hire and Fire." Effective Manager Seminar Series: Nightingale-Conant Corporation, 1988.

[102] Siegel, David. "A More Humane Approach to Firing." Harvard Business Review. Published Aug. 2018; Accessed March 2019: https://hbr.org/2018/08/a-more-humane-approach-to-firing-people.

[103] *Id.*

[104] Friedman, Thomas. "The 'Next America.'" New York Times. Published Dec. 2018; Accessed March 2019: https://www.nytimes.com/2018/12/04/opinion/the-next-america.html.

[105] *Id.*

[106] Branson, Richard. "Quotes." Goodreads. Accessed March 2019: https://www.goodreads.com/quotes/7356284-clients-do-not-come-first-employees-come-first-if-you.

[107] Lipman, Victor. "Take Care of Your People and They Will Take Care of You." Forbes. Published Sept. 2012; Accessed March 2019: https://www.forbes.com/sites/victorlipman/2012/09/08/take-care-of-your-people-and-theyll-take-care-of-you/#673587846e1a.

[108] *Id.*

[109] Sinek, Simon. "Why good leaders make you feel safe." TED2014. Accessed March 2019: https://www.ted.com/talks/simon_sinek_why_good_leaders_make_you_feel_safe.

[110] Dyer, Wayne. As quoted in Habits for Wellbeing: "20 Quotes to Inspire Responsibility." Accessed Jan. 2020: https://www.habitsforwellbeing.com/20-quotes-to-inspire-responsibility/.

[111] Young, Owen. Forbes Quotes: "Responsibility." Accessed Jan. 2020: https://www.forbes.com/quotes/theme/responsibility/.

[112] Stamp, J. Forbes Quotes: "Responsibility." Accessed Jan. 2020: https://www.forbes.com/quotes/theme/responsibility/.

[113] Marais, Dina. "Nine Ways to Take Responsibility for Your Life." Thrive Global. Published Mar. 2018; Accessed Jan. 2020: https://thriveglobal.com/stories/9-ways-to-take-responsibility-for-your-life/.

[114] ADP 6-22. Army Leadership and The Profession (2019). Department of the Army United States of America. Accessed Jan. 2020: https://armypubs.army.mil/ProductMaps/Pubform/Details.aspx?PUB_ID=1007609.

[115] Wilson, Woodrow. Forbes Quotes: "Responsibility." Accessed Jan. 2020: https://www.forbes.com/quotes/theme/responsibility/.

[116] Kistner, Robert. Business Leadership Interview. January 2020.

[117] Covey, Stephen. As quoted in Habits for Wellbeing: "20 Quotes to Inspire Responsibility." Accessed Jan. 2020: https://www.habitsforwellbeing.com/20-quotes-to-inspire-responsibility/.

[118] Kistner, Robert. Business Leadership Interview. January 2020.

[119] *Id.*

[120] *Id.*

[121] Svare, Harland. Forbes Quotes: "Responsibility." Accessed Jan. 2020: https://www.forbes.com/quotes/theme/responsibility/.

[122] Nicholson, Nigel. "How to Motivate Your Problem People." Harvard Business Review. Published Jan. 2003; Accessed Feb. 2020: https://hbr.org/2003/01/how-to-motivate-your-problem-people.

[123] *Id.*

[124] *Id.*

[125] Welch, Jack. As quoted by AZ Quotes, "Leadership Vision." Accessed Feb. 2020: https://www.azquotes.com/quotes/topics/leadership-vision.html.

[126] Churchill, Winston. As quoted in Habits for Wellbeing: "20 Quotes to Inspire Responsibility." Accessed Jan. 2020: https://www.habitsforwellbeing.com/20-quotes-to-inspire-responsibility/.

[127] Welch, Jack. As quoted by AZ Quotes, "Leadership Vision." Accessed Feb. 2020: https://www.azquotes.com/quotes/topics/leadership-vision.html.

[128] Jobs, Steve. As quoted on Pass it On. Accessed Feb. 2020: https://www.passiton.com/inspirational-quotes/6652-if-you-are-working-on-something-exciting-that.

[129] Nizar, Louis. As quoted in Habits for Wellbeing: "20 Quotes to Inspire Responsibility." Accessed Jan. 2020: https://www.habitsforwellbeing.com/20-quotes-to-inspire-responsibility/.

[130] Williamson, Marianne. As quoted in Habits for Wellbeing: "20 Quotes to Inspire Responsibility." Accessed Jan. 2020: https://www.habitsforwellbeing.com/20-quotes-to-inspire-responsibility/.

[131] Rohn, Jim. As quoted in Habits for Wellbeing: "20 Quotes to Inspire Responsibility." Accessed Jan. 2020: https://www.habitsforwellbeing.com/20-quotes-to-inspire-responsibility/.

[132] Wikipedia. "Seat belt use rates in the United States." Accessed Jan. 2020: https://en.wikipedia.org/wiki/Seat_belt_use_rates_in_the_United_States.

[133] Edgar Snyder. "Seat Belt Statistics." Accessed Jan. 2020: https://www.edgarsnyder.com/car-accident/defective-products/seat-belts/seat-belts-statistics.html.

[134] Wikipedia. "Seat belt use rates in the United States." Accessed Jan. 2020: https://en.wikipedia.org/wiki/Seat_belt_use_rates_in_the_United_States.

[135] ADP 6-22. Army Leadership and The Profession (2019). Department of the Army United States of America. Accessed Jan. 2020: https://armypubs.army.mil/ProductMaps/Pubform/Details.aspx?PUB_ID=1007609.

[136] Lucas, George. As quoted by Leonard, Michael. "Seven Amazing Focus Quotes That Will Help You Accomplish Your Goals." Fearless Motivation. Published May 2018; Accessed Feb. 2020: https://www.fearlessmotivation.com/2018/05/03/focus-quotes-goals/.

[137] Tracy, Brian as quoted by Marcus, Bonnie. "Lessons in Management from Brian Tracy: How to Motivate and Inspire Your Team." Forbes. Published Apr. 2011; Accessed Feb. 2020: https://www.forbes.com/sites/bonniemarcus/2011/04/25/lessons-in-management-from-brian-tracy-how-to-motivate-and-inspire-your-team/#4d383ce93883.

[138] *Id.*

[139] ADP 6-22. Army Leadership and The Profession (2019). Department of the Army United States of America. Accessed Jan. 2020: https://armypubs.army.mil/ProductMaps/Pubform/Details.aspx?PUB_ID=1007609.

[140] *Id.*

[141] *Id.*

[142] *Id.*

[143] *Id.*

[144] *Id.*

[145] *Id.*

[146] *Id.*

[147] Tracy, Brian as quoted by Marcus, Bonnie. "Lessons in Management from Brian Tracy: How to Motivate and Inspire Your Team." Forbes. Published Apr. 2011; Accessed Feb. 2020: https://www.forbes.com/sites/bonniemarcus/2011/04/25/lessons-in-management-from-brian-tracy-how-to-motivate-and-inspire-your-team/#4d383ce93883.

[148] ADP 6-22. Army Leadership and The Profession (2019). Department of the Army United States of America. Accessed Jan. 2020: https://armypubs.army.mil/ProductMaps/Pubform/Details.aspx?PUB_ID=1007609.

[149] Collier, Robert. As quoted by Martin. "97 Quotes to Inspire Your Life and Business." Accessed Feb. 2020: https://www.cleverism.com/97-quotes-to-inspire-success-in-your-life-and-business/.

[150] Carlyle, Thomas. "Thomas Carlyle Quotes." BrainyQuote. Accessed Feb. 2020: https://www.brainyquote.com/quotes/thomas_carlyle_156155.

[151] Kistner, Robert. Business Leadership Interview. January 2020.

[152] Frohlinger, Carol as quoted in "Women and Negotiation: Why Men Should Come to the Table." Oxford Leadership. Published Aug. 2016; Accessed Aug. 2018: http://www.oxfordleadership.com/women-negotiation-men-come-table/.

[153] Brooks, Alison W. "Emotion and the art of negotiation." Harvard Business Review. Published Dec. 2015; Accessed Aug. 2018: https://hbr.org/2015/12/emotion-and-the-art-of-negotiation.

[154] *Ibid.*

[155] Nelson, Mark. Unpublished interview regarding negotiation. August 2018.

[156] Kennedy, John F. "Inaugural Address." John F. Kennedy Presidential Library and Museum. Speech made Jan. 1961; Accessed Aug. 2018: https://www.jfklibrary.org/Research/Research-Aids/Ready-Reference/JFK-Quotations/Inaugural-Address.aspx.

[157] Mamas, Michael. "5 Steps to master the art of negotiation." Entrepreneur. Published Dec. 2015; Accessed Aug. 2018: https://www.entrepreneur.com/article/253074.

[158] Voss, Christopher as quoted in "Hostage negotiation techniques that will get you what you want." Published June 2013; Accessed Aug. 2018: https://www.bakadesuyo.com/2013/06/hostage-negotiation/.

[159] Tribby, MaryEllen. "The art of negotiation: learn it and watch your business grow!" HuffPost. Published Sept. 2013; Accessed Aug. 2018: https://www.huffingtonpost.com/maryellen-tribby/negotiation_b_3605194.html.

[160] Zohar, Ilana. "The art of negotiation: leadership skills required for negotiation in the time of crisis." Science Direct. Published 2015; Accessed Aug. 2018: www.sciencedirect.com.

[161] Morrow, Lance as quoted in Chris Anderson. "Negotiation tips: how to get what you want." Published May 2013; Accessed Aug. 2018: http://smartbusinesstrends.com/negotiation-tips-how-to-get-what-you-want/.

162 Coleman, Bill as quoted in "117 inspirational quotes for a prosperous new year." American Genius. Published Jan. 2018; Accessed Aug. 2018: https://theamericangenius.com/lists/117-inspirational-quotes-for-a-prosperous-new-year/.

163 Court, Robert as quoted in "117 inspirational quotes for a prosperous new year." American Genius. Published Jan. 2018; Accessed Aug. 2018: https://theamericangenius.com/lists/117-inspirational-quotes-for-a-prosperous-new-year/.

164 Harroch, Richard. "15 tactics for successful business negotiations." Forbes. Published Sept. 2016; Accessed Aug. 2018: https://www.forbes.com/sites/allbusiness/2016/09/16/15-tactics-for-successful-business-negotiations/#295654dc2528.

165 Brooks, Alison W. "Emotion and the art of negotiation." Harvard Business Review. Published Dec. 2015; Accessed Aug. 2018: https://hbr.org/2015/12/emotion-and-the-art-of-negotiation.

166 Nelson, Mark. Unpublished interview regarding negotiation. August 2018.

167 Brooks, Alison W. "Emotion and the art of negotiation." Harvard Business Review. Published Dec. 2015; Accessed Aug. 2018: https://hbr.org/2015/12/emotion-and-the-art-of-negotiation.

168 Kennedy, John F. "Radio and television report to the American people on the Berlin crisis." Delivered July 1961; Accessed Aug. 2018: https://www.jfklibrary.org/Research/Research-Aids/JFK-Speeches/Berlin-Crisis_19610725.aspx.

169 Nelson, Mark. Unpublished interview regarding negotiation. August 2018.

170 Landry, Lauren. "The Importance of Creativity in Business." Published Nov. 2017; Accessed April 2019: https://www.northeastern.edu/graduate/blog/creativity-importance-in-business.

171 Tracy, Brian. *The Creative Manager*. Effective Manager Seminar Series. Nightingale-Conant Corporation, 1988.

172 Morr, Kelly. "What is creativity? The ultimate guide to understanding today's most important ability." 99designs. Published Dec. 2018; Accessed April 2019: https://99designs.com/blog/creative-thinking/what-is-creativity.

173 Culture of the United States Marines. Wikipedia. Accessed April 2019: https://en.wikipedia.org/wiki/Culture_of_the_United_States_Marine_Corps.

174 Tracy, Brian. *The Creative Manager*. Effective Manager Seminar Series. Nightingale-Conant Corporation, 1988.

175 Morr, Kelly. "What is creativity? The ultimate guide to understanding today's most important ability." 99designs. Published Dec. 2018; Accessed April 2019: https://99designs.com/blog/creative-thinking/what-is-creativity.

176 Csikszentmihalyi, Mihaly. *Creativity—Flow and the Psychology of Discovery and Invention*. As cited by California State University Northridge. Accessed April 2019: https://www.csun.edu/~vcpsy00h/creativity/define.htm.

177 Franken, Robert. *Human Motivation*. As cited by California State University Northridge. Accessed April 2019: https://www.csun.edu/~vcpsy00h/creativity/define.htm.

178 Tracy, Brian. *The Creative Manager*. Effective Manager Seminar Series. Nightingale-Conant Corporation, 1988.

179 *Id.*

180 Amabile, T. and Khaire, M. "Creativity and the Role of the Leader." Harvard Business Review. Published Oct. 2008; Accessed April 2019: https://hbr.org/2008/10/creativity-and-the-role-of-the-leader.

181 *Id.*

182 Brace, Louise. "The Seven Principles of Managing for Creativity." Published April 2016; Accessed April 2019: https://management30.com/blog/the-seven-principles-of-managing-for-creativity.

183 *Id.*

184 *Id.*

185 Amabile, T. and Khaire, M. "Creativity and the Role of the Leader." Harvard Business Review. Published Oct. 2008; Accessed April 2019: https://hbr.org/2008/10/creativity-and-the-role-of-the-leader.

186 Moran, Gwen. "Six Habits of Creative Managers." Fast Company. Published May 2016; Accessed April 2019: https://www.fastcompany.com/3059779/6-habits-of-creative-managers.

187 *Id.*

[188] Brace, Louise. "The Seven Principles of Managing for Creativity." Published April 2016; Accessed April 2019: https://management30.com/blog/the-seven-principles-of-managing-for-creativity.

[189] McLeod, Saul. "Social Identity Theory." Simply Psychology. Published 2008; Accessed April 2019.

[190] Amabile, T. and Khaire, M. "Creativity and the Role of the Leader." Harvard Business Review. Published Oct. 2008; Accessed April 2019: https://hbr.org/2008/10/creativity-and-the-role-of-the-leader.

[191] Id.

[192] Brace, Louise. "The Seven Principles of Managing for Creativity." Published April 2016; Accessed April 2019: https://management30.com/blog/the-seven-principles-of-managing-for-creativity.

[193] Trapp, Roger. "Five Steps to Business Creativity." Forbes. Published Oct. 2013; Accessed April 2019: https://www.forbes.com/sites/rogertrapp/2013/10/21/five-steps-to-business-creativity/#955039d249d7.

[194] Landry, Lauren. "The Importance of Creativity in Business." Published Nov. 2017; Accessed April 2019: https://www.northeastern.edu/graduate/blog/creativity-importance-in-business.

[195] Bahcall, Safi. "The most important breakthroughs are the ones most likely to be shot down." Published March 2019; Accessed April 2019: https://www.linkedin.com/pulse/most-important-breakthroughs-ones-likely-shot-down-safi-bahcall.

[196] Id.

[197] Kistner, Robert. Business Leadership Interview. 2019.

[198] Landry, Lauren. "The Importance of Creativity in Business." Published Nov. 2017; Accessed April 2019: https://www.northeastern.edu/graduate/blog/creativity-importance-in-business.

[199] Tracy, Brian. *The Creative Manager*. Effective Manager Seminar Series. Nightingale-Conant Corporation, 1988.

[200] Uchtdorf, Dieter as quoted by Mikesh, Kimberly. "10 Positive Quotes to Inspire Creativity." Accessed April 2019: https://www.happier.com/87ublog/10-positive-quotes-to-inspire-creativity.

[201] Angelou, Maya as quoted by Mikesh, Kimberly. "10 Positive Quotes to Inspire Creativity." Accessed April 2019: https://www.happier.com/blog/10-positive-quotes-to-inspire-creativity.

[202] Einstein, Albert as quoted by Mikesh, Kimberly. "10 Positive Quotes to Inspire Creativity." Accessed April 2019: https://www.happier.com/blog/10-positive-quotes-to-inspire-creativity.

[203] De Bono, Edward as quoted by Mikesh, Kimberly. "10 Positive Quotes to Inspire Creativity." Accessed April 2019: https://www.happier.com/blog/10-positive-quotes-to-inspire-creativity.

[204] Morr, Kelly. "What is creativity? The ultimate guide to understanding today's most important ability." 99designs. Published Dec. 2018; Accessed April 2019: https://99designs.com/blog/creative-thinking/what-is-creativity.

[205] Id.

[206] Trapp, Roger. "Five Steps to Business Creativity." Forbes. Published Oct. 2013; Accessed April 2019: https://www.forbes.com/sites/rogertrapp/2013/10/21/five-steps-to-business-creativity/#955039d249d7.

[207] Amabile, T. and Khaire, M. "Creativity and the Role of the Leader." Harvard Business Review. Published Oct. 2008; Accessed April 2019: https://hbr.org/2008/10/creativity-and-the-role-of-the-leader.

[208] Id.

[209] Id.

[210] Tracy, Brian. *The Creative Manager*. Effective Manager Seminar Series. Nightingale-Conant Corporation, 1988.

[211] Amabile, T. and Khaire, M. "Creativity and the Role of the Leader." Harvard Business Review. Published Oct. 2008; Accessed April 2019: https://hbr.org/2008/10/creativity-and-the-role-of-the-leader.

[212] Bahcall, Safi. *Loonshots: How to Nurture the Crazy Ideas that Win Wars, Cure Diseases, and Transform Industries*. Accessed April 2019: https://www.goodreads.com/work/quotes/61659659-loonshots-how-to-nurture-the-crazy-ideas-that-win-wars-cure-diseases.

[213] Id.

214 *Id.*

215 EdX. "Innovation and Creativity Management." Accessed April 2019: https://www.edx.org/course/innovation-creativity-management-rwthx-mti003x.

216 Daily News. "The Steve Jobs Nobody Knew." Published Oct. 2011; Accessed April 2019: https://web.archive.org/web/20120425233149/http://india.nydailynews.com/article/3ea39bee2a29179c3406250afd01c526/the-steve-jobs-nobody-knew.

217 Love, Dylan. "16 Examples of Steve Jobs Being a Huge Jerk." Published Oct. 2011; Accessed April 2019: https://www.businessinsider.com/steve-jobs-jerk-2011-10.

218 NY Daily News. "The Steve Jobs Nobody Knew." Published Oct. 2011; Accessed April 2019: https://web.archive.org/web/20120425233149/http://india.nydailynews.com/article/3ea39bee2a29179c3406250afd01c526/the-steve-jobs-nobody-knew.

219 *Id.*

220 Kistner, Robert. Business Leadership Interview. 2019.

221 Stanford News. "You've got to find what you love." Commencement Address by Steve Jobs June 2005; Accessed April 2019: https://news.stanford.edu/2005/06/14/jobs-061505.

222 *Id.*

223 *Id.*

224 *Id.*

225 Vonnegut, Kurt as quoted by Mikesh, Kimberly. "10 Positive Quotes to Inspire Creativity." Accessed April 2019: https://www.happier.com/blog/10-positive-quotes-to-inspire-creativity.

226 Tracy, Brian. *The Creative Manager.* Effective Manager Seminar Series. Nightingale-Conant Corporation, 1988.

227 *Id.*

228 Stanford News. "You've got to find what you love." Commencement Address by Steve Jobs June 2005; Accessed April 2019: https://news.stanford.edu/2005/06/14/jobs-061505.

229 McCarthy, Dan. "Learn the Ways Leaders Encourage Innovation." Published Aug. 2017; Accessed March 2018: https://www.thebalance.com/encourage-innovation-from-employees-2275816.

230 Australian Government. "Business Innovation." Published Nov. 2017; Accessed March 2018: https://www.business.gov.au/info/run/innovation.

231 Amabile, T. & Khaire, M. "Creativity and the Role of the Leader." Harvard Business Review. Published Oct. 2008; Accessed March 2018: https://hbr.org/2008/10/creativity-and-the-role-of-the-leader.

232 Robert W. Woodruff Foundation. Accessed March 2018: http://woodruff.org/about-the-foundation/robert-w-woodruff/.

233 Cashman, K. "7 Ways Leaders can Foster Innovation." Forbes Leadership. Published Aug. 2013; Accessed March 2018: https://www.forbes.com/sites/kevincashman/2013/08/21/7-ways-leaders-can-foster-innovation/#546075fc29a9.

234 *Id.*

235 Berkus, Dave. "The five kinds of risk in building your business." Published June 2015; Accessed March 2018: https://berkonomics.com/?p=2286.

236 McCarthy, Dan. "70 Awesome Coaching Questions for Managers." Published Aug. 2017; Accessed March 2018: https://www.thebalance.com/coaching-questions-for-managers-2275913.

237 Amabile, T. & Khaire, M. "Creativity and the Role of the Leader." Harvard Business Review. Published Oct. 2008; Accessed March 2018: https://hbr.org/2008/10/creativity-and-the-role-of-the-leader.

238 Eurostat Statistics Explained. "Share of enterprises that had product innovations, 2012-2014." Accessed March 2018: http://ec.europa.eu/eurostat/statistics-explained/index.php/File:Share_of_enterprises_that_had_product_innovations,_2012%E2%80%932014_(%25)_YB17.png.

239 Amabile, T. & Khaire, M. "Creativity and the Role of the Leader." Harvard Business Review. Published Oct. 2008; Accessed March 2018: https://hbr.org/2008/10/creativity-and-the-role-of-the-leader.

240 Hoque, F. "How to Create a Culture of Innovation." Fast Company. Published June 2014; Accessed March 2018: https://www.fastcompany.com/3031092/how-to-create-a-culture-of-innovation-in-the-workplace.

241 Entrepreneurs' Organization. "6 Ways to Encourage Innovation at Your Company." Published Sept. 2015; Accessed March 2018: https://www.inc.com/entrepreneurs-organization/6-ways-to-encourage-innovation-at-your-company.html.

242 Horth, D. & Vehar, J. "Innovation—how leadership makes the difference." Center for Creative Leadership. Accessed March 2018: https://www.ccl.org/articles/white-papers/innovation-how-leadership-makes-the-difference/.

243 Conroy, K. "Encouraging Employees to Innovate." Edward Lowe Foundation. Accessed March 2018: http://edwardlowe.org/encouraging-employees-to-innovate/.

244 Cashman, K. "7 Ways Leaders Can Foster Innovation." Forbes Leadership. Published Aug. 2013; Accessed March 2018: https://www.forbes.com/sites/kevincashman/2013/08/21/7-ways-leaders-can-foster-innovation/#546075fc29a9.

245 Personal communication with MAJ (CA) Mark F. Nelson. March 2018.

246 Groysbert, B., Lee, J., Price, J. and Cheng, J. "The Leader's Guide to Corporate Culture." Harvard Business Review. Published Jan. 2018; Accessed July 2022: https://hbr.org/2018/01/the-leaders-guide-to-corporate-culture.

247 Id.

248 Id.

249 Doerr, John. Measure What Matters. Portfolio/Penguin. New York: 2018; p. 212.

250 Overy, Richard as quoted by Venable, Heather. "More Than Meets the Eye." Army War College. Published Dec. 2020; Accessed July 2022: https://warroom.armywarcollege.edu/special-series/dusty-shelves/why-the-allies-won/.

251 Groysbert, B., Lee, J., Price, J. and Cheng, J. "The Leader's Guide to Corporate Culture." Harvard Business Review. Published Jan. 2018; Accessed July 2022: https://hbr.org/2018/01/the-leaders-guide-to-corporate-culture.

252 Id.

253 Id.

254 Tarver, Evan. "Corporate Culture." Investopedia. Published Sept. 2021; Accessed July 2022: https://www.investopedia.com/terms/c/corporate-culture.asp.

255 Doerr, John. Measure What Matters. Portfolio/Penguin. New York: 2018; p. 230.

256 Indeed Editorial Team. "3 Examples of Great Organizational Culture – And How to Develop It." Published April 2021; Accessed July 2022: https://www.indeed.com/lead/build-great-organizational-culture?gclid=EAIaIQobChMIoIb92rmn-QIVyiCtBh1upQBJEAAYASAAEgKodfD_BwE&aceid.

257 Id.

258 Id.

259 Id.

260 Tarver, Evan. "Corporate Culture." Investopedia. Published Sept. 2021; Accessed July 2022: https://www.investopedia.com/terms/c/corporate-culture.asp.

261 Groysbert, B., Lee, J., Price, J. and Cheng, J. "The Leader's Guide to Corporate Culture." Harvard Business Review. Published Jan. 2018; Accessed July 2022: https://hbr.org/2018/01/the-leaders-guide-to-corporate-culture.

262 Doerr, John. Measure What Matters. Portfolio/Penguin. New York: 2018; p. 215.

263 Id. at 213.

264 Seidman, Dov as quoted by Doerr, John. Measure What Matters. Portfolio/Penguin. New York: 2018; p. 220.

265 Indeed Editorial Team. "3 Examples of Great Organizational Culture – And How to Develop It." Published April 2021; Accessed July 2022: https://www.indeed.com/lead/build-great-organizational-culture?gclid=EAIaIQobChMIoIb92rmn-QIVyiCtBh1upQBJEAAYASAAEgKodfD_BwE&aceid.

266 Id.

267 Doerr, John. Measure What Matters. Portfolio/Penguin. New York: 2018; p. 213.

268 Cunningham, Keith. As cited in "Summary of The Road Less Stupid." Published Dec. 2019; Accessed July 2022: https://waiyancan.com/summary-the-road-less-stupid-by-keith-j-cunningham/.

[269] Tenney, Matt. "The Best Company Culture in the World -- 2022." Business Leadership Today. Accessed July 2022: https://businessleadershiptoday.com/what-is-the-best-company-culture/.

[270] Doerr, John. *Measure What Matters*. Portfolio/Penguin. New York: 2018; p. 219.

[271] *Id.* at 220.

[272] Indeed Editorial Team. "3 Examples of Great Organizational Culture – And How to Develop It." Published April 2021; Accessed July 2022: https://www.indeed.com/lead/build-great-organizational-culture?gclid=EAIaIQobChMIoIb92rmn-QIVyiCtBh1upQBJEAAYASAAEgKodfD_BwE&aceid.

[273] *Id.*

[274] *Id.*

[275] Tenney, Matt. "The Best Company Culture in the World—2022." Business Leadership Today. Accessed July 2022: https://businessleadershiptoday.com/what-is-the-best-company-culture/.

[276] *Id.*

[277] *Id.*

[278] *Id.*

[279] Katzenbach, Jon et. al. "Cultural Change that Sticks." Harvard Business Review. Published July 2012; Accessed August 2022: https://hbr.org/2012/07/cultural-change-that-sticks.

[280] Walker, Bryan and Soule, Sarah. "Changing Company Culture Requires a Movement, not a Mandate." Harvard Business Review. Published June 2017; Accessed August 2022: https://hbr.org/2017/06/changing-company-culture-requires-a-movement-not-a-mandate.

[281] Katzenbach, Jon et. al. "Cultural Change that Sticks." Harvard Business Review. Published July 2012; Accessed August 2022: https://hbr.org/2012/07/cultural-change-that-sticks.

[282] Cunningham, Keith. *The Road Less Stupid*. As quoted on Goodreads. Accessed July 2022: https://www.goodreads.com/author/quotes/203293.Keith_J_Cunningham.

[283] Groysbert, B., Lee, J., Price, J. and Cheng, J. "The Leader's Guide to Corporate Culture." Harvard Business Review. Published Jan. 2018; Accessed July 2022: https://hbr.org/2018/01/the-leaders-guide-to-corporate-culture.

[284] Doerr, John. *Measure What Matters*. Portfolio/Penguin. New York: 2018; p. 212.

[285] Tracy, Brian. "Brian Tracy Quotes." Brainy Quote. Accessed April 2021: https://www.brainyquote.com/authors/brian-tracy-quotes.

[286] Doerr, John. *Measure What Matters*. Portfolio/Penguin. New York: 2018; p. 229.

[287] Groysbert, B., Lee, J., Price, J. and Cheng, J. "The Leader's Guide to Corporate Culture." Harvard Business Review. Published Jan. 2018; Accessed July 2022: https://hbr.org/2018/01/the-leaders-guide-to-corporate-culture.

[288] Groysbert, B., Lee, J., Price, J. and Cheng, J. "The Leader's Guide to Corporate Culture." Harvard Business Review. Published Jan. 2018; Accessed July 2022: https://hbr.org/2018/01/the-leaders-guide-to-corporate-culture.

[289] Cunningham, Keith. *The Road Less Stupid*. Keys to the Vault, 2018: USA; 145.

[290] Cunningham, Keith. *The Road Less Stupid*. Keys to the Vault, 2018: USA; 146.

[291] *Id.*

[292] Kistner, Robert. "Leadership Quotes." Business Leadership Interview.

[293] Doerr, John. *Measure What Matters*. Portfolio/Penguin. New York: 2018; p. 221.

[294] *Id.* at 216.

[295] *Id.* at 217.

[296] *Id.* at 217.

[297] *Id.*

[298] Doerr, John. *Measure What Matters*. Portfolio/Penguin. New York: 2018; p. 228.

[299] Cunningham, Keith. As cited in "Summary of The Road Less Stupid." Published Dec. 2019; Accessed July 2022: https://waiyancan.com/summary-the-road-less-stupid-by-keith-j-cunningham/.

[300] Doerr, John. *Measure What Matters*. Portfolio/Penguin. New York: 2018; p. 212.

[301] Groysbert, B., Lee, J., Price, J. and Cheng, J. "The Leader's Guide to Corporate Culture." Harvard Business Review. Published Jan. 2018; Accessed July 2022: https://hbr.org/2018/01/the-leaders-guide-to-corporate-culture.

[302] Jacobsen, Darcy. "Five Companies Whose Great Cultures Saved Their Bacon." Workhuman. Published April 2014; Accessed August 2022: https://www.workhuman.com/resources/globoforce-blog/5-companies-whose-great-cultures-saved-their-bacon.

[303] *Id.*

[304] *Id.*

[305] Harman, Wendy. "Twitter Faux Pas." Red Cross Chat. Published Feb. 2011; Accessed August 2022: https://redcrosschat.org/2011/02/16/twitter-faux-pas/.

[306] *Id.*

[307] Doerr, John. Quoting Andy Grove. *Measure What Matters.* Portfolio/Penguin. New York: 2018; p. 31.

[308] Brown, Brené. "Vulnerability is the birthplace of innovation, creativity and change." TED2012. Published March 2012; Accessed September 2022: https://blog.ted.com/vulnerability-is-the-birthplace-of-innovation-creativity-and-change-brene-brown-at-ted2012/.

[309] Doerr, John. *Measure What Matters.* Portfolio/Penguin. New York: 2018; p. 228.

[310] *Id.*

[311] *Id.*

[312] Razzetti, Gustavo. "12 Examples of Companies with Powerful Cultures." Culture Design Canvas. Published Dec. 2020; Accessed August 2022: https://www.fearlessculture.design/blog-posts/11-examples-of-companies-with-powerful-cultures.

[313] *Id.*

[314] Groysbert, B., Lee, J., Price, J. and Cheng, J. "The Leader's Guide to Corporate Culture." Harvard Business Review. Published Jan. 2018; Accessed July 2022: https://hbr.org/2018/01/the-leaders-guide-to-corporate-culture.

[315] Doerr, John. *Measure What Matters.* Portfolio/Penguin. New York: 2018; p. 215.

[316] Collins, Jim as quoted by Doerr, John. *Measure What Matters.* Portfolio/Penguin. New York: 2018; p. 223.

[317] Doerr, John. *Measure What Matters.* Portfolio/Penguin. New York: 2018; p. 227.

[318] Cunningham, Keith. *The Road Less Stupid.* Keys to the Vault, 2018: USA; 42.

[319] *Id.* at 45.

[320] Doerr, John. *Measure What Matters.* Portfolio/Penguin. New York: 2018; p. 216.

[321] Cunningham, Keith. *The Road Less Stupid.* Keys to the Vault, 2018: USA; 46.

[322] Jacobsen, Darcy. "Five Companies Whose Great Cultures Saved Their Bacon." Workhuman. Published April 2014; Accessed August 2022: https://www.workhuman.com/resources/globoforce-blog/5-companies-whose-great-cultures-saved-their-bacon.

[323] *Id.*

[324] *Id.*

[325] Cunningham, Keith. *The Road Less Stupid.* Keys to the Vault, 2018: USA; 42.

[326] Huang, Chieh. "Confessions of a Recovering Micromanager." TED Lecture Oct. 2018; Accessed Dec. 2018: https://www.ted.com/talks/chieh_huang_confessions_of_a_recovering_micromanager.

[327] *Id.*

[328] *Id.*

[329] Burg, Bob. Conant Leaders. "52 Quotes about Trust and Leadership." Published June 2015; Accessed Dec. 2018: https://conantleadership.com/52-quotes-about-trust-and-leadership/.

[330] Covey, Stephen. "Stephen Covey Quotes." Brainy Quote. Accessed Dec. 2023: https://www.brainyquote.com/quotes/stephen_covey_450798.

[331] Horsager, David. "You Can't be a Great Leader Without Trust—Here's How You Build It." Forbes. Published Oct. 2018; Accessed Dec. 2018: https://www.forbes.com/sites/forbesleadershipforum/2012/10/24/you-cant-be-a-great-leader-without-trust-heres-how-you-build-it/#8c3cec44ef7a.

[332] *Id.*

[333] *Id.*

[334] Conant Leaders. "52 Quotes about Trust and Leadership." Published June 2015; Accessed Dec. 2018: https://conantleadership.com/52-quotes-about-trust-and-leadership/.

[335] Covey, Stephen. Accessed Dec. 2023: https://quotefancy.com/quote/909532/Stephen-R-Covey.

[336] Bush, George. "Advice to Young People." Accessed Dec. 2023: https://www.goodreads.com/quotes/9259493-my-advice-to-young-people-might-be-as-follows.

[337] *Id.*

[338] *Id.*

[339] *Id.*

[340] *Id.*

[341] *Id.*

[342] *Id.*

[343] *Id.*

[344] Stimson, Henry L. Brainy Quote. Accessed Dec. 2023: https://www.brainyquote.com/quotes/henry_l_stimson_176996.

[345] Powell, Colin. Conant Leaders. "52 Quotes about Trust and Leadership." Published June 2015; Accessed Dec. 2018: https://conantleadership.com/52-quotes-about-trust-and-leadership/.

[346] Geleta, Bekele. "What is Stewardship, and should all great leaders practice it?" NY Times. Accessed Dec. 2018: https://nytimesineducation.com/spotlight/what-is-stewardship-and-should-all-great-leaders-practice-it/.

[347] Nardizzi, Steven. "Leadership Through Stewardship." NY Times. Accessed Dec. 2018: https://nytimesineducation.com/spotlight/leadership-through-stewardship-a-foundation-for-organizational-success-across-cultures/.

[348] Warren, Rick. "A Life of Purpose." TED Lecture 2006; Accessed Dec. 2018: https://www.ted.com/talks/rick_warren_on_a_life_of_purpose.

[349] *Id.*

[350] *Id.*

[351] *Id.*

[352] Barnes, Brenda. Conant Leaders. "52 Quotes about Trust and Leadership." Published June 2015; Accessed Dec. 2018: https://conantleadership.com/52-quotes-about-trust-and-leadership/.

[353] Warren, Rick. "A Life of Purpose." TED Lecture 2006; Accessed Dec. 2018: https://www.ted.com/talks/rick_warren_on_a_life_of_purpose.

[354] Kistner, Robert. Private Interview. Dec. 2018.

[355] Wilde, Oscar. Conant Leaders. "52 Quotes about Trust and Leadership." Published June 2015; Accessed Dec. 2018: https://conantleadership.com/52-quotes-about-trust-and-leadership/.

[356] Warren, Rick. "A Life of Purpose." TED Lecture 2006; Accessed Dec. 2018: https://www.ted.com/talks/rick_warren_on_a_life_of_purpose.

[357] *Id.*

[358] Burg, Bob and Mann, John D. *The Go-Giver*. Portfolio: 2015.

[359] *Id.*

[360] Little, P. Private Letter. Nov. 2018.

[361] *Id.*

[362] *Id.*

[363] Ayala, L. Private Letter. Nov. 2018.

[364] Hamel, Gary. "Leaders as Stewards." Leadership Excellence. Published Aug. 2012; Accessed Dec. 2018: http://www.ila-net.org/members/directory/downloads/LE/le0812.pdf.

[365] Horsager, David. "You Can't be a Great Leader Without Trust—Here's How You Build It." Forbes. Published Oct. 2018; Accessed Dec. 2018: https://www.forbes.com/sites/forbesleadershipforum/2012/10/24/you-cant-be-a-great-leader-without-trust-heres-how-you-build-it/#8c3cec44ef7a.

[366] Ben-Shahar, Tal. "The Secret to Happiness." Jerusalem U. Published March 2016; Accessed Feb. 2019: https://www.youtube.com/watch?v=YbTJBwBBs2k&feature=youtu.be&t=21.

[367] Bergland, Christopher. "The Neurochemicals of Happiness." Psychology Today. Published Nov. 2012; Accessed Feb. 2019: https://www.psychologytoday.com/us/blog/the-athletes-way/201211/the-neurochemicals-happiness.

[368] Bennett, Nick. "The Secret of Success." Forbes. Published Nov. 2018; Accessed Feb. 2019: https://www.forbes.com/sites/nickbennett1/2018/11/18/the-secret-of-success-is-it-happiness/#68ddcc286aa9.

[369] Ben-Shahar, Tal. "The Secret to Happiness." Jerusalem U. Published March 2016; Accessed Feb. 2019: https://www.youtube.com/watch?v=YbTJBwBBs2k&feature=youtu.be&t=21.

[370] Morris, George. "Slow is Smooth. Smooth is Fast." Medium. Published May 2023; accessed Dec. 2023: https://gm3.medium.com/slow-is-smooth-smooth-is-fast-1c33b37a5960.

[371] As cited in: Bennett, Nick. "The Secret of Success." Forbes. Published Nov. 2018; Accessed Feb. 2019: https://www.forbes.com/sites/nickbennett1/2018/11/18/the-secret-of-success-is-it-happiness/#68ddcc286aa9.

[372] Ben-Shahar, Tal. *The Pursuit of Perfect: How to Stop Chasing Perfection.* 2009.

[373] *Id.*

[374] Tracy, Brian. "Making Course Corrections." Accessed Feb. 2019: https://www.briantracy.com/blog/brians-words-of-wisdom/making-course-corrections/.

[375] Covey, Steven R. "How to Develop Your Personal Mission Statement." Goodreads. Accessed Feb. 2019: https://www.goodreads.com/work/quotes/6909067-how-to-develop-your-personal-mission-statement.

[376] Tracy, Brian. "Making Course Corrections." Accessed Feb. 2019: https://www.briantracy.com/blog/brians-words-of-wisdom/making-course-corrections/.

[377] Bradt, Steve. "Wandering mind not a happy mind." Published Nov. 2010; Accessed Feb. 2019: https://news.harvard.edu/gazette/story/2010/11/wandering-mind-not-a-happy-mind/.

[378] Gelles, David. "How to be more mindful at work." New York Times. Accessed Feb. 2019: https://www.nytimes.com/guides/well/be-more-mindful-at-work.

[379] *Id.*

[380] *Id.*

[381] Holmes, Cassie M. "What Kind of Happiness Do People Value Most?" Harvard Business Review. Published Nov. 2018; Accessed Feb. 2019: https://hbr.org/2018/11/what-kind-of-happiness-do-people-value-most.

[382] *Id.*

[383] Tracy, Brian. "Four Essentials for Happiness." Accessed Feb. 2019: https://www.briantracy.com/blog/personal-success/four-essentials-for-happiness/.

[384] *Id.*

[385] Tracy, Brian. "How to be Happy: Five Steps to Living a Life You Love." Accessed Feb. 2019: https://www.briantracy.com/blog/personal-success/happiness-in-life-you-deserve-it/.

[386] Tal, Ben-Shahar. "Be Happier: How to Enjoy Lasting Change." Happy & Well. Published March 2018; Accessed Feb. 2019: https://www.youtube.com/watch?v=9-NWpw_bpdQ.

[387] "124 Best Gratitude Quotes and Sayings." Accessed Feb. 2019: https://www.developgoodhabits.com/gratitude-quotes/.

[388] *Id.*

[389] *Id.*

[390] Greater Good in Action: Science-based Practices for a Meaningful Life. "Gratitude Journal." Accessed Feb. 2019: https://ggia.berkeley.edu/practice/gratitude_journal.

[391] Tracy, Brian. "How to be Happy: Five Steps to Living a Life You Love." Accessed Feb. 2019: https://www.briantracy.com/blog/personal-success/happiness-in-life-you-deserve-it/.

[392] *Id.*

[393] Tracy, Brian. "Four Essentials for Happiness." Accessed Feb. 2019: https://www.briantracy.com/blog/personal-success/four-essentials-for-happiness/.

[394] Kondo, Marie. "The Life-Changing Magic of Tidying Up Quotes." Goodreads. Accessed Feb. 2019: https://www.goodreads.com/work/quotes/41711738.

[395] *Id.*

[396] Tracy, Brian. "How to be Happy: Five Steps to Living a Life You Love." Accessed Feb. 2019: https://www.briantracy.com/blog/personal-success/happiness-in-life-you-deserve-it/.

[397] Selhub, Eva. "Love Response, Stress, and Neuroscience." Sivananda Ashram. Published Feb. 2018; Accessed Feb. 2019: https://www.youtube.com/watch?v=Z_UTsIs6Tf4. Quotations in this document are taken from similar works.

398 Brown, Brene. "Quotes." Goodreads. Accessed Feb. 2019: https://www.goodreads.com/author/quotes/162578.Bren_Brown.

399 Brown, Brene. *Daring Greatly: How the Courage to be Vulnerable Transforms the Way We Live, Love, Parent and Lead*. New York: Avery, 2011.

400 Williams, David. "The Best Leaders are Vulnerable." Forbes. Published July 2013; Accessed Feb. 2019: https://www.forbes.com/sites/davidkwilliams/2013/07/18/the-best-leaders-are-vulnerable/#45e006f13c1d.

401 Brown, Brene. "Quotes." Goodreads. Accessed Feb. 2019: https://www.goodreads.com/author/quotes/162578.Bren_Brown.

402 As cited in Davies, William. *The Happiness Industry*. London: Verso, 2015.

403 Spicer, Andre and Cederstrom. "The Research We've Ignored About Happiness at Work." Harvard Business Review. Published July 2015; Accessed Feb. 2019: https://hbr.org/2015/07/the-research-weve-ignored-about-happiness-at-work.

404 Bruckner, Pascal. *Perpetual Euphoria: On the Duty to Be Happy*. New Jersey: Princeton University Press, 2000.

405 Tracy, Brian. "How to be Happy: Five Steps to Living a Life You Love." Accessed Feb. 2019: https://www.briantracy.com/blog/personal-success/happiness-in-life-you-deserve-it/.

406 *Id.*

407 McFerrin, Bobby. "Don't Worry Be Happy." Accessed Nov. 2023: https://genius.com/Bobby-mcferrin-dont-worry-be-happy-lyrics.

408 Ben-Shahar, Tal. *The Pursuit of Perfect: How to Stop Chasing Perfection*. 2009.

409 Tolle, Eckhart. *Stillness Speaks*. New World Library, California: 2003, p. 13.

410 James, Alfred. "Understanding the Monkey Mind." Pocket Mindfulness. Accessed July 2019: https://www.pocketmindfulness.com/understanding-monkey-mind-live-harmony-mental-companion/.

411 Hansen, Drew. "A Guide to Mindfulness at Work." Forbes. Published Oct. 2012; Accessed July 2019: https://www.forbes.com/sites/drewhansen/2012/10/31/a-guide-to-mindfulness-at-work/#9305f4725d28.

412 *Id.*

413 *Id.*

414 Tolle, Eckhart. "Eckhart Tolle Quotes." Accessed July 2019: https://www.eckharttollenow.com/eckhart-tolle-quotes/p31/.

415 Pert, Candace. As cited by Suzanne Heyn. "How the Body Stores Emotions." Accessed July 2019: https://suzanneheyn.com/the-body-stores-emotions/.

416 Tolle, Eckhart. "Eckhart Tolle Quotes." Accessed July 2019: https://www.eckharttollenow.com/eckhart-tolle-quotes/p31/.

417 Hansen, Drew. "A Guide to Mindfulness at Work." Forbes. Published Oct. 2012; Accessed July 2019: https://www.forbes.com/sites/drewhansen/2012/10/31/a-guide-to-mindfulness-at-work/#9305f4725d28.

418 Weber, Jill. "The Power of Your Internal Dialogue." Psychology Today. Published July 2017; Accessed July 2019: https://www.psychologytoday.com/us/blog/201707/the-power-your-internal-dialogue.

419 Tolle, Eckhart. "Eckhart Tolle Quotes." Accessed July 2019: https://www.eckharttollenow.com/eckhart-tolle-quotes/p31/.

420 Brendel, David. "There are Risks to Mindfulness at Work." Harvard Business Review. Published Feb. 2015; Accessed July 2019: https://hbr.org/2015/02/there-are-risks-to-mindfulness-at-work.

421 *Id.*

422 Carter, Jacqueline and Gimian, James. "How Mindfulness Makes You a Better Leader." Published Nov. 2018; Accessed Aug. 2019: https://www.mindful.org/how-mindfulness-make-you-a-better-leader/.

423 Weiner, Jeff, as cited by Schwartz, Tony. "How to be Mindful in an 'Unmanageable World." Harvard Business Review. Published Feb. 2013; Accessed Aug. 2019: https://hbr.org/2013/02/how-to-be-mindful-in-an-unmana.

424 *Id.*

425 Huffington, Arianna. *Thrive: The Third Metric to Redefining Success and Creating a Life of Well-being, Wisdom, and Wonder.* Quoted by GoodReads.com. Accessed Aug. 2019: https://www.goodreads.com/work/quotes/32695230-thrive-the-third-metric-to-redefining-success-and-creating-a-life-of-we.

426 Private Interview. Names Withheld.

427 Feloni, Richard. "After interviewing 140 people at the top of their fields, Tim Ferriss realizes that almost all of them share the same habit." Business Insider. Published Nov. 2017; Accessed Aug. 2019: https://www.businessinsider.com/tim-ferriss-meditation-mindfulness-2017-11.

428 Ferriss, Tim. As quoted by Feloni, Richard. "After interviewing 140 people at the top of their fields, Tim Ferriss realizes that almost all of them share the same habit." Business Insider. Published Nov. 2017; Accessed Aug. 2019: https://www.businessinsider.com/tim-ferriss-meditation-mindfulness-2017-11.

429 Feloni, Richard. "After interviewing 140 people at the top of their fields, Tim Ferriss realizes that almost all of them share the same habit." Business Insider. Published Nov. 2017; Accessed Aug. 2019: https://www.businessinsider.com/tim-ferriss-meditation-mindfulness-2017-11.

430 Hanh, Thich N. Excerpt from *At Home in the World*. Posted Nov. 2018; Accessed Aug. 2019: https://plumvillage.org/news/memories-from-the-root-temple-washing-dishes/.

431 *Id.*

432 Baldelomar, Raquel. "Want to Be a Better Leader? Take Five Minutes to Meditate." Forbes. Published June 2016; Accessed July 2019: https://www.forbes.com/sites/raquelbaldelomar/2016/06/17/want-to-be-a-better-leader-take-five-minutes-to-meditate/#21d44ad53aea.

433 Hafenbrack, Andrew C. et al. "Debiasing the Mind through Meditation: Mindfulness and the Sunk Cost Bias." Sage Journals. Published Dec. 2013; Accessed Aug. 2019: http://pss.sagepub.com/content/early/2013/12/06/0956797613503853.

434 *Id.*

435 Seppala, Emma. "How Meditation Benefits CEOs." Harvard Business Review. Published Dec. 2015; Accessed Aug. 2019: https://hbr.org/2015/12/how-meditation-benefits-ceos.

436 Seppala, Emma. "How Meditation Benefits CEOs." Harvard Business Review. Published Dec. 2015; Accessed Aug. 2019: https://hbr.org/2015/12/how-meditation-benefits-ceos.

437 DeMers, Jason. "Five successful business leaders that have used meditation to improve productivity, creativity, and business acumen." Published April 2018; Accessed July 2019: https://www.businessinsider.com/5-successful-leaders-that-have-used-meditation-to-be-more-productive-2018-4. Citing Schwartz, Tony. "How to be Mindful in an 'Unmanageable' World." Published Feb. 2013; Accessed July 2019: https://hbr.org/2013/02/how-to-be-mindful-in-an-unmana.

438 Hanh, Thich Nhat. As quoted by "10 Inspirational Meditation Quotes." Published Feb. 2019; Accessed Aug. 2019: https://flaxseedsandfairytales.com/inspirational-meditation-quotes-thich-nhat-hanh/.

439 Winfrey, Oprah. As quoted in, "Eight motivational quotes that show empathy is the key to great leadership." Published Apr. 2018; Accessed Aug. 2019: https://yourstory.com/2018/04/motivational-quotes-empathy-key-great-leadership.

440 Freedman, Joshua. As quoted in, "Eight motivational quotes that show empathy is the key to great leadership." Published Apr. 2018; Accessed Aug. 2019: https://yourstory.com/2018/04/motivational-quotes-empathy-key-great-leadership.

441 *Id.*

442 Burke, Miles. "Meditation Can Make You a Better Leader." Accessed Aug. 2019: https://inside.6q.io/meditation-can-make-you-a-better-leader/.

443 Kistner, Robert. Business Leadership Interview. 2019.

444 Schwartz, Tony. "Relax! You'll be More Productive." Published Feb. 2013; Accessed July 2019: https://www.nytimes.com/2013/02/10/opinion/sunday/relax-youll-be-more-productive.html.

445 Goodreads Quotes. Accessed Aug. 2019: https://www.goodreads.com/quotes/83633-give-me-six-hours-to-chop-down-a-tree-and.

446 Goodreads Quotes. Accessed Aug. 2019: https://www.goodreads.com/quotes/35269-i-have-so-much-to-do-that-i-shall-spend.

447 Covey, Franklin. "HABIT 7: SHARPEN THE SAW." Accessed Aug. 2019:
https://www.franklincovey.com/the-7-habits/habit-7.html
448 Hooke, William. "Living on the Real World." Accessed Aug. 2019:
https://www.livingontherealworld.org/habit-7-sharpen-the-saw/
449 "Nationwide survey reveals widespread use of mind and body practices." National Center for
Complementary and Integrative Health. Published Feb. 2015; Accessed July 2019:
https://nccih.nih.gov/news/press/02102015mb.
450 Huffington, Arianna. *Thrive: The Third Metric to Redefining Success and Creating a Life of Well-Being,
Wisdom, and Wonder.* As quoted on Good Reads. Accessed Aug. 2019:
https://www.goodreads.com/work/quotes/32695230-thrive-the-third-metric-to-redefining-
success-and-creating-a-life-of-we.
451 Dass, Ram. As quoted by Tracy Kennedy. "How to Listen to Your Inner Voice for Greater
Fulfillment." LifeHack. Published and Accessed July 2019:
https://www.lifehack.org/804051/inner-voice.
452 Kornfield, Jack. "Walking Meditation." Accessed Aug 2019:
https://jackkornfield.com/walking-meditation-2/.
453 Tomaine, Gina. "Why You Should Try Meditating While Running (and How to Do It)."
Accessed Aug. 2019: https://www.runnersworld.com/health-injuries/a20838122/why-you-
should-try-meditating-while-running-and-how-to-do-it/.
454 Juntti, Melaina. "The Insane Power of Combining Exercise and Meditation." Accessed Aug.
2019: https://www.mensjournal.com/health-fitness/the-insane-power-of-combining-exercise-
and-meditation-20160301/.
455 Gonzalez, Maria. "Your Car Commute Is a Chance to Practice Mindfulness." Accessed Aug.
2019: https://hbr.org/2014/11/your-car-commute-is-a-chance-to-practice-mindfulness.
456 DeMers, Jason. "Five successful business leaders that have used meditation to improve
productivity, creativity, and business acumen." Published April 2018; Accessed July 2019:
https://www.businessinsider.com/5-successful-leaders-that-have-used-meditation-to-be-more-
productive-2018-4.
457 Tolle, Eckhart. *Stillness Speaks.* Namaste: California, 2003.
458 Carter, Jacqueline and Gimian, James. "How Mindfulness Makes You a Better Leader."
Published Nov. 2018; Accessed Aug. 2019: https://www.mindful.org/how-mindfulness-make-
you-a-better-leader/.
459 Burke, Miles. "Meditation Can Make You a Better Leader." Accessed Aug. 2019:
https://inside.6q.io/meditation-can-make-you-a-better-leader/.
460 Seppala, Emma. "How Meditation Benefits CEOs." Harvard Business Review. Published Dec.
2015; Accessed Aug. 2019: https://hbr.org/2015/12/how-meditation-benefits-ceos.
461 Krockow, Eva. "How Many Decisions Do We Make Each Day?" Psychology Today. Published
Sept. 2018; Accessed Dec. 2022: https://www.psychologytoday.com/us/blog/stretching-
theory/201809/how-many-decisions-do-we-make-each-day.
462 Cunningham, Keith. *The Road Less Stupid.* The Keys to the Vault. USA; 2018: p. 1.
463 *Id.* at 2.
464 Manson, Mark. "Personal Values." Accessed Jan. 2023: https://markmanson.net/personal-
values.
465 *Id.*
466 Manson, Mark. "The Most Important Question of Your Life." Accessed Jan. 2023:
https://markmanson.net/question.
467 Manson, Mark. "Three Reasons Why You Make Terrible Decisions (And How to Stop)."
Accessed Jan. 2023: https://markmanson.net/decision-making.
468 Cunningham, Keith. *The Road Less Stupid.* The Keys to the Vault. USA; 2018: p. 5.
469 Moran, Gwen quoting Noreena Hertz. "Seven Ways to Stop Making Bad Decisions." Fast
Company. Published March 2014; Accessed Jan. 2023:
https://www.fastcompany.com/3027160/7-ways-to-stop-making-bad-decisions.
470 Cunningham, Keith. *The Road Less Stupid.* The Keys to the Vault. USA; 2018: p. 5.

[471] Danzinger, S., Levav, J. and Avnaim-Pesso, L. "Extraneous factors in judicial decisions." PNAS. Published April 2011; Accessed Jan. 2023: https://www.pnas.org/doi/10.1073/pnas.1018033108.

[472] *Id.*

[473] Clear, James. "How Willpower Works: How to Avoid Bad Decisions." Accessed Jan. 2023: https://jamesclear.com/willpower-decision-fatigue.

[474] Berg, Sara. "What doctors wish patients knew about decision fatigue." AMA. Published Nov. 2021; Accessed Jan. 2023: https://www.ama-assn.org/delivering-care/public-health/what-doctors-wish-patients-knew-about-decision-fatigue.

[475] Danzinger, S., Levav, J. and Avnaim-Pesso, L. "Extraneous factors in judicial decisions." PNAS. Published April 2011; Accessed Jan. 2023: https://www.pnas.org/doi/10.1073/pnas.1018033108.

[476] Guy-Evans, Olivia. "Frontal lobe function, location in brain, damage, more." Simply Psychology. Published May 2021; Accessed Jan. 2023: www.simplypsychology.org/frontal-lobe.html.

[477] Tracy, Brian. Goodreads. Accessed Jan. 2023: https://www.goodreads.com/author/quotes/22033.Brian_Tracy.

[478] Guy-Evans, Olivia. "Amygdala function and location." Simply Psychology. Published May 2021; Accessed Jan. 2023: www.simplypsychology.org/amygdala.html.

[479] Troncale, Joseph. "Your Lizard Brain." Psychology Today. Published April 2014; Accessed Feb. 2023: https://www.psychologytoday.com/us/blog/where-addiction-meets-your-brain/201404/your-lizard-brain.

[480] *Id.*

[481] Whitman, Walt. "Song of Myself." Accessed Feb. 2023: https://poets.org/poem/song-myself-3.

[482] Erwin, Mike. "Six Reasons We Make Bad Decisions, and What to Do About Them." Harvard Business Review. Published Aug. 2019; Accessed Jan. 2023: https://hbr.org/2019/08/6-reasons-we-make-bad-decisions-and-what-to-do-about-them.

[483] Kistner, Robert. "Leadership Quotes." Business Leadership Interview.

[484] Brach, Tara. "RAIN: A Practice of Radical Compassion." Accessed Feb. 2023: https://www.tarabrach.com/rain/.

[485] Tracy, Brian. "Brian Tracy Quotes." Brainy Quote. Accessed April 2021: https://www.brainyquote.com/authors/brian-tracy-quotes.

[486] Tracy, Brian. As quoted by AZ Quotes. Accessed Jan. 2023: https://www.azquotes.com/quote/1385253.

[487] Cunningham, Keith. *The Road Less Stupid*. The Keys to the Vault. USA; 2018: p. 9.

[488] Snowden, David and Boone, Mary. "A Leader's Framework for Decision Making." Harvard Business Review. Published Nov. 2007; Accessed March 2023: https://hbr.org/2007/11/a-leaders-framework-for-decision-making.

[489] *Id.*

[490] *Id.*

[491] *Id.*

[492] Cunningham, Keith. *The Road Less Stupid*. The Keys to the Vault. USA; 2018: p. 9.

[493] *Id.* at 11.

[494] *Id.* at 10.

[495] *Id.* at 10.

[496] *Id.* at 11.

[497] Snowden, David and Boone, Mary. "A Leader's Framework for Decision Making." Harvard Business Review. Published Nov. 2007; Accessed March 2023: https://hbr.org/2007/11/a-leaders-framework-for-decision-making.

[498] Cunningham, Keith. *The Road Less Stupid*. The Keys to the Vault. USA; 2018: p. 11.

[499] Wilding, Melody. "How to Stop Overthinking and Start Trusting Your Gut." Harvard Business Review. Published March 2022: Accessed March 2023: https://hbr.org/2022/03/how-to-stop-overthinking-and-start-trusting-your-gut.

500 *Id.*

501 *Id.*

502 National Library of Medicine. Brain and behavior. Published June 2014; Accessed March 2023: https://www.ncbi.nlm.nih.gov/pmc/articles/PMC4086365/.

503 Wilding, Melody. "How to Stop Overthinking and Start Trusting Your Gut." Harvard Business Review. Published March 2022: Accessed March 2023: https://hbr.org/2022/03/how-to-stop-overthinking-and-start-trusting-your-gut.

504 Cunningham, Keith. *The Road Less Stupid.* The Keys to the Vault. USA; 2018: p. 12.

505 *Id.* at 12.

506 *Id.* at 12.

507 *Id.* at 14.

508 *Id.* at 15.

509 *Id.* at 15.

510 *Id.* at 15.

511 *Id.* at 16.

512 Tracy, Brian. As quoted by AZ Quotes. Accessed Jan. 2023: https://www.azquotes.com/quote/1385253.

513 Cunningham, Keith. *The Road Less Stupid.* The Keys to the Vault. USA; 2018: p. 12.

514 *Id.* at 17.

515 *Id.* at 17.

516 Greenan, Harold. As quoted by "Get Smart: Three Ways of Thinking to Make Better Decisions and Achieve Results." Farnam Street Media. Accessed March 2023: https://fs.blog/get-smart-brian-tracy/.

517 "Get Smart: Three Ways of Thinking to Make Better Decisions and Achieve Results." Farnam Street Media. Accessed March 2023: https://fs.blog/get-smart-brian-tracy/.

518 Tracy, Brian. From "How the Best Leaders Lead." As quoted by: AZ Quotes, "Brian Tracy Quotes about Decisions." Accessed March 2023: https://www.azquotes.com/author/21943-Brian_Tracy/tag/decision.

519 Cunningham, Keith. *The Road Less Stupid.* The Keys to the Vault. USA; 2018: p. 19.

520 Snowden, David and Boone, Mary. "A Leader's Framework for Decision Making." Harvard Business Review. Published Nov. 2007; Accessed March 2023: https://hbr.org/2007/11/a-leaders-framework-for-decision-making.

521 *Id.*

522 Tracy, Brain. As quoted by "Get Smart: Three Ways of Thinking to Make Better Decisions and Achieve Results." Farnam Street Media. Accessed March 2023: https://fs.blog/get-smart-brian-tracy/.

523 *Id.*

524 Cunningham, Keith. *The Road Less Stupid.* The Keys to the Vault. USA; 2018: p. 18.

525 *Id.* at 21.

526 *Id.* at 22.

527 Lincoln, Abraham. As quoted by "Get Smart: Three Ways of Thinking to Make Better Decisions and Achieve Results." Farnam Street Media. Accessed March 2023: https://fs.blog/get-smart-brian-tracy/.

528 *Id.*

529 Kistner, Robert. "Leadership Quotes." Business Leadership Interview.

530 Snowden, David and Boone, Mary. "A Leader's Framework for Decision Making." Harvard Business Review. Published Nov. 2007; Accessed March 2023: https://hbr.org/2007/11/a-leaders-framework-for-decision-making.

531 *Id.*

532 *Id.*

533 *Id.*

534 *Id.*

535 Tracy, Brian. From "How the Best Leaders Lead." As quoted by: AZ Quotes, "Brian Tracy Quotes about Decisions." Accessed March 2023: https://www.azquotes.com/author/21943-Brian_Tracy/tag/decision.

[536] Fernandez, Rich. "Five Ways to Boost Your Resilience at Work." Harvard Business Review. Published June 2016; Accessed Dec. 2019: https://hbr.org/2016/06/627-building-resilience-ic-5-ways-to-build-your-personal-resilience-at-work.

[537] *Id.*

[538] *Id.*

[539] *Id.*

[540] *Id.*

[541] Wikipedia. "Psychological Resilience." Accessed Dec. 2019: https://en.wikipedia.org/wiki/Psychological_resilience.

[542] Fernandez, Rich. "Five Ways to Boost Your Resilience at Work." Harvard Business Review. Published June 2016; Accessed Dec. 2019: https://hbr.org/2016/06/627-building-resilience-ic-5-ways-to-build-your-personal-resilience-at-work.

[543] *Id.*

[544] Tracy, Brian. "The Roots of Resilience." Brian Tracy International. Accessed Dec. 2019: https://s3.amazonaws.com/media.briantracy.com/downloads/pdf/roots_of_resilience.

[545] Wikipedia. "Psychological Resilience." Accessed Dec. 2019: https://en.wikipedia.org/wiki/Psychological_resilience.

[546] *Id.*

[547] Edison, Thomas. Brainy Quotes. Accessed Jan. 2020: https://www.brainyquote.com/quotes/thomas_a_edison_132683.

[548] Philip, Davie. "Resilience Revisited." Positive Life. Published March 2014; Accessed Jan. 2010: http://www.positivelife.ie/2014/03/resilience-revisited-communities-springing-forward-with-davie-philip/.

[549] Lincoln, Abraham. "Across the Land." Published Aug. 2015; Accessed Jan. 2020: https://jackfussellacrosstheland.wordpress.com/2015/08/15/abraham-lincoln-never-quit/.

[550] Heraclitus. "Who Said 'the Only Thing Constant is Change?" Reference. Accessed Jan. 2020: https://www.reference.com/world-view/said-only-thing-constant-change-d50c0532e714e12b.

[551] Toffler, Alvin of Future Shock as quoted by Scroggins, Clay. How to Build Resilience." Accessed Dec. 2019: https://subsplash.com/northpointministries/lb/mi/+tsp66vf.

[552] Angelou, Maya as quoted by Pennock, Seph. "19 Resilience & Adversity Quotes That Will Inspire and Empower You." Positive Psychology. Published Oct. 2019; Accessed Dec. 2019: https://positivepsychology.com/resilience-quotes/.

[553] U.S. Marine Corps. GoodReads. Accessed Jan. 2020: https://www.goodreads.com/quotes/815428-improvise-adapt-and-overcome---usmc-unofficial.

[554] Tracy, Brian. "The Roots of Resilience." Brian Tracy International. Accessed Dec. 2019: https://s3.amazonaws.com/media.briantracy.com/downloads/pdf/roots_of_resilience.

[555] Kistner, Robert. Business Leadership Interview. Dec. 2019.

[556] Tracy, Brian. "The Roots of Resilience." Brian Tracy International. Accessed Dec. 2019: https://s3.amazonaws.com/media.briantracy.com/downloads/pdf/roots_of_resilience.

[557] Jobs, Steve. "18 Powerful Steve Jobs Quotes That Just Might Change Your Life." Published July 2017; Accessed Jan. 2020: https://www.fearlessmotivation.com/2017/07/19/steve-jobs-quotes/.

[558] Fernandez, Rich. "Five Ways to Boost Your Resilience at Work." Harvard Business Review. Published June 2016; Accessed Dec. 2019: https://hbr.org/2016/06/627-building-resilience-ic-5-ways-to-build-your-personal-resilience-at-work.

[559] Jordan, Michael. Brainy Quote. Accessed Jan. 2020: https://www.brainyquote.com/quotes/michael_jordan_127660.

[560] Tracy, Brian. "The Roots of Resilience." Brian Tracy International. Accessed Dec. 2019: https://s3.amazonaws.com/media.briantracy.com/downloads/pdf/roots_of_resilience.

[561] Thatcher, Margaret as quoted by Pennock, Seph. "19 Resilience & Adversity Quotes That Will Inspire and Empower You." Positive Psychology. Published Oct. 2019; Accessed Dec. 2019: https://positivepsychology.com/resilience-quotes/.

562 Mandela, Nelson as quoted by Pennock, Seph. "19 Resilience & Adversity Quotes That Will Inspire and Empower You." Positive Psychology. Published Oct. 2019; Accessed Dec. 2019: https://positivepsychology.com/resilience-quotes/.

563 Ross, Elizabeth K. as quoted by Scroggins, Clay. How to Build Resilience." Accessed Dec. 2019: https://subsplash.com/northpointministries/lb/mi/+tsp66vf.

564 Scroggins, Clay. How to Build Resilience." Accessed Dec. 2019: https://subsplash.com/northpointministries/lb/mi/+tsp66vf.

565 Carucci, Ron. "The Better You Know Yourself, the More Resilient You'll Be." Harvard Business Review. Published Sept. 2017; Accessed Dec. 2019: https://hbr.org/2017/09/the-better-you-know-yourself-the-more-resilient-youll-be.

566 Uchtdorf, Dieter F. as quoted by Pennock, Seph. "19 Resilience & Adversity Quotes That Will Inspire and Empower You." Positive Psychology. Published Oct. 2019; Accessed Dec. 2019: https://positivepsychology.com/resilience-quotes/.

567 Fernandez, Rich. "Five Ways to Boost Your Resilience at Work." Harvard Business Review. Published June 2016; Accessed Dec. 2019: https://hbr.org/2016/06/627-building-resilience-ic-5-ways-to-build-your-personal-resilience-at-work.

568 Id.

569 Rowling, J. K. Inspirational Quotes. Pass It On. Accessed Dec. 2019: https://www.passiton.com/inspirational-quotes/6595-rock-bottom-became-the-solid-foundation-on.

570 Oliver, Mary as quoted by Pennock, Seph. "19 Resilience & Adversity Quotes That Will Inspire and Empower You." Positive Psychology. Published Oct. 2019; Accessed Dec. 2019: https://positivepsychology.com/resilience-quotes/.

571 Redmoon, Ambrose as quoted by Pennock, Seph. "19 Resilience & Adversity Quotes That Will Inspire and Empower You." Positive Psychology. Published Oct. 2019; Accessed Dec. 2019: https://positivepsychology.com/resilience-quotes/.

572 Tracy, Brian. "How to Negotiate – Skills You Need to Succeed." Accessed May 2023: https://www.briantracy.com/blog/brians-words-of-wisdom/making-course-corrections/.

573 Masahide, Mizuta. "Barn's burnt down." Wikipedia. Accessed Dec. 2019: https://en.wikipedia.org/wiki/Mizuta_Masahide.

574 Tracy, Brian. "Making Course Correction." Accessed Jan. 2020: https://www.goodreads.com/quotes/50795-i-am-not-what-happened-to-me-i-am-what.

575 Fernandez, Rich. "Five Ways to Boost Your Resilience at Work." Harvard Business Review. Published June 2016; Accessed Dec. 2019: https://hbr.org/2016/06/627-building-resilience-ic-5-ways-to-build-your-personal-resilience-at-work.

576 Picoult, Jodi as quoted by Pennock, Seph. "19 Resilience & Adversity Quotes That Will Inspire and Empower You." Positive Psychology. Published Oct. 2019; Accessed Dec. 2019: https://positivepsychology.com/resilience-quotes/.

577 Fernandez, Rich. "Five Ways to Boost Your Resilience at Work." Harvard Business Review. Published June 2016; Accessed Dec. 2019: https://hbr.org/2016/06/627-building-resilience-ic-5-ways-to-build-your-personal-resilience-at-work.

578 Achor, Shawn and Gielan, Michelle. "Resilience is about how you recharge, not how you Endure." Harvard Business Review. Published June 2016; Accessed Dec. 2019: https://hbr.org/2016/06/resilience-is-about-how-you-recharge-not-how-you-endure.

579 Id.

580 Carucci, Ron. "The Better You Know Yourself, the More Resilient You'll Be." Harvard Business Review. Published Sept. 2017; Accessed Dec. 2019: https://hbr.org/2017/09/the-better-you-know-yourself-the-more-resilient-youll-be.

581 Greene, Susan. "Compassion in Business." Forbes. Accessed Dec. 2019: https://www.forbes.com/sites/forbescoachescouncil/2019/05/31/compassion-in-business/#204edb7c5fd8.

582 Seppala, Emma. "Why Compassion in Business Makes Sense." Greater Good Magazine. Published Apr. 2013; Accessed Dec. 2019: https://greatergood.berkeley.edu/article/item/why_compassion_in_business_makes_sense

583 Id.

[584] Fernandez, Rich. "Five Ways to Boost Your Resilience at Work." Harvard Business Review. Published June 2016; Accessed Dec. 2019: https://hbr.org/2016/06/627-building-resilience-ic-5-ways-to-build-your-personal-resilience-at-work.

[585] Carucci, Ron. "The Better You Know Yourself, the More Resilient You'll Be." Harvard Business Review. Published Sept. 2017; Accessed Dec. 2019: https://hbr.org/2017/09/the-better-you-know-yourself-the-more-resilient-youll-be.

[586] *Id.*

[587] Lombardi, Vince. "Picture Quotes." Accessed Jan. 2020: https://www.quoteswave.com/picture-quotes/60909.

[588] Carucci, Ron. "The Better You Know Yourself, the More Resilient You'll Be." Harvard Business Review. Published Sept. 2017; Accessed Dec. 2019: https://hbr.org/2017/09/the-better-you-know-yourself-the-more-resilient-youll-be.

[589] Gates, Bill. "Brainy Quote. Accessed Jan. 2020: https://www.brainyquote.com/quotes/bill_gates_385735.

[590] Tracy, Brian. "Resilience! How to Bounce Back from Any Problem or Adversity." Accessed Dec. 2019: https://www.briantracy.com/catalog/resilience.

[591] *Id.*

[592] Rojo, David. Private Communication. 2022.